REFLECTIONS

ON LEADERSHIP

AND CAREER

DEVELOPMENT

On the Couch with Manfred Kets de Vries

On the Couch with Manfred Kets de Vries offers an overview of the author's work spanning four decades, a period in which Manfred F. R. Kets de Vries has established himself as the leading figure in the clinical study of organizational leadership.

The three books in this series contain a representative selection of Kets de Vries's writings about leadership from a wide variety of published sources. They cover three major themes: character and leadership in a global context; career development; and leadership in organizations. The original essays were all written or published between 1976 and 2008. Updated where appropriate and revised by the author, they present a digest of the work of one of today's most influential management thinkers.

Published Titles
Reflections on Character and Leadership
Reflections on Leadership and Career Development

Forthcoming Titles
Reflections on Organizations

REFLECTIONS ON LEADERSHIP AND CAREER DEVELOPMENT

Manfred F. R. Kets de Vries

JOSSEY-BASS
A Wiley Imprint
www.josseybass.com

Library of Congress Cataloging-in-Publication Data

Kets de Vries, Manfred F. R.
   Reflections on leadership and career development : on the couch with Manfred Kets de Vries / Mafred F.R. Kets de Vries.
       p. cm.
   ISBN 978-0-470-74246-4
1. Leadership.   2. Leadership–Psychological aspects   I. Title.
   HD57.7.K484 2010
   658.4'092–dc22

                                                           2009038962

British Library Cataloguing in Publication Data
A catalogue record for this book is available from the British Library

ISBN 978-0-470-74246-4

Typeset in 10.5/12 pt Bembo by Toppan Best-set Premedia Limited
Printed and bound in Great Britain by TJ International Ltd, Padstow, Cornwall.

To Elisabet—
who knows that patience is a major companion of wisdom.

CONTENTS

INTRODUCTION

An autobiography is only to be trusted when it reveals something disgraceful. A man who gives a good account of himself is probably lying, since any life when viewed from the inside is simply a series of defeats.

—*George Orwell*

I write fiction and I'm told it's autobiography, I write autobiography and I'm told it's fiction, so since I'm so dim and they're so smart, let them decide what it is or it isn't.

—*Philip Roth*

I don't think anyone should write their autobiography until after they're dead.

—*Samuel Goldwyn*

Many of the major themes of this book—the relationship between leaders and followers, leadership archetypes, the enigma of Russia, and the challenges we all face at midlife and beyond—have marked formative experiences in my own life. Reviewing material that I have worked on over the course of 30 years I revisited many memories, some archaic ones, others more recent, which have informed my interest in these themes.

BULLIES AND NARCISSISTS

One of my earliest memories is of being lost. However, because I was very young, I have never been sure whether it is a real memory or an implanted memory that I inadvertently internalized as the story was told to me over and over again by my mother. It is possible that these 'memories' were implanted—but in my mind's eye, I see myself doing these things from a first person perspective.

I was born and spent the first 11 years of my life in the outskirts of a small village called Huizen, on the Zuiderzee (now the Ijsselmeer), a large lake in the center of Holland, a place where people still wore traditional regional dress. The women wore very large white caps, while the men looked like crows, all dressed in black. The village was surrounded by endless meadows where cattle were raised. One day, it seems, I wandered off with my cousin and could not be found. My mother panicked and warned the authorities in the village. When there were important announcements or emergencies (like trying to find out what had happened to two small boys), the people in charge of the town hall sent a person armed with a rattle to bicycle around and make announcements. In this instance, the alarm was sounded and the whole village was alerted that two small boys had gone missing. Eventually, the two of us were found. From the dubious safety of one side of a small ditch, I was busily throwing stones at a big bull that was getting madder and madder. I still wonder whether I was trying to drive the bull away or was I the instigator of its fury—probably the latter. I don't remember why I was doing what I was doing. Luckily, the cavalry arrived in the shape of a farmer who saved us from what would have been an extremely unfortunate incident. This story was repeated to me many times over the years by my mother, who saw it as a metaphor for my attitude toward authority and 'bullies'—less sympathetically, my rebelliousness.

BEING AN EXPLORER

Some things never change. All my life, I have obeyed the impulse to court danger. As a child, I always wanted to be an explorer—I wanted to go into the jungles in the heart of Africa or the Amazon, or to the deserts of the Sahara or Outer Mongolia, climb mountains in Asia or Canada, or be at the North Pole. The call of the wild was always with me. Moving from the center of the village where I lived during World War II to the countryside helped to deal with my adventurous bent. It was a great area to play in. Stalking birds, animals, and fish became a popular pastime. Luckily, our neighbor had a whole menagerie of creatures. Turtles, ducks, chickens, turkeys, pigeons, rabbits, dogs, and cats all roamed the garden. The most imposing creatures, however, were the geese, which, when they felt threatened, would raise their necks, make a lot of noise, and run after me, trying to peck me. All these animals made up part of my inner life. My explorations in the heather, the forest, and the meadows became a transitional world where geese would magically transform into buffalos, cats into lions, and pike into piranhas and sharks. These outdoor activities continued when we moved to an apartment by the North Sea. The sea and the dunes were even more exciting playgrounds.

What added to the theme of adventure in my inner world was my fascination for the novels of Karl May, a German writer of adventure stories. In particular, I would dream my way through his novels set in the American West—as he described it, a dangerous territory populated by cowboys and Indians. I was fascinated by May's characterization of Winnetou, the wise chief of the Apache, and Old Shatterhand, Winnetou's white blood brother (and May's alter ego). These armchair 'thrills and regressions' were followed by Hergé's comic strip Tintin, describing the exploits of a young Belgian reporter in all parts of the world, including space. To add to this sense of (sublimated) adventure, there were also cartoon strips of Tom Puss and Oliver B. Bumble ('Tom Poes' and 'Olivier B. Bommel' in Dutch), an anthropomorphic cat and bear, written by Marten Toonder. Their adventures and misadventures helped to quench my thirst for exploration. In addition, I was fascinated by the historically oriented voyages in a Viking ship of the cartoonist Hans Kresse's Eric de Noorman (Eric the Norseman). I remember clearly his many expeditions to uphold what was right. His exploits took him to Russia, China, Mongolia, Britain, North America, and even Atlantis. These adventures filled my imagination, and were acted out through various games in the forests, heather, and dunes.

At university I became fascinated by the Russian novelists and playwrights, triggered by discovering Ivan Turgenev's book *Sketches from a Hunter's Album*, a collection of short stories based on his own observations while hunting at his mother's estate. I loved that book, which fed my passion for the outdoors. In it, Turgenev also described the abuse of the peasants and the injustices of the system that constrained them. At the time, a Dutch publisher was translating all the Russian classics into Dutch, a series to which I subscribed. In this way, I found other Russian writers, like Alexander Pushkin, Mikhail Lermontov, Nikolai Gogol, Ivan Alexandrovich Goncharov, Leo Tolstoy, Anton Chekhov, Fyodor Dostoevsky, Isaac Babel, and Alexander Solzhenitsyn. It is little wonder that Russia has remained an area of continuing interest to me.

Sadly, on reaching adulthood, I realized that there's not much left to explore, but in my adult life—like the heroes of my youth—I've managed it by going on strange expeditions, usually combined with climbing, fishing, and hunting. After glasnost, I was one of the first to travel to previously forbidden regions of the Russian Federation. I liked to explore the country's wild places, from Kamchatka, to Siberia, to the High Altai. I also went to the old republics, like Tajikistan, Kazakhstan, and Kirghizistan. I get great pleasure from going to totally out of the way places where nobody else has been.

To pursue my anthropological bent, I like to better understand the indigenous people in those regions. I don't have any special training—I've spent time with the Inuit in the Arctic, the Indians in the Amazon, and the pygmies in the rain forest and I've relied on their special skills to find my way back. Being with these people gives me a sense of humility—realizing how knowledgeable they are in their natural environment. It also helps me appreciate the simple things of life—a good antidote of the luxuries to be found in the center of Paris.

During my exploits I've been seriously frightened on rare occasions, but those were usually the most exciting. Once on the Alaska Peninsula, early in the morning, a hungry Kodiak bear tried to get into my tent, an incident worth remembering. At another time, in the same area, I climbed a mountain with a guide, to look for two bears that I had seen at the top. Climbing up, we tracked them closer and closer until I suddenly spotted the two of them lying beside each other, not far from us, at which point it dawned on me that it was the mating season. I wanted to take a picture but when I went to take my camera out of my backpack, one of the bears caught the movement, and came straight for me. I dropped my camera, grabbed my gun, and was preparing to shoot when the guide who was with me stood up, waved his arms to make himself look as big as possible and yelled at the bear, which stopped dead in its tracks, and turned less than ten meters from us.

On another occasion, I had crossed the border between Tajikistan and Afghanistan, dressed as a Russian soldier—the only way to get in, as the Soviet war with that country was at its peak. There was bombing on the adjacent mountain. I will never forget my guide—as we climbed the mountain, hanging with our nails on the steepest cliffs I had ever seen—saying that we were '*сумасшедший*', or crazy. Not only was there the danger of breaking our necks, but there were also the muja-hideen to watch out for, who had their own ideas of what to do with our necks. On our return to Tajikistan, following the course of a river at night, in a jeep, four sharp, penetrating lights suddenly appeared: Russian tanks. We were very lucky not to be shot to smithereens.

These stories say a great deal about my attitudes to independence and personal safety. I have never shaken off the impulse to explore, test, challenge, and ask questions. In my work, when trying to build better teams and organizations, some describe me as the 'Lord High Executioner' of asking questions of all and sundry—whatever their position. I may do so, but I do it—I hope—with very good intentions.

Those attitudes of rebelliousness and adventure have inevitably influenced the way I have dealt with leader–follower relationships throughout my life. We are all leaders and followers, in whatever sphere we operate—social, professional, and personal. Although academic institutions are not the simplest types of organizations, they are the professional context in which I have made my career and have had to make sense of the relationship between leaders and followers, first, as a student in Amsterdam, Harvard, and Montreal, and later in my role as a professor *vis-à-vis* various deans. As a follower, I have sometimes had to engage in a delicate dance with my leaders. Of course, like everyone else, the way I manage that dance originates in my relationship with my father and mother. As I have suggested, my rebelliousness toward authority and need for independence were established very early in my life. They informed my interest in entrepreneurship and pointed me to the road I took to becoming a psychoanalyst, a professor, a consultant—and a fly fisherman and hunter.

However, my earliest impressions of leadership were also colored—much more darkly—by my vague memories of life in Nazi-occupied Holland, and the stories I heard about the activities of the Nazis party in our country. Here I must have absorbed something of my family's (and particular my mother's) rebellious attitude toward bullies. During World War II, my maternal grandfather—who was a good carpenter—sheltered '*onderduikers*' (Jews and others who were hiding from the Nazis). He had built a double wall in the house to create a remarkable hiding place. The entrance to that place was underneath a carpet. Off and on, up to 20 people hid in his farmhouse, including a 12-year-old boy who had walked all the way from Poland with his sister. Feeding these 'non-existent' people, with strict wartime food rationing, was a major endeavor for my father and mother.

Understandably, being not allowed to go outside the house, the *onderduikers* (including my Jewish paternal grandparents) were all very bored and used to make a huge fuss of me. But the dangers of hiding people and possible discovery were enormous. The most likely punishment was death in a concentration camp. It would have been so easy for a small child to say or do the wrong thing. Although I have no clear memory of it, I must have been told not to talk about the people hidden in the house. But I do remember my mother, who was born in Germany and spoke fluent German, being very assertive—and fearless—with the *Grüne Polizei* (the Nazi police force) when they interrogated people in the house, looking for *onderduikers* and her heroic feat of getting my father out of one of the transition camps—a temporary holding place for one of the death camps. The winter of 1944 was very harsh and Holland was empty of supplies; everything was siphoned off to Germany. My mother made many excursions with her sister into the countryside, on bicycles with hard rubber tires, to trade with farmers to obtain food. Now, the names of my mother and her parents are listed among those of other 'righteous Gentiles'—people who saved lives—at the Holocaust Museum in Washington.

If my early childhood experiences taught me a lot about the darker side of leader–follower relationships, I was also fast becoming aware of the many facets of narcissism. Like many young boys (and adults), I was no stranger to attention-seeking. I discovered a spectacular way of impressing all and sundry. For a while my brother and I, determined to trump the other boys in the neighborhood, specialized in falling out of trees. We had a very tall conifer in our garden, with plenty of well-spaced branches to enable a controlled fall, and we could make the exercise look a great deal more dramatic than it was. The worst aspect was being badly scratched—but it was worth the excitement. What made it even better was that no one else (with the exception of my brother) dared to do it. I can still remember the enormous fright of my grandfather, who caught us in the act. Attention-seeking though this kind of entertainment was, it was essentially innocent and comfortably at the healthy end of the narcissistic spectrum. The opposite extreme of narcissism run mad was being played out around me in the larger world.

CAREER DEVELOPMENT

As I grew older, and saw the people around me aging, I became more and more interested in the adult life cycle. When I started teaching, much had been written about the early stages of human development, starting with Freud's *Three Essays on Sexuality*. This famous work had established the foundation—but what about the stages of adult life? At that time, one of the leading figures in human development, Erik Erikson, was teaching the most popular course at Harvard University. I was lucky enough to be able to follow his classes; I met him, and became deeply interested in his work. I once remember sitting in a taxi in New York with Erikson and a very close friend and colleague, Sudhir Kakar— now a leading scholar and psychoanalyst. We were returning from a ceremony held by the International Psychoanalytic Association to honor Erikson for his work on the human life cycle. The taxi driver drove like a maniac, screaming and yelling, and commenting on all the 'idiots' on the road. At one point, he asked us if we knew what made people 'tick.' We glanced at each other and kept quiet—it was clearly a rhetorical question—while he treated us all, including the giant in the field of human behavior, to a lecture on human psychology. It was an unforgettable and very funny moment.

Ironically, I wrote the articles about retirement, on which the chapters in the final part of this book are based, long before I reached the age when many people tend to retire. When I revisited them for this book, having now come closer to that point in my life, I was struck by how little I wanted to change them. I believe my impulse to write about a life stage that still lay in the distant future was related to my father's unhappiness about being forced to retire, and the disorientation he experienced.

My father joined a family firm in Amsterdam when he was 16 and remained with the firm throughout his working life. When the owner died after World War II, my father promised him on his deathbed that he would take care of his wife and children. And he did so by dramatically expanding the business, making them all wealthy in the process. But children grow up. Unfortunately, these children didn't have my father's entrepreneurial capabilities. Although he received a good salary throughout his career with the company, my father was neither given (nor asked for) shares. At 65, he was pushed out—one of the sons-in-law (the most capable) wanted to become president. This change in position was a catastrophe for my father, as, like many entrepreneurial types, the company was his life. Interestingly enough, after my father's exit, the family members started to fight among themselves and the company went down the drain. It was hard for my father to see so many people, who had worked with him for a lifetime, lose their job.

My father, to save his own sanity, and I imagine in a spirit of some defiance, after he was pushed out, decided to start his own entrepreneurial company rather than retire. He is not the type to plant roses. This made an enormous impression on me. I had already learned not to be dependent on other people and the value of my own independence: now I saw at first-hand the proof of the value of those ideals—and, through my father's example, to reject the arbitrariness of society's expectations of age-appropriate behavior.

An entrepreneur in my own way, and differently than my father, I have been an academic entrepreneur. Not only does my work involve teaching, writing, and playing with ideas, at INSEAD, I have also developed one of the largest leadership coaching centers in the world. And, to hedge my bets, I also have my own consulting firm. I am well aware that there are some people who start their retirement long before they stop working but that way of behaving has never been attractive to me. I don't want to retire from something before I have something to retire to. I am always interested in doing new things. Furthermore, I also believe that age is only a number—a means of keeping track. As I play many roles in life, as long as my mind is functioning, I certainly will not retire. How can I retire from life? I know that sooner or later, I will die, but 'retirement' is not part of the package. There are still too many things and places left to explore. As the comedian George Burns said, 'You can't help getting older, but you don't have to get old.'

ABOUT THIS BOOK

To start off this book, I take an in-depth look at the way basic psychological processes operate on individual and organizational performance and analyze these in the context of case studies of leaders and organizations. In the second part, I look at various leadership styles, including a lengthy study of Vladimir Putin, as 'CEO of Russia, Inc.' The third part of the book examines the career life cycle and how leaders and executives cope (or fail to cope) with *rites de passage* like succession and retirement.

Part 1 The Origins of Leadership examines the qualities that characterize great leaders and the interactions, both positive and dysfunctional, between leaders and followers. Taking a psychological perspective, I describe the processes at work in leader–follower relationships and leadership coaching and counselling interventions.

Part 2 Leadership and Personality builds on the clinical orientation introduced in Part 1. In these chapters I introduce a range of character types and leadership archetypes, examining how they operate within organizations, and how to deal with them as bosses, colleagues, and consultants.

Part 3 Leadership and Career Development is an examination of the issues, anxieties and opportunities that we face at midlife and beyond, a critical time both personally and professionally, as we confront changes in family life and our career trajectory changes direction.

In the **Conclusion**, I explore the ways in which change can be embraced to alter our perspective on life, giving us the opportunity to become 'twice-born.'

Manfred Kets de Vries
Paris 2009

ACKNOWLEDGEMENTS

This is the second book in a three-part series, *On the Couch with Manfred Kets de Vries*, a collection of essays about leadership and career development that I have written over the last 30 years. Most of the chapters in this book are based on previously published material that has been revised and updated. The chapters in Part 3, 'Leadership and Career Development,' conflate a number of shorter articles published in various journals and extracts from some of my books. I would like to thank my editor, Sally Simmons, and her colleagues Carol Schaessens and Mary Conochie at the Cambridge Editorial Partnership, for their help in reshaping such a large amount of material. Sally has managed to keep her sense of the ridiculous throughout. It is her way of dealing with life's absurdities.

In addition, I am particularly grateful to Stanislav Shekshnia for his advice and collaboration in the original article about Vladimir Putin on which Chapter 5 is based, and for which he was co-author. Stanislav added a lot of contextual material to my psychological inferences. I would also like to thank Elizabeth Florent-Treacy for her support during this project.

As always, I owe special thanks to my assistant, Sheila Loxham, who protects me from others with determination and great good humor, and from myself with great difficulty.

THE ORIGINS OF LEADERSHIP

INTRODUCTION

The search for the origins of leadership seems to preoccupy a lot of us. There are over five million entries for 'origins of leadership' in Google, so plenty of people have obviously tried hard to identify them. In their most basic form, the origins of leadership, like so many other aspects of human nature, are probably to be found in our fundamental needs systems. These in turn are a function of our earliest experiences, which determine the roles we will play in our human drama. Some of us are marked out as leaders, others as followers, and our success in either of these roles depends on our finding the right position on this stage.

The first chapter in this book is about narcissism—an inescapable aspect of human nature—and leadership. Everyone knows the myth of Narcissus, the beautiful boy who rejected all his would-be lovers only to lose his heart to his own reflection, and pine away to death, grieving over the impossibility of consummating his passion. But the real hero of the story is the prophet Tiresias. When he was born, Narcissus' mother, fearful that her son was too beautiful to live, consulted Tiresias about the boy's future. The seer first prophesized a long life for Narcissus. But his prophecy carried a warning: 'If Narcissus ever truly knows himself, he will die.' In making this prophecy, Tiresias set the scene for the dramatization of one of our greatest challenges as human beings: for our psychological health we have to outgrow our childhood narcissism, which puts us at the center of everyone's existence. If we do not, we will sentence ourselves to a lifetime of isolation and illusion. Narcissus' inability to separate himself from the object of his own affection brought him an early death. Even as he was rowed over the Styx to Hell, he couldn't resist taking a last glimpse of himself in the river. The myth ends with Narcissus' metamorphosis into a spring flower—the ultimate symbol of the transience of beauty and existence.

Leaders, not surprisingly, tend to have a large dose of narcissism—but as I explain in the opening chapter of this book, narcissism has generally had a bad press. There is such a thing as a healthy dose and it lies somewhere on a wide spectrum that ranges from grandiosity and showmanship to denigration and coldness. My successive 'couches' have been well warmed by narcissistic leaders and from my observations, I have identified three main types of narcissistic orientation that operate in leadership situations, all of which have their origins in early childhood experiences and relationships. I term these various forms reactive, self-deceptive and constructive narcissism and in the second part of this chapter, I examine how these different orientations work within organizations. All will be recognizable: but how can their narcissism be managed? What measures can be taken to control their behavior and to protect the people with whom they work?

In Chapter 2, I take a closer look at 'the influence game.' We all think we know a leader when we see one, but what characteristics and qualities do effective leaders have? What is it leaders do, to make people want to be part of their team? Without digressing too far into the psychology of followership, I take the examples of some formidable, more 'heroic' types of leader in the worlds of politics and business (including Charles de Gaulle, General MacArthur, Winston Churchill, Henry Ford and Walt Disney) and examine how their leadership behavior puts them at the top of the influence game. As well as their more intangible skills— their ability to provide focus, their gift for empathy, their appreciation and manipulation of symbolism, their sense-making—their effectiveness largely derives from their capacity for sheer hard graft. They need to know their stuff, and they need the stamina to persevere in getting what they want. Churchill's public rhetoric was universally inspirational but his personal motto was much more prosaic: Keep Buggering On. Perhaps more than anything, however, effective leaders possess the kinds of qualities actors have—but actors who are directing their own script as they go along. For them, authenticity, consistency of character and performance is critical: one false step and it could be a company or an entire country, not just a performance, which is brought to a standstill.

At its best, organizational play is lively, playful and mutually beneficial: when it goes wrong, it shades into collusion, what I term 'a neurotic form of collaboration.' I extend the metaphor of the organizational theater in Chapter 3 but the approach I take to what goes on in the leader-follower relationship is drawn from a very different field of study—couple therapy, which I have discovered is eminently applicable to work settings. The organizational leader is an actor–director, selecting members of the cast and assigning roles. This requires a substantial quantity of integrity and trustworthiness. It is very easy to typecast some people and put them in roles where they will give what you want rather

than perform their part creatively. Once the insidious and largely unconscious process of projective identification—pushing our personal short-
falls onto others—takes hold, a huge amount of psychic energy is
generated and wasted. Leaders and followers locked in collusive relationships experience high levels of stress, not least from the mutual need to
maintain the equilibrium of a dysfunctional relationship. Chapter 3
offers some typical dysfunctional scenarios within organizations, tracing
them to their roots in childhood development, and makes some initial
recommendations about how individuals and 'organizational detec-
tives'—consultants and professional counselors—can intercept and reveal
these processes, allowing repair work to be done.

One of these is encouraging the ability to pick up on subliminal and
non-verbal forms of communication, by 'listening with the third ear,'
which I describe in detail in Chapter 4 as one of the key skills the therapist, leadership coach, and consultant bring to individual and organizational interventions. I wrote this chapter from the perspective of a
management consultant or leadership coach who has some clinical training. My approach to my work with organizations is the application of a
clinical paradigm of intervention, drawn not only from psychotherapy
but also from cognitive theory, family systems theory, group dynamics,
motivational interviewing, neuropsychiatry, and developmental psychology. In this chapter I look at a key element of all psychotherapeutic
interventions—countertransference. In Book 1 in this series (*Reflections
on Character and Leadership*) I wrote about transference, a process first
identified by Sigmund Freud, who became aware that patients were
transferring archaic feelings for others to him during interventions.
Transference is an inappropriate repetition, in the present, of a relationship that was important in a person's childhood. All human relationships
are mixtures of realistic and transference reactions.

Freud initially considered transference a nuisance, then realized that
it provided a tool to deep understanding for both patient and therapist—
indeed, we all transfer these archaic feelings to significant people and
situations throughout our lives. The other side of this particular coin is
countertransference, where the response of the consultant or therapist to
the client is informed by the archaic feelings the patient evokes in the
therapist. Countertransference is a useful tool for the therapist to uncover
deep meaning and significance in an individual's inner theater—and
incidentally, one reason why all would-be therapists would do well to
undergo therapy themselves.

Part 1 ends on this analytical note and in Part 2, I put some leaders
'on the couch,' illustrating the many ways leadership personality works
within organizations.

CHAPTER 1

NARCISSISM AND LEADERSHIP[1]

If each of us were to confess his most secret desire, the one that inspires all his deeds and signs, he would say, 'I want to be praised.' Yet none will bring himself to do so, for it is less dishonorable to commit a crime than to announce such a pitiful and humiliating weakness arising from a sense of loneliness and insecurity, a feeling that afflicts both the fortunate and the unfortunate with equal intensity. No one is sure of who he is, or certain of what he does. Full as we may be of our own worth, we are gnawed by anxiety and, to overcome it, ask only to be mistaken in our doubt, to receive approval from no matter where or no matter whom

—Corian, Désir et honneur de la gloire

Whoever loves becomes humble. Those who love have, so to speak, pawned a part of their narcissism.

—Sigmund Freud

LEADERS AND FOLLOWERS

We still know little about what makes a good leader, though not for any lack of research on the subject. The late scholar of leadership, Ralph Stogdill, made the discouraging statement that 'there are almost as many definitions of leadership as there are persons who have attempted to define the concept' (Bass, 1981, p. 7). In his classic *Handbook of Leadership*, Stogdill reviewed 72 definitions proposed by scholars between 1902 and 1967.

[1] Some material in this chapter has previously appeared in published form in the following: Kets de Vries, M.F.R. and Miller, D. 'Narcissism and leadership: An object relations perspective,' *Human Relations,* 1985, 38 (6), 583–601.

The proliferation of literature on leadership is reflected by the increase in the number of articles listed in the *Handbook*: in the 1974 edition of the *Handbook* 3000 studies were referred to but seven years later, the number exceeded 5000. And the latest count will not be the end of it.

Thus competing theories clearly abound. We find Great Man theories, trait theories, environmental theories, person–situation theories, interaction–expectation theories, humanistic theories, exchange theories, behavioral theories, and perceptual and cognitive theories. This confused state of affairs caused some scholars to abandon the subject altogether and focus on more specific problems such as power or motivation. Other researchers, however, are less pessimistic, anticipating that the wealth of results constitutes some basis for a cogent theory of leadership. They attempt to escape the labyrinth of contradictory findings and theories of leadership by proposing a contingency paradigm (House and Baetz, 1979). Some try to explain the discrepancies in the research, noting that 'leadership has an effect under some conditions and not under others and also that the causal relationships between leader behavior and commonly accepted criteria of organizational performance are two-way' (House and Baetz, 1979, p. 348).

Despite the quantity of material on leadership we would argue that far richer characterizations of leadership are still needed: those taking into consideration both its cognitive and affective dimensions. Such characterizations are suggested by the psychoanalytic and psychiatric literature. Using these orientations to analysis, the inner world of leaders can be analyzed and their personalities and characters related to their behavior and situation. Research that aims to decipher intrapsychic thought processes and resulting actions thus involves the study of 'psycho-political drama' (Zaleznik and Kets de Vries, 1975; Kets de Vries, 2001, 2006), which relates managerial personality both to role behavior and to administrative setting.

In my view what most leaders seem to have in common is the ability to reawaken primitive emotions in their followers. When under the spell of certain types of leader, their followers often feel powerfully grandiose and proud, or helpless and acutely dependent. Max Weber (1947) used the term *charisma* to elucidate the strange influence of some leaders over followers which, for him, consisted of:

> a certain quality of an individual personality by virtue of which he is set apart from ordinary men and treated as endowed with supernatural, super-human, or at least specifically exceptional powers or qualities. These are such as are not accessible to the ordinary person, but are regarded as of divine origin or as exemplary, and on the basis of them, the individual concerned is treated as a leader (pp. 358–359).

We might not want to go so far as Weber, but whatever strange quality leaders possess, some have the power to induce regressive behavior among their followers by exploiting (not necessarily in full awareness) unconscious feelings of their subordinates. In this process, some followers may try to embrace an idealized, omnipotent leader, one who will fulfill their dependency needs, which may lead to the destructive suspension of their own rational faculties.

In spite of the regressive potential of some leaders, there are, however, others who are prepared to transcend their personal agenda, who are able to create a climate of constructiveness, involvement, and care, who engender initiative, and spur creative endeavors. This is the kind of person Zaleznik (1977) had in mind when he wrote:

> One often hears leaders referred to in adjectives rich in emotional content. Leaders attract strong feelings of identity and difference, or of love and hate. Human relations in leader-dominated structures often appear turbulent, intense, and at times even disorganized. Such an atmosphere intensifies individual motivation and often produces unanticipated outcomes (p. 74).

James MacGregor Burns (1978) probably had similar thoughts when he compared 'transactional' with 'transformational' leadership. While the first type of leader motivates followers by exchanging rewards for services rendered (whether economic, political, or psychological), the latter type recognizes and exploits an existing need or demand of a potential follower. But, beyond that, the successful transformational leader looks for potential motives in followers, seeks to satisfy their higher needs, and engages their full potential. The result of the most adept transformational leadership is a relationship of mutual stimulation and elevation that converts followers into leaders and leaders into moral agents (Burns, 1978, p. 4).

To conclude, leadership can be pathologically destructive or intensely inspirational. But what is it about the leaders themselves that causes them to be one or the other? I believe the answer lies in the degree of narcissism in the personality of the leader in question.

THE NARCISSISTIC DISPOSITION IN LEADERS

Narcissists live with the assumption that they cannot reliably depend on anyone's love or loyalty. They feel they must rely on themselves rather than on others for the gratification of life's needs. While pretending to be self-sufficient, in the depth of their being they experience a sense of deprivation and emptiness. To cope with these feelings and, perhaps, as a cover for their insecurity, narcissists become preoccupied with establishing their adequacy—whether in terms of power, beauty, status, prestige, or superiority. At that same time, narcissists expect others to accept the high esteem in which they hold themselves, and to cater to their needs. What is striking in the behavior of these people is their interpersonal exploitativeness. Narcissists live under the illusion that they are entitled to be served, that their own wishes take precedence over those of others. They think that they deserve special consideration in life.

It must be emphasized, however, that these characteristics occur with different degrees of intensity. A certain dose of narcissism is necessary in all humans in order to function effectively and so we all at times show signs of narcissistic behavior. Among individuals who possess only limited narcissistic tendencies, we find those who are very talented and capable of making great contributions to society. Those who gravitate toward the extreme, however, give narcissism its pejorative reputation. Here we find preoccupation with self, excessive rigidity, narrowness, resistance, and discomfort in dealing with the external environment. The leadership implications of destructive narcissism can be extremely dramatic.

Although the narcissistic type of personality has long been recognized, only relatively recently has it come under critical scrutiny. For example, the latest version of the *Diagnostic and Statistical Manual of Mental Disorders* (American Psychiatric Association, 2000) lists a large number of diagnostic criteria to describe narcissistic personality disorders. Many of these characteristics are also applicable, albeit in smaller measure, to narcissistic individuals who adopt a more 'normal' mode of functioning. According to the manual, these people have 'a pervasive pattern of grandiosity (in fantasy or behavior), need for admiration, and lack of empathy, beginning in early adulthood and present in a variety of contexts, as indicated by five (or more) of the following:

has a grandiose sense of self-importance (e.g., exaggerates achievements and talents, expects to be recognized as superior without commensurate achievements)

is preoccupied with fantasies of unlimited success, power, brilliance, beauty, or ideal love

believes that he or she is 'special' and unique and can only be understood by, or should associate with, other special or high-status people (or institutions)

requires excessive admiration

has a sense of entitlement, i.e., unreasonable expectations of especially favorable treatment or automatic compliance with his or her expectations

is interpersonally exploitative, i.e., takes advantage of others to achieve his or her own ends

lacks empathy: is unwilling to recognize or identify with the feelings and needs of others

is often envious of others or believes that others are envious of him or her

shows arrogant, haughty behaviors or attitudes.' *(American Psychiatric Association, 2000, p. 661.)*

The reason I dwell on narcissism is that if there is one personality constellation that best fits most leaders it is the narcissistic one. Freud (1921) identified this in his study of the relationship between leaders and followers, stating that 'the leader himself need love no one else, he may be of a masterful nature, absolutely narcissistic, self-confident and independent' (pp. 123–124). Later, he introduced a 'narcissistic libidinal personality,' an individual whose main interest is self-preservation, who is independent and impossible to intimidate. This individual may also show significant aggressiveness, which sometimes manifests itself in a constant readiness for activity. People belonging to this type impress others as being strong personalities. They are especially situated to act as moral ideological bastions for others—in short, as true leaders (Freud, 1921, p. 257).

In a similar context, Wilhelm Reich referred to a 'phallic-narcissistic character,' which he portrayed as 'self-confident, often arrogant, elastic, vigorous and often impressive ... The outspoken types tend to achieve leading positions in life and resent subordination ... If their vanity is hurt, they react either with cold reserve, deep depression or lively aggression' (Reich, 1949, p. 201).

Narcissism became a particularly important topic for study when new developments in psychoanalytic theory occurred in this area. The introduction of object relations theory in the 1940s and self psychology in the 1970s was especially fruitful. The most important revisions concerning narcissism were formulated by clinicians such as Otto Kernberg (1975) and Heinz Kohut (1971). I will not dwell here on the theoretical controversies about whether narcissism is a result mainly of developmental arrest or regression, or whether it possesses its own developmental lines. My aim is to explore the relationships between narcissism and leadership, a connection recognized by both Kernberg and Kohut. For example, Kernberg states that because 'narcissistic personalities are often driven by intense needs for power and prestige to assume positions of authority and leadership, individuals with such characteristics are found rather frequently in top leadership positions' (Kernberg, 1979, p. 33). Kohut, in focusing on leaders as objects of identification, mentions that 'certain types of narcissistically fixated personalities with their apparently absolute self-confidence and certainty lend themselves specifically to this role' (Kohut, 1971, p. 316).

Narcissism is often the driving force behind the desire to obtain a leadership position. Perhaps individuals with strong narcissistic personality features are more willing to undertake the arduous process of attaining a position of power.

THREE TYPES OF NARCISSIST

I will now consider three types of narcissistic orientation, beginning with the most pernicious or pathological, and proceeding toward the more adaptive or functional: these I call *reactive, self-deceptive,* and *constructive.* Each type is illustrated using examples from my clinical experiences, which demonstrate how executives with different formative backgrounds manifest narcissistic behavior in various leadership situations. However, I begin by briefly looking at where narcissism stems from in a child's early experiences, as explained by object-relations theory—one of the orientations we find in psychoanalytic theory.

As children grow from infants into adulthood over time, they develop relatively stable ways of representing their experience of themselves and others. They do this in terms of developing psychic representations in their private inner world, known as 'internal objects,' which represent accumulated perceptions. These are composed of fantasies, ideals, thoughts, and images that combine to create a person's cognitive map of the world (Klein, 1948; Fairbairn, 1952; Jacobson, 1964; Guntrip, 1969; Mahler, Pine, and Bergman, 1975; Kernberg, 1976). Naturally, the earliest 'objects' are the parents, whose degree of nurturing of the child gives rise to different kinds of 'internal world' in that child. The term 'object relations' thus refers to theories, or aspects of theories, concerned with exploring the relationships between real, external people, the mental images retained of these people, and the significance of these mental residues for psychological functioning (Greenberg and Mitchell, 1983). Thus our interactions with actual people depend not only on how we view them, but also on our views of internalized others. These psychic representations profoundly influence our affective states as well as our behavior.

Good internal objects serve as a source of sustenance in dealing with life's adversities. They constitute the underpinnings of healthy functioning. But in the absence of good internal objects, various dysfunctions accrue. Therein lies the genesis of pathological narcissism. This can be displayed in three different forms, ranging in degree of pathology.

Reactive narcissism

In describing messianic and charismatic leaders, Kohut (1978) attributes their pathological narcissistic development to their failure during early childhood to integrate two important spheres of the self, namely 'the grandiose self' and 'the idealized parental image.' The first construct refers to early feelings of omnipotence, when a child wishes to display its evolving capabilities and to be admired for them. The second construct refers to the child's desire to experience a sense of merger with an idealized person. Typically, the child's 'I am perfect and you admire me,' gradually changes to 'You are perfect and I am part of you.'

Clinical studies indicate that these early experiences (which are a part of everyone's maturation process) become mitigated and neutralized through phase-appropriate development (Winnicott, 1975). By this process, the child is gradually able to reduce frustration from the inevitable failure of parents to live up to his or her archaic expectations and, through experience, comes gradually to understand the difference between the ideal of perfection and just being good enough. The child learns that the parent is neither completely good nor completely bad. A more balanced and integrated image of the parent is internalized to make for a more realistic appreciation. This fusion of originally split good and bad objects is said to be essential for the development of trust in the permanence, constancy, or reliability of the parental figures (Klein, 1948). In turn, this early success in creating secure interpersonal attachments makes for confident self-esteem and for stable relationships. Kohut (1971) believes this process to be the basis of the development of a permanent and durable psychic structure.

Unfortunately, phase-appropriate development does not always take place. When parents are insufficiently sensitive to the needs of the growing child, their behavior may be experienced as cold and unempathic, even at the earliest stage of development. In these cases, children acquire a defective sense of self and are unable to maintain a stable level of self-esteem. Consequently, childhood needs are not modified or neutralized, but continue to prevail. This, in turn, results in a persistent longing and a search for narcissistic recognition throughout adulthood.

The stage is thus set for 'reactive narcissism.' In a classic article, Kohut and Wolf (1978) refer to the fragmented self that results from too few stimulating and integrating parental responses during childhood.

The legacy of such deficient interactions for the child may be a lingering sense of inadequacy. To cope with such feelings some individuals create for themselves a self-image of 'specialness' as a compensatory, reactive refuge against an ever-present feeling of never having been loved by the parent. This illusion of uniqueness will vitally affect how the individual deals with his or her external environment. Any discrepancies between capacities and wants are likely to contribute to anxiety and to impaired reality testing (the inability to distinguish wish from perception or, in other words, 'inside' from 'outside'). Individuals with this reactive kind of orientation will frequently distort outside events and resort to primitive defense mechanisms to prevent a sense of loss and disappointment. If they are in a position of leadership—when they are acting on a public stage—this can have grave consequences. Thus we can classify reactive narcissism, caused by emotionally unresponsive, rejecting parents, as the severest type of narcissism.

In making these inferences, we should bear in mind that early experiences in themselves rarely have a direct, final, causal impact on adult functioning. There are many mediating experiences during everyone's life and humankind is very resilient. Early experiences do, however, play a substantial role in shaping the core personality, which then influences the kind of environment sought out by the individual. This has an effect on experience and, in turn, will influence personality. We are thus talking about an interactive cycle of personality, behavior, and situation (Erikson, 1963; McKinley Runyan, 1982).

Self-deceptive narcissism

There is also a second type of early childhood development that leads to a different kind of narcissism. Leaders with this background were once led by one or both parents to believe that they were completely lovable and perfect, regardless of their actions. Unfortunately, what may appear as indulgence on the part of the parents is, in fact, exactly the opposite. The parents use their children to take care of their own needs, overburdening them with their implicit desires. When parents impose their unrealistic hopes on their children, they engender delusions. They confuse the children about their true abilities. Self-deceptive leaders probably suffer from what Kohut and Wolf (1978) describe as an 'over-stimulated' or 'overburdened' self. Because the responses of the figures of early childhood were inappropriate, given the child's age, the child never really learns to moderate the grandiose self-images or its idealized parental images. These ideals of perfection have been too demanding to allow the child to internalize soothing, stabilizing internal objects. These children become the proxies of their parents, entrusted with the mission to fulfill many unrealized parental hopes. All too often, this turns out to be 'mission impossible.'

Sometimes these people's unrealistic beliefs may act as an impetus that then differentiates them from others and does indeed make them successful. Perhaps Freud (1917, p. 156) had this in mind when he noted that 'if a man has been his mother's undisputed darling, he retains throughout life the triumphant feeling, the confidence in success, which not seldom brings actual success along with it.' In those rare instances when such encouragements work out, the child may be sufficiently talented to live up to the parents' exaggerated expectations. A person who in more normal circumstances might have led an ordinary life, has used the expectations imposed on him as a child as a basis for excellence.

Self-deceiving narcissists are likely to suffer from interpersonal difficulties due to their desire to live up to the now internalized parental illusions of self-worth. They tend to demonstrate emotional superficiality and poverty of affect. Their behavior has an 'ideal-hungry' quality resulting from difficulties in identity formation.

Conceptually, it is fairly easy to differentiate between the etiology of the reactive and self-defective modes of narcissism. In practice, however, a distinction is more difficult to make because each parent might have responded differently toward the developing child. One parent might have taken a cold, hostile, rejecting attitude, while the other might have been supportive. Moreover, as I pointed out earlier, learning experiences later in life may also have buffering effects on an individual's personality development.

Constructive narcissism

In describing the childhood object-relations of healthy or constructive narcissists, Miller (1981) stated:

> Aggressive impulses [were] neutralized because they did not upset the confidence and self-esteem of the parents. ... Strivings toward autonomy were not experienced [by parents] as an attack. ... The child was allowed to experience and express 'ordinary' impulses (such as jealousy, rage, defiance) because his parents did not require him to be 'special', for instance,

to represent their own ethical attitudes. ... There was no need to please anybody (under optimal conditions), and the child could develop and exhibit whatever was active in him during each developmental phase. ... Because the child was able to display ambivalent feelings, he could learn to regard both himself and the subject [the other] as 'both good and bad', and did not need to split off the 'good' from the 'bad' object (pp. 33–34).

Constructive narcissists do not behave in a reactive or self-deceptive manner. They do not feel the same need to distort reality to deal with life's frustrations. Nor are they so prone to anxiety. They make less frequent use of primitive defenses, and are less estranged from their feelings, wishes, or thoughts. In fact, they often generate a sense of positive vitality that derives from confidence about their personal worth. Such people have internalized relatively stable and benign objects, which sustain them in the face of life's adversities. They are willing to express their wants and to stand behind their actions, irrespective of the reactions of others. When disappointed, they do not act spitefully, but are able to engage in reparative action. That is, they have the patience to wait, to search out the moment when their talents will be needed (Erikson, 1978). Boldness in action, introspection, and thoughtfulness are common.

DEFENSIVE SYSTEMS IN NARCISSISTS

So how do these three types of narcissistic leaders use their defensive systems? What strikes one most in observing their behavior is how primitive the defenses of the first two types tend to be (Kernberg, 1975). At the core of the defensive system is the mental process 'splitting'. All other defenses can be seen as derivatives of this very primitive mechanism.

Splitting is the tendency to see everything as either ideal (all good) or persecutory (all bad). When the individual has not sufficiently integrated the opposite qualities of internal objects, these representations are kept separate to avoid contamination of good or bad. Individuals with a strong tendency toward splitting possess affective and cognitive representations of themselves and others that are dramatically oversimplified. They fail to appreciate the real ambiguity of human relationships. Relationships are polarized between unbridled hatred, fear, or aggression on the one hand, and over-idealization on the other. Splitting thus avoids conflicts and preserves an illusory sense of one's self as being all good. All evil is ascribed to others. The price of maintaining this illusory sense of goodness is, of course, an impaired conception of reality.

Closely related to this defense are the primitive defenses of *idealization* and *devaluation*. First, there is need to create unrealistic, all-good, all-powerful representations of others. This process can be viewed as a protection against persecutory objects. A sense of intense helplessness and insignificance creates the need for all-powerful protectors. In the long run, however, no one can sustain these exaggerated expectations. Thus, a vengeful devaluation of the idealized figure then occurs when needs are not met.

Other derivatives of splitting are *projection* and *projective identification* (Ogden, 1982). Both projection and projective identification reduce anxiety by allowing the expression of unwanted unconscious impulses or desires without letting the conscious mind recognize them. The main difference, however, between projection and projective identification is that the former belongs to intrapsychic dynamics, while the latter applies to interpersonal dialogue.

Projection implies attributing our own feelings, thoughts, and motives to others and usually involves unacceptable or undesirable impulses. For example, an executive, unable to accept her competitive or hostile feelings toward a colleague, says that she doesn't like him. In contrast, projective identification describes a very primitive, pre-verbal mode of communicating and relating. The archetypical model of projective identification is the mother-child interface. Infants cannot say how they feel; instead, they make the mother experience the same feeling. And although projective identification can be viewed as a very archaic psychological process, it is also thought to be the basis of more mature psychological processes, like empathy and intuition.

For the receiver, projective identification is far more disturbing and more difficult to deal with than simple projection. In both defense mechanisms, however, there is never any sense of personal responsibility. Instead, there are distortions of reality. The frequency, severity, and intensity of these defensive mechanisms vary between the types of narcissism. The reactive type shows the highest frequency and intensity, the constructive type, the lowest. (In Chapter 4, I elaborate further on projective identification.)

NARCISSISTS WITHIN ORGANIZATIONS

I detailed the clinical indicators of narcissism earlier but it is important to stress that the first two types of narcissistic leaders show these indicators to a different extent. In my experience, reactive narcissists tend to be cold, ruthless, grandiose, and exhibitionistic. They may show a desire to dominate and control and can be extremely exploitative. Self-deceptive narcissists are milder; they want to be liked and are much less abrasive. However, they still lack empathy, are obsessed mainly with their own needs, and are given to discreetly Machiavellian behavior. Their behavior has an 'as if' quality, because they lack a strong sense of inner conviction and identity (Deutsch, 1965). Finally, constructive narcissistic leaders are also ambitious and can be manipulative and hyper-sensitive to criticism. But they have enough self-confidence, adaptability, and humor to stress real achievements. They get on well with others because of their insights into relationships.

I will now describe two managerial situations in which I have seen the two personalities in operation. The first is in *leadership* or interpersonal relations. The second relates to how they try *to make sense* of their external environment and how they make *decisions*.

The reactive narcissist at work

The reactive narcissist (RN) can be an extremely demanding taskmaster. The arguments of others are ignored if they run counter to the boss's ideas. Only solicitous subordinates are tolerated by a reactive narcissist; all others are 'expelled.' The followers play politics simply to survive. Caring little about hurting and exploiting others in pursuit of their own advancement, RN leaders surpass all other types in their formidable lack of empathy. Their fluctuations in attitude toward their people will be extreme, and, consequently, the level of employee turnover in organizations they lead tends to be very high. Projects that require teamwork or subordinate initiative are seriously jeopardized.

RN leaders exhibit characteristic dysfunctions when making important decisions for the organization. They tend to do very little scanning or analysis of the internal and external environment before making decisions, feeling that the environment is somehow beneath them, and poses no challenges that cannot easily be met. RNs' grandiosity, exhibitionism, and preoccupation with fantasies of unlimited success cause them to undertake extremely bold and adventurous projects often doomed to fail. The quality of their leadership style is transformational rather than transactional. They want to attract the attention of an invisible audience, to demonstrate their mastery and brilliance.

First, their overblown scale reflects the personal desires of the leader more than the realities of the situation, and too many resources are placed at risk for too little reason. Second, RN leaders are not the type to really listen to their advisors, peers, or subordinates. They truly believe that they alone are sufficiently informed to make judgments. A potentially crucial forum to help in decision-making is thereby lost. Third, even when it is clear that things are not going well with a project, RN leaders are reluctant to admit the evidence. They believe strongly in their infallibility. They will not own up to having made any errors and become especially rigid and sensitive to criticism. Thus, they initiate a momentum that is difficult to reverse (Miller and Friesen, 1980, 1984). When these leaders finally realize how fast the situation is deteriorating, their penchant for splitting causes them to blame others, never seeing themselves as being responsible for anything at all negative.

The self-deceptive leader

These individuals have many of the traits of reactive executives, but they are less evident in a managerial situation. As leaders, self-deceptive (SD) executives are much more approachable than their RN counterparts. They care more about their subordinates, are more given to listening to the opinions of others, and are much less exploitative than the RNs. However, they also show a hypersensitivity to criticism, extreme insecurity, and a strong need to be loved. SD leaders, however, are more tolerant of dissenting opinions in that they may seem to react sympathetically when the opinions are expressed. But they tend to bear grudges, to be less available to habitual critics and to promote weaker-willed subordinates over their more vocal peers.

However, while SD leaders will often express interest in their subordinates' preoccupations, this will be out of a desire to appear sympathetic rather than out of a genuine sense of concern. They will want to do the right thing, but will not really feel very enthusiastic about it. An exception to this pattern occurs in cases where leaders become attached to a subordinate whom they come to idealize. They will do all in their power to 'bind' this person, to develop and bring him or her along in their own image. It is not surprising, of course, that this treasured subordinate generally idolizes the boss and is not usually a very strong individual—certainly not very strong within the sphere of his or her boss. If the subordinate were to show personal initiative, it could be interpreted as treason. The leader's idealization would then quickly change into devaluation, and even rage, with predictable results for the subordinate's future in the organization.

SD leaders, in contrast to their RN counterparts, may be eager to discover opportunists, and particularly threats, in their environment.

They are insecure and therefore spend a considerable amount of time analyzing the internal and external environment to make sure that they will be able to neutralize threats and avoid costly mistakes. Competitors are watched, customers are interviewed, and information systems are established. A good deal of analysis and assessment takes place, so much so that it may paralyze action.

In making strategic decisions, SD leaders have a degree of performance anxiety. They want to do the best job they possibly can so that they will be respected and admired, but they worry about their ability to do so. Being afraid of failure tends to make them much more conservative than the reactive executive. SD executives study the situation very thoroughly and solicit the opinions of others. Decision-making is done in response to exchanges of various types, in contrast to the pernicious transformational style of the reactive leader. SD leaders' orientation is predominantly transactional. Conservative (like-minded) executives are much more likely to be given a receptive hearing than more adventurous executives. SD narcissists have a general tendency to procrastinate, and their perfectionism and hesitancy can give rise to organizational stagnation. Note that RN narcissists work to impress the broader political or business community, to be revered, to fulfill bold, impossible, visionary dreams. SD narcissists just want to be loved and admired by the people with whom they interact. Their symptoms will wax and wane, corresponding to the degree of anxiety they are experiencing, to a greater extent than those of the RN leader.

The constructive leader

Constructive leaders are no strangers to manipulation and not beyond occasional acts of opportunism. But they are generally able to get on fairly well with their subordinates. Constructive narcissists have a high degree of confidence in their abilities. Being highly task-oriented they may sometimes come across as lacking in warmth or consideration.

Although constructive leaders enjoy being admired, they have a sufficiently realistic appreciation of their abilities and limitations to recognize the competence of others. Constructive leaders can be good listeners and appreciate the opinions of their subordinates, even though they are content to assume the ultimate responsibility for collective actions.

These leaders possess a sense of inner direction and self-determination that gives them confidence. They radiate a sense of authenticity. They have the ability to inspire others and to create a common cause, transcending petty self-interest. Their inner directedness, however, can also be reflected by coldness, arrogance, or a stubborn insensitivity to the needs of others. Abstract concerns, such as 'the good of the company' or 'helping the worker,' may replace reciprocity in interpersonal relations and the building of a team. In general, however, constructive narcissists have a sense of humor, which makes it possible for them to put things in perspective. Their independence can make for the creativity and vision necessary to energize subordinates to engage in ambitious endeavors. Since it lacks the rigidity of the other two types, the dominant leadership style of these people has both a transformational and transactional quality.

   Constructive leaders vary a good deal in their decision-making styles, which are more reflections of the situation facing the firm than the personal foibles of the executive. Their adaptability allows them to do a good deal of analysis, environmental scanning, and consultation before making strategic decisions of far-reaching consequences. But it also enables them to handle more routine situations with dispatch, entrusting matters to subordinates. Thy also tend to avoid extremes of boldness and conservatism, operating more in the 'middle range.'

MANAGING NARCISSISTIC LEADERS

Clearly, constructive narcissistic leaders pose relatively few problems for organizations. But what can a firm's more healthy executives do when faced with the two more dysfunctional types of leader? Where the organization is centralized and the narcissistic leader is dominant, poor performance and subsequent dismissal by a strong, watchful board of non-executive directors may be the only effective catalysts for change. And even these mutative influences are ruled out when a leader has strong financial control—like being in an ownership position. However, the outlook is much brighter where organizational power is more broadly distributed or where the narcissist occupies a less elevated position (Kets de Vries and Miller, 1984).

   In fact, there are a number of organizational measures that can be taken to minimize the damage done by narcissistic leaders working at a lower level. The first might be simply to try to become aware of their existence. In this pursuit, it may be useful to bear in mind that single indicators of each of these types are not sufficient to warrant a diagnosis of narcissism. But when these combine to form a syndrome this may indicate trouble.

It must be emphasized that it is not easy to change a narcissist's personality. Although we can engage in a dose of behavior modification—making narcissists aware of the implications of their actions, and demonstrating other ways of handling specific situations—the core of the personality will retain its dominance. If behavior modification doesn't work, the focus should be on transferring the individual out of harm's way or reducing his or her influence. A number of structural devices can be used to accomplish the latter. For example, power can be more broadly distributed in the organization so that many people become involved in strategic decisions, and lower-level executives are allowed to take responsibility for more routine concerns. Cross-functional committees, task forces, and executive committees can provide a useful forum in which a multitude of executives can express their viewpoint, providing opportunities for the narcissistic leaders (and especially their subordinates) to learn from, and have their influence mitigated by, others. Monolithic and unrealistic perspectives are thereby discouraged.

Regular executive appraisals or multi-party (360-degree) feedback activities, in which subordinates have a chance to express their opinions about their superior to other parties, can also be useful. Where a consensus of dissatisfaction emerges, particularly if it coincides with poor unit performance, it might be time to engage in some form of leadership development, or transfer, and eventually dismiss the leader. In fact, the existence of such assessment policies might inhibit any overtly narcissistic exploitation.

When the top decision-makers in an organization become aware of the narcissistic proclivities of some of the organization's executives, they can use this information in carrying out their leader and leadership development activities. This is especially true when assigning subordinates to a narcissistic leader. One of the greatest dangers lies in engaging insecure, inexperienced executives to work for the narcissist. As the African saying goes, 'Under a great tree grows very little.' While it can be seen as a great learning experience, these employees will have too little strength or resolve to be able to cope, and still less potential to act as useful counterbalancing forces. It is therefore useful to assign strong, confident, and secure personalities to work with the narcissistically inclined executive, those who are not afraid to express their opinions and can help to introduce more 'reality' into the decision-making process.

It is particularly important, also, to look for signs of excessive narcissism when recruiting and making promotions. Psychological assessments by trained clinicians or leadership coaches and interviews with a candidate's previous superiors and subordinates might flag up a narcissistic leader. However, there is no doubt that the easiest way to deal with these executives is to avoid hiring them altogether, or failing that, to refrain from giving them much power. The writer, Oscar Wilde—no stranger to narcissism himself—once said, 'To love oneself is the beginning of a life-long romance.' And a romance it is, but at what price!

CHAPTER 2

WHY FOLLOW THE LEADER?[1]

He was a great thundering paradox of a man, noble and ignoble, inspiring and outrageous, arrogant and shy, the best of men the worst of men, the most protean, most ridiculous, and most sublime. No more baffling, exasperating soldier ever wore a uniform. Flamboyant, imperious, and apocalyptic, he carried the plumage of a flamingo, could not acknowledge errors, and tried to cover up his mistakes with sly, childish tricks. Yet he was also endowed with great personal charm, a will of iron, and a soaring intellect. Unquestionably he was the most gifted man-at-arms this nation has produced.

—*Manchester*

Thus reads the opening paragraph of William Manchester's biography of the American General, Douglas MacArthur. Manchester describes a giant of a man, not easily disregarded. We find ourselves face to face with someone who knows the ins and outs of the influence game. MacArthur looms larger than life. It was hard to remain indifferent to him: those who knew him either admired or disliked him. Whatever reservations anyone had about MacArthur's behavior—his exhibitionism, his haughtiness or his inconsistencies—no one could doubt his leadership qualities. As one of his officers said, 'I'd follow that man—anywhere—blindfolded' (Manchester, 1978, p. 5).

There is an element of immediacy in descriptions such as that of MacArthur: our imaginations are swiftly stimulated. Unfortunately, the same cannot be said of research writing about leadership. For example, reading through Stogdill's gargantuan *Handbook of Leadership* (Bass, 1981)

[1] Material for this chapter has appeared in print under the same title in: Kets de Vries, Manfred F. R. 'Why Follow the Leader,' *Bedrijfskunde*, 1987, 3, 197–207. Another version appeared in Kets de Vries, Manfred, F. R. *Prisoners of Leadership*. New York: Wiley, 1989.

is a sobering and bewildering experience. Even the casual reader will quickly discover that finding one's way in the domain of leadership is like walking on quicksand. One political scientist commented wryly: 'All paths to the study of leadership end up swallowing their subject matter' (Wildavsky, 1980, p. 12). Although it can be hard to define or measure effective leadership it is not difficult to recognize it when we see it. True leaders know how to motivate us. Truly effective leaders transcend a mere managerial role, and put themselves in a different league (Zaleznik, 1976). Such leaders play a transformational role (MacGregor Burns, 1978). The best demonstration of how effective leaders operate is seen in the way they deal with the people and events around them. However, one student of leadership noted that 'there is a startling lack of evidence on what leaders actually do' (McCall, 1976, p. 139). This makes direct observation and first-hand reports even more important.

Assessment of the qualities of effective leadership is difficult, however, because of the interaction of three sets of variables. Obviously, leadership is not only a function of the leader but is also made up of a complex interaction process that consists of leader, followers, and the context in which they are operating, the latter sometimes being called the 'historical moment' (Erikson, 1978). In this chapter my main emphasis will therefore be on the actual behavior of the leader, and my conclusions will, I hope, be complementary to previous work done on personal dimensions associated with leadership (Stogdill, 1948; Bass, 1981). Through interpretation of behavior and actions I hope to define some of the qualities that make for leaders' effectiveness, using examples of business and political leaders taken from the public domain (MacGregor Burns, 1978; Levinson, 1980; Tucker, 1981; Kets de Vries, 1987, 2001). Since this will produce a kind of 'shopping list' of a number of the possible qualities desirable in a leader, it is highly unlikely that many leaders will possess them all. Astute leaders, however, know that they can't do whatever needs to be done alone. They know how to build great teams. They recognize the importance of complementarity in talent, thus creating executive role constellations.

My conjectures about leader behavior are based on information provided by a large number of observations of senior executives, augmented by historical data about leaders. Naturally, given this relatively limited database, my comments should be treated as a series of inferences about effective leadership rather than a rigid framework.

LEADER OR PUPPET?

In leadership literature we come across both 'great man' theories (Borgatta, Couch, and Bales, 1954; Jennings, 1960) and 'environmental' theories (Mumford, 1909; Murphey, 1941; Pfeffer and Salancik, 1978). The former emphasize the impact of leaders on their environment, while the latter transform the leader 'into a bus driver whose passengers will leave him unless he takes them in the direction they wish to go' (Simon, 1967, p. 134). According to this view, it does not make much of a difference who is in charge; societal constraints will determine the kind of action that is taken (Pfeffer, 1977). Herbert Simon is somewhat more generous about the influence of leaders. He suggests that leaders can have 'minor discretion as to the road to be followed' (1967, p. 134). My own observations differ, however. In my experience, leaders can, in fact, be more than a bus driver and leadership is not merely the outcome of various social forces. For sure, leaders are influenced by events but they can also be catalysts for events. To borrow a metaphor from Robert Tucker, 'The leader is not merely an actor (however great) in a play but the playwright as well' (Hoffman, 1967, p. 109). Certain situations, like crises, may facilitate leaders' rise to pre-eminence, but leaders make a difference through their action—or perhaps lack of action—at many important moments. But a debate about the primacy of person versus situation, however, is like the nature–nurture conflict, ultimately bound to end in stalemate. Nonetheless, in order properly to understand the intricacies of leadership we have to look at the person–situation interface (Bass, 1981).

LEADERS AND THEIR FOLLOWERS

Willner (1984) explores some key issues about what happens between followers and leaders in her discussion of charismatic leadership. She suggests that many leader–follower relationships have the following properties:

- The leader is perceived by the followers as somehow superhuman.
- The followers blindly believe the leader's statements.
- The followers unconditionally comply with the leader's directives for action.
- The followers give the leader unqualified emotional support (p. 8).

Although Willner is referring to truly transformational leaders (using examples from Third World countries) such factors as 'leader-image,' idea acceptance, compliance, and emotional commitment seem to play a significant role in any form of leadership.

WHAT MAKES AN EFFECTIVE LEADER?

A few decades ago, Charles de Gaulle, a transformational leader himself, wrote:

> '... [T]here can be no prestige without mystery, for familiarity breeds contempt ... In the designs, the demeanor and the mental operations of a leader there must be always a 'something' which others cannot altogether fathom, which puzzles them, stirs them, and rivets their attention ... if one is to influence men's minds, one must observe them carefully and make it clear that each has been marked out from among his fellows ...
>
> This attitude of reserve demands, as a rule, a corresponding economy of words and gestures ... There would even seem to be some relationship between a man's inner force and his outward seeming ... the great leaders have always carefully stage-managed their effects.'
>
> *(De Gaulle, 1975, pp. 58–59).*

De Gaulle also lists other characteristics of leadership:

- 'a readiness to launch great undertakings and a determination to see things through to the end' (p. 46).
- the leader 'must aim high, show that he has vision, act on the grand scale' (p. 64).
- the effective leader needs to be well informed of the details of specific situations and not just think in abstractions or vague, generalized theories (p. 80).
- a leader 'must outbid his rival in self-confidence' (p. 140).

Charles de Gaulle knew what he was talking about—he had ample opportunity to test out his ideas. His perception of leadership didn't allow for mediocrity. He himself was a charismatic leader (Weber, 1964), a type that holds a spellbinding power over his followers, a type that becomes a transforming agent, able to 'shape and alter and elevate the motives and values and goals of followers' (MacGregor Burns, 1978).

Many years of training as a soldier and resistance fighter prepared De Gaulle for his role as France's guide and head of state. When the opportunity eventually came for power, he rose to the occasion. De Gaulle was a master in the influence game, knowing how to sustain his power base through direct, dramatic appeals to the people. Crisis management—for example, his handling of the Algerian situation—was his forte. He was decisive and courageous in difficult situations. In spite of the damage to their self-esteem that the loss of this long-cherished dominion entailed for the French, De Gaulle was able to unite the nation behind him. His style, his skills in stagecraft and the self-confidence he radiated made many of his otherwise highly unpopular actions palatable.

When we analyze his statements carefully we can discern a number of themes, which are also echoed by other leaders in action.

The 'dream'

As de Gaulle indicated, effective leaders have a vision of the future that they make highly compelling to others. They are extremely effective in providing focus. De Gaulle was not alone in doing so. For example, we have Franklin Delano Roosevelt, whose concept of the 'New Deal' became his weapon against the Great Depression in the 1930s. Adolf Hitler had a vision of a new Germany, described in his autobiography *Mein Kampf*, where he predicts the coming of the Thousand-Year Reich. Mohandas Gandhi imagined an independent India after the British where Hindus and Moslems would live in harmony. Martin Luther King Jr's 'dream' of harmony between blacks and whites was of a similar visionary nature. More recently, we have seen Barack Obama on stage, articulating impassionedly that 'A new era of engagement has begun ... It is time for America to lead again.' In describing their dreams, leaders often use the imagery of a journey: of a path to follow, or of being at a crossroads.

Each of these leaders' magnificent obsessions created a focus that enabled them to mobilize their followers to pursue a course of action to its successful conclusion. Such leaders seem to be able to mold the images in their internal, private world in such a way that these become acceptable to the external, public stage. What differentiates these people from others is that they possess starkly pronounced internal scripts (mental codes for representing experiences) that guide their behavior and that can be transmitted to their followers in such a way that they create a shared reality (Kets de Vries and Miller, 1984; Zaleznik and Kets de Vries, 1985; Kets de Vries, 2009). We can hypothesize that these scripts are based on the way these individuals interpret early relationships of the self with significant others. They become the 'sustaining myth' or set of myths, which gives the people composing the societies a sense of what it means to be a member. Eventually such scripts provide the building blocks for action.

General Douglas MacArthur is a good case in point. Reading his *Reminiscences* we realize the extent to which his internal world was populated with the heroic images of his grandfather, father, and older brother. His life's task became to emulate a father described by his comrades in arms as 'magnificent ... afraid of nothing ... who would fight a pack of tigers in the jungle ... who became the hero of the regiment' (MacArthur, 1964, p. 9). Such exalted imagery was combined with the confidence created by a mother who would tell him: 'You'll win if you don't lose your nerve. You must believe in yourself ... or no one else will believe in you. Be self-confident, self-reliant, and even if you don't make it, you will know you have done your best' (MacArthur, 1964, p. 18). With such a support system of reliable, dependable figures incorporated in his inner world, it's no wonder that MacArthur became the leader he was. Moreover, and not surprisingly in the light of his specific background, part of his destiny was 'to return' and be the liberator of the Philippines (a country that his father had once ruled as governor general) from its Japanese invaders.

In the business realm, we can observe similar processes at work. For example, a major theme in car manufacturer Henry Ford's 'inner world' was to engage—in a psychological sense—in some form of reparative effort vis-à-vis the farmer. The 'vehicle' for achieving this became the Model T, the 'farmer's car' (Jardim, 1970). The dream of DeWitt Wallace, the founder of *Reader's Digest,* once the world's most widely read magazine, was to present books and articles in a simplified form to uplift and ameliorate the lives of its readers. Walt Disney had a vision of family togetherness through wholesome entertainment for the entire family.

Manipulation of symbols

Another essential part of effective leadership is communication. Leaders need to be able to articulate their dreams to their followers. They often do this through evoking and emulating historical and mythological figures, tapping into people's cultural roots and through ceremonies, symbols, and settings. Here leadership and stagecraft join forces. Effective leaders possess great oratorical skills and know how to make use of humor, irony, and colloquialisms. What differentiates effective leaders from others is that they know how to talk directly to their listeners' unconscious, employing figurative language such as similes and metaphors, which facilitates identification by their followers. Their sense of timing often seems uncanny. They are masters in the creation of suspense.

The unsettling emotional nature of these symbolic methods of communication induces reactions of dependency, regression, and transference in their followers (Kets de Vries and Miller, 1984; Kets de Vries, 2006). Leaders, in one way or another, create in their followers a desire and need to be taken care of. Having raised certain expectations, they then seem to be the logical caretakers to fulfill these.

Leaders reawaken past relationships of dominance and submission. In this transferential process significant individuals from childhood become intertwined with contemporary figures. The leader becomes the depository of the followers' fantasies. And even incompetent leaders are often given the benefit of the doubt and thus profit from this psychological process.

Freud compared the peculiar psychological relationship between leaders and followers with that of a hypnotist and his subject (Freud, 1921, p. 81). Dialogues between these two parties typically involve simplification, stark contrast and extremes; dramatization is essential. Truly effective leaders know how to use simple language so their message comes across easily.

We can see how the rhetoric of political leaders like Winston Churchill ('I have nothing to offer but blood, toil, tears, and sweat') and John Kennedy ('Ask not what your country can do for you; ask what you can do for you country') could motivate their audience.

On a less grandiose scale, business leaders use comparable imagery. The first Henry Ford's decision to pay his workers five dollars a day (almost double the existing rate of pay) temporarily made him the savior of the working man. IBM's real founder Thomas Watson Sr's almost religious attention to service became legendary. The builder of McDonald's, Ray Kroc, would stress the themes of quality, service, cleanliness, and value.

Emotional empathy

The ability to summon positive emotions, especially during periods of intense stress, lies at the heart of effective leadership. Effective leaders possess great interpersonal skills: not only are they master communicators on mass scale but also at a more intimate level. Usually it has been the support of a core group of dedicated followers that helps them reach their position of power. Those who rise to the top are very skilled in influencing, controlling, and manipulating their followers. They seem to be able to deal with emotionally tough situations. They figure out what kind of guidance their key people need. They are able to interpret what drives them. They are also capable of providing holding environments, managing to contain their followers' emotions. The more effective leaders are very sensitive to other people and possess the ability to listen, and to understand others' points of view. As McCall, Morgan, and Lombardo (1983) discovered in their findings on successful and unsuccessful business leaders, 'the most frequent cause for derailment (along the path to the executive suite) was insensitivity to other people' (p. 28). In their study, ineffective leaders turned out to be the ones who were abrasive, intimidating, and unwilling to participate in the give and take of the influence game. My observations of leadership pathology point in the same direction (Kets de Vries, 2006).

Network building activity

Effective leaders are also masters at creating and maintaining organizational networks for interacting with and monitoring the activities of their key subordinates (Kotter, 1982; Luthans, Rosenkrantz, and Hennessey, 1985). They are very aware of those on whom they are dependent, and vice versa, and manage their relationships with them very carefully. Hiring, firing, and promoting are their network maintenance tools. The resource-allocation process, including the management of information, is another way of fostering these interdependencies.

Franklin Delano Roosevelt's skills in network building and manipulation were legendary. One of the first things he did after taking office was to develop an organizational intelligence system to prevent him from becoming a captive of the complex official bureaucracy of Washington. A well-known analyst of his presidency, Richard Neustadt, recorded:

> Not only did he keep his organization overlapping and divide authority among them, but he also tended to put men of clashing temperaments, outlooks, ideas, in charge of them. Competitive personalities mixed with competing jurisdictions was Roosevelt's formula for putting pressure on himself, for making his subordinates push up to him the choices they could not take for themselves. It also made them advertise their punches; their quarrels provided him with not only heat but information ...
> *(Neustadt, 1960, pp. 157–158.)*

Sense-making

The ability of effective leaders to organize patterns and relationships among seemingly disjointed events has repeatedly been emphasized

(Isenberg, 1984). Leaders are masters of sense-making, of bringing order to the chaos that tends to surround them. Effective decision-makers possess the cognitive ability to sort relevant from irrelevant information. They also know how to prevent themselves being swamped by sensory and informational overloads They are what have been called 'reducers' (as opposed to 'augmenters'), that is, they have the ability to limit the degree to which stimulation impinges on them (Lipowski, 1975). This characteristic enables them to deal with complex, novel and interesting situations without impaired task performance, cognitive disorganization, or health problems (Petrie, 1967). They know how to weave connections through selective combination and selective comparison. This makes them highly skilled in putting together isolated pieces of information. Effective leaders are strong in the ability to manage conceptual complexity. They are also flexible in the cognitive differentiation and integration of information, so that data can be processed according to the needs of a situation (Suedfeld and Rank, 1976). If simple information processing is required, dissonant information will be rejected. But if the situation warrants it, effective leaders will integrate and combine multiple points of view simultaneously and look for novel solutions.

Many of the more effective business leaders whom I have encountered differ from other people in their tolerance for high levels of arousal. To paraphrase Kipling, they keep their head when all about them are losing theirs. They deal successfully with crisis situations without feeling overcommitted or experiencing a sense of discomfort and exhaustion.

Empowerment

Effective leaders communicate high-performance expectations to their followers and show confidence in their ability to meet them (House, 1977). They motivate their followers by making them feel significant. They know how to inspire them. Their high expectations seem to enhance their followers' sense of self-esteem and feelings of competence, influencing their effectiveness. Effective leaders know how to create commitment. By harnessing the energies of their followers and translating intention into sustained reality, they encourage them to attain unexpected results.

We don't have to look far to find examples in the political sphere of how to transcend followers' more pedestrian preoccupations. When Barack Obama won the Democratic presidential nomination in 2008, his reiteration of one simple phrase—'Yes, we can!'—in reference to contemporary challenges and difficulties in the US, was widely inspirational. Many years before, one of his predecessors, John Kennedy, had induced the same effect in his listeners: 'We stand today on the edge of a new frontier.' Charles de Gaulle expressed the same kind of confidence in his followers when he stated at the beginning of World War II that 'France has lost the battle but she has not lost the war.' More than a hundred years before him, his predecessor Napoleon Bonaparte proclaimed confidently, 'Every French soldier carries in his cartridge-pouch the baton of the marshal of France.' What all these leaders had in common was the ability to create an atmosphere of excitement, enthusiasm, and motivation among their followers. They knew how to get the best out of their followers; how to create performance beyond expectations.

Competence

Stogdill's Handbook of Leadership (Bass, 1981) lists technical skills as a very important factor in effective leadership. Leaders need to be familiar with the substance of the matter—they have to know what they are talking about. If not, they will quickly lose credibility. Winging it will only work for so long. Not only is it essential that leaders recognize the big picture, they also need to be familiar with the specifics of the situation: this will enable them to be realistic in making recommendations. Some familiarity is therefore needed with the exact nature of the work that has to be done.

Lee Iacocca, former chairman of the Chrysler Corporation, has been is a good example. In the 1980s, his dramatic skills were essential in reviving the ailing corporation (Iacocca appeared in the company's TV advertisements and even in popular entertainment programs). Without them, the company would not have been given financial assistance from the government, received backing from the unions to accept a pay cut, or persuaded consumers to buy their cars. One other key factor, however, was his intimate familiarity with the ins and outs of the car industry. He knew what it meant to build an automobile. He understood how different segments of the production process interacted. He knew how to use control systems to pull together the disparate fiefdoms that made up Chrysler. It was this specific knowledge that made him so effective when articulating his vision about organizational renewal. Iacocca left the company in 1992. Unfortunately, since then, much water has passed under the bridge—and not to the benefit of Chrysler.

Hardiness, perseverance, and consistency

To be a leader one definitely requires a certain amount of resilience or 'hardiness' (Kobasa, 1979) as considerable endurance is needed to cope with the stresses and strains of a rapidly changing environment. Effective leaders know how to manage stress, and what differentiates these people from others is that they possess a positive and stable self-image (Kets de Vries and Miller, 1987). They firmly believe that they can control what affects their life (Rotter, 1966) and see change as a challenge (Kobasa, 1979).

Alongside hardiness come perseverance and consistency. As has been said, it is hard to beat a person who never gives up. True leaders do not give up easily; they keep on trying and insisting that their demands are met. They will stick to their original objective despite all the difficulties. At times, their preoccupations can make them sound like a broken record but they are convinced that their persistence will eventually bear fruit. Furthermore, if required, they are prepared to sit and wait for the right moment. The salient themes in their inner scripts keep them going. They emanate integrity and trust. Their actions are characterized by consistency and predictability, making it easier for others to work with them.

In the life histories of many entrepreneurs and builders of institutions, the two factors of consistency and perseverance appear over and over again. In his memoirs, the architect of European integration, Jean Monnet, wrote:

> I am not an optimist. I am simply persistent. If action is necessary, how can one say that it is impossible, so long as one has not tried it? ... Events that strike me and occupy my thoughts lead me to general conclusions about what has to be done... I can wait a long time for the right moment. In Cognac, they are good at waiting. It is the only way to make good brandy.
>
> *(Monnet, 1976, p. 44.)*

William DeWitt Wallace, the founder of *Reader's Digest* is an example of this from the business world. Although he met with general discouragement for his particular formula for a magazine, his persistence made his venture an ultimate success. And in a similar vein, it took a long time for distributors to become interested in Walt Disney's animated mouse. Only after he added sound to his first two rejected mouse films did he grab their attention. However, persistence, consistency, and hardiness alone are not good enough; they have to be combined with action, or enactment.

Enactment

Many people have lots of ideas, but that is the stage at which they stay—there's no progression from idea to implementation. As we all know, the road to hell is paved with good intentions. But effective leaders are different. They go one step further; they are the doers, creating their own environment (Weick, 1979). Such people have a great ability to initiate and sustain interaction with others. They know how to come up with new ideas and make them viable.

Enactment is triggered by intense motivation to achieve, the need to do something better than has been done before. This high need for achievement is very characteristic of effective leaders, who strive to make things happen, and have strong entrepreneurial talents. They are willing to take calculated risks. However, they are also capable of recognizing when risk-taking can become excessive (McClelland, 1961).

CONCLUSIONS

In this chapter, I have aimed to delineate some of the major qualities that have to be taken into consideration in distinguishing effective leadership. Although I acknowledge the importance of social setting, and the psychology of followers, here I have not considered these dimensions.

Leaders are symbols. They are outlets of identification for their followers and will serve as scapegoats when things go wrong. Throughout history, we can observe the repeated rise and fall of leaders. In this interactive process, power becomes the binding force between leaders and followers, the currency on which most of these relationships will depend. Unfortunately, effective leadership and the wise exercise of power do not necessarily go together. In the leader–follower dialogue, regressive group pressure and delusions of grandeur are always present and may lead to the abuse of power and eventually to the leader's fall. The truly effective leader, however, is the one who knows how to balance reflection and action by using self-insight as a restraining force when the sirens of power start singing. And to quote Lao Tsu, 'He who controls others may be powerful, but he who has mastered himself is mightier still.'

CHAPTER 3

THE DANCE OF LEADERS AND FOLLOWERS[1]

'Hallo!' said Piglet, 'what are you doing?'
'Hunting,' said Pooh.
'Hunting what?'
'Tracking something,' said Winnie-the-Pooh very mysteriously.
'Tracking what?' said Piglet, coming closer.
'That's just what I ask myself. I ask myself, What?'
'What do you think you'll answer?'
'I shall have to wait until I catch up with it,' said Winnie-the-Pooh.

—*A. A. Milne,* **Winnie-the-Pooh**

On August 24, 1994, Jeffrey Katzenberg, head of Walt Disney Studios, resigned. His acrimonious departure came as a shock after his 18-year collaborative relationship with Michael Eisner, the chairman of Disney. Katzenberg's defection sent ripples through the entertainment industry and became front page news. Most industry analysts saw Katzenberg's exit as a major loss to the company. He was perceived as the architect of a whole series of highly successful animated films (including the fabulously profitable *Lion King*), which were the primary engine for Disney's growth. Katzenberg's departure endangered a smooth succession process, following the accidental death of company president Frank Welch (particularly in light of the fact that Eisner had recently had a quadruple coronary bypass operation). In addition, Katzenberg soon became a partner in a new company called DreamWorks SKG, creating a serious competitor for Disney (Auletta, 1994; Huy, 1995).

[1] Part of this material has appeared in Kets de Vries, Manfred F.R. (1999) 'What's Playing in the Organizational Theatre? Collusive Relationships in Management,' *Human Relations*, 52 (6), 745–773.

Ten years earlier in 1984, after leaving Paramount together, Eisner and Katzenberg had taken over a moribund Disney that had relatively disappointing revenues of $1.4 billion. By 1993, Disney's revenues had reached the level of $8.5 billion. Pretax profits of the film studio (which was Katzenberg's responsibility) had risen from $2 million in 1984 to about $800 million in 1994. No film studio had reported greater profits over the previous decade. Given Disney's financial success, the Eisner-Katzenberg break-up does not seem to have been a simple question of finance but rather one where human factors played an important role. What went wrong with the chemistry between the two men? What soured their 18-year collaboration? What really happened?

The story of the break-up has all the elements of a marriage gone bad. In this messy public divorce it became hard to know what was reality. Observers took sides and depending on their perspective assigned one man the villain's role and the other the hero's. Each protagonist was accused of being an abrasive megalomaniac by the other's supporters. Some people felt that Katzenberg was claiming undeserved credit for Disney's success, while others faulted Eisner for only tolerating yes-men and leading the company in a disastrous direction.

Going beyond fault-finding, the conjecture can be made that the manifest and latent demands of the relationship seemed to have gotten out of sync. The various descriptions of the 'divorce' make it sound like a tale of dependence and counterdependence, autonomy and control, narcissism and emotions. It appeared that as long as both parties played their appropriate roles in the partnership a kind of equilibrium existed. But when Katzenberg tried to change that situation and assert himself, requesting the number two job in the organization (after Frank Welch's death), Eisner's hackles seemed to rise.

According to people familiar with the two protagonists, Eisner had always remained rather aloof toward his star performer. These observers would remark that Eisner was slow to give credit for a job well done. Even worse, some noted that he seemed to have become more arrogant and tougher over the years. They suggested that he liked keeping Katzenberg in the one-down position, always searching for approval, playing the role of supplicant. On the other hand, others commented that Katzenberg was not exactly Mr Nice Guy. According to them he had a reputation for playing hardball, but had started trying to change his image by presenting a more softened, conciliatory side at times (Grover, 1994).

From the information given we can hypothesize that when Katzenberg made it clear to Eisner that he wanted to be a more equal partner, the equilibrium seemed to be shaken. Apparently, Eisner was not prepared to give in to Katzenberg's demands. It looked like a change in their working relationship was unacceptable to Eisner; he appeared unwilling to compromise. He may have felt that Katzenberg had become too pushy. Whatever the 'glue' had been between the two of them, it seemed to be no longer holding.

Unfortunately, we may postulate that neither parties ever understood the real nature of this 'glue.' In spite of the many years that they worked together, they appeared to have very little insight about their interpersonal chemistry. They didn't seem to be very clear about their roles. Thus the 'tragedy' ran its inevitable course. As Ken Auletta wrote in the *New Yorker*, 'Katzenberg left a job that he loved and Disney lost a talented executive that it didn't want to lose. Primal forces were at work, which could not be controlled by the mind' (page 69).

Who was to blame? Who was the major culprit? Could the outcome have been avoided? What can be said about the roles Eisner and Katzenberg played in this drama? What kind of psychodynamic forces were at play?

In a fundamental way, we are all actors. We are all on stage. We love playing theater, and what is more, we like to get others involved in our plays. Wherever we look around us, we can see various cameo performances: comedies, tragedies, romances—you name it! This is part and parcel of daily functioning in both private and organizational life.

Within organizations, as in private life, great masterpieces are continuously being performed. Organizational leaders—Disney is a good example—are partially in the theater business. As I mentioned in Chapter 2, some form of play-acting is an important part of their job. It is a way of influencing their subordinates. Leaders have to inspire their followers, get them to share their vision of where the company should be going, and enlist their help in enacting the leaders' ideas. To accomplish those tasks, leaders find that a dose of impression management is essential. They need their subordinates to play along, to help them to get things done.

Spontaneous as all these forms of interaction between senior executives and their subordinates (or even colleagues) may appear, the truth of the matter can be quite different. Some of the 'plays' we witness at the office are not as spontaneous as they seem at first glance. Perceptive observers will soon notice that there is a certain regularity to some of these superior-subordinate encounters. Closer scrutiny reveals that the ways particular superiors and subordinates deal with each other may fall into specific set patterns—ways of interacting that tend to harden over time. Moreover, the participants in these organizational psychodramas sometimes become stuck in a vicious circle of repetitive behavior pat-

terns that can contribute to various forms of organizational malfunctioning. This is not, of course, to imply that there are no constructive
interpersonal operational modes. In most office relationships, executives'
ways of interacting with each other, if occasionally stressful, lead to
further maturation, creativity, peak experiences or flow, transformation,
and change; many relationships possess the qualities of intimacy and
autonomy that set the stage for further development. But in some
situations this is not the case.

In this chapter, I look at some of the collusive interaction patterns
that can be found in organizations. To understand the origin of these
sorts of patterns, I use concepts taken from psychodynamically oriented
couple therapy and identify the most frequent types of collusions and
their consequences, taking different character types as points of departure (Reich, 1949; Shapiro, 1965; Storr, 1979; Millon, 1981; Kets de
Vries and Perzow, 1991; McWilliams, 1994). Finally, I will make some
observations about how to recognize and manage these dysfunctional
behavior patterns.

THE MESHING OF FANTASIES

Collusive arrangements begin with a sort of 'courtship' during which
the future partners assess each other's suitability for these projective
processes. In organizational terms this courtship display is acted out
during the selection and socialization process of new people into the
organization. Training and development programs, during which
employee behavior is shaped, as well as a person's initial entry into an
organization, are important occasions for assessing a newcomer's preparedness to participate in the particular interaction patterns enacted by the
key players in the organization—the actors who set the tone and define
the corporate culture. During this time of courtship, both parties,
through the process of projective identification (as described in Chapter
1), give off conscious or unconscious signals that are received by the
other party. Each partner may recognize in the other disowned, denied,
or projected parts of the self; each searches the other for an (unconscious)
preparedness to participate in the prevailing 'script.' Provisionally, the
question explored is to what extent each of the players will be a good
'container' for the other's projective identifications. The exact content
of this script, however, is not openly expressed. The signs given are much
more subtle. But these tentative feelers often constitute the beginning
of a kind of secret alliance or collusion. These are times of exploration during which the person–organization fit is being determined.

Newcomers who do not have the 'right' personality makeup will eventually have no choice but to leave the organization.

The word 'collusion' is used to signify the way in which the players of these games become stuck in these mutual projective identifications that may hamper future growth and development. Collusion in this context should be understood as an out-of-awareness, repetitive pattern of interaction between people, instigated and maintained in such a way as to manage and master anxiety about certain past conflictual experiences. The psychiatrist Jürg Willi defines the collusion principle as 'the unconscious interplay of two partners who are looking for each other in the hope of coming to terms *together* with those conflicts and frustrations in their lives which they have not yet managed to resolve' (1982, Preface).

These collusions, which can be seen as a neurotic form of collaboration, often take up an enormous amount of psychic energy. They occur when certain behavior patterns resonate between the partners in the play. Usually, one of the partners keeps the other bound to a set of complementary reactions. There is a great insistence to get from the other what the initiating partner feels is missing inside him- or herself. Thus, through this process of projective identification, the initiator uses the partner as a vehicle for those aspects of his or her own personality that the initiator would like to integrate within him- or herself. And in organizations—given the dynamics of power—employees who are not willing to 'play' with the senior executive are not likely to last.

Such unhealthy collusions contrast sharply with more playful encounters that leave both parties a considerable amount of transitional space where new learning can take place and where new solutions to problems can be discovered (Winnicott, 1975). In the latter situations, the outcome is not predetermined; the players do not find themselves stuck in frozen positions; new permutations and combinations are possible. The partners are involved in a process of further growth and development.

Usually, the invitation to participate in collusive activities operates at three different levels of awareness. The first level is the one most often verbalized. At a person's entry into an organization, much effort is exerted by the organization to make the new employee aware of the unique features of the prevailing corporate culture: its preferred interpersonal style and way of relating to others. More specifically, an attempt is made to articulate the kind of partnership arrangement the person will be subjected to. This verbalization does not always mean that the receiver truly understands the message, of course. The process of projective identification is prone to distortion. There can be a substantial difference between one's understanding of such a message at a cognitive level and one's understanding at an emotional level. As a consequence, the new person does not always react as expected to the signals given.

At the next level of awareness, one of the parties is conscious (at least subliminally) of the 'contract'—what it means to be associated with the other—but has not articulated it for fear of a negative reaction. Some aspects of the expected role will come into question, such as who will be in power and control, what is going to be the degree of closeness versus distance, and who will play the more active and who will play the more passive role. Only gradually is the other party made aware of what 'signing up' is all about.

The last level of the 'contract' contains those aspects that are mostly completely outside conscious awareness. Occasionally, the themes in each party's inner theater that will dominate the relationship in the future will be close to the surface, giving the parties in question a fleeting sense of the prevailing themes; however, those will quickly be pushed aside. For example, the 'contract' may concern unexpressed, almost ritualistic wishes centered around dependent, narcissistic, or sadistic needs. At this level, the many subtleties of the 'script' specifying how the parties will relate to each other come to the fore. No longer is it a question of the generalities of the 'play'; now an exact description of each person's role during the different acts is outlined. Here repetition plays a major role as disavowed, denied, or projected parts of the self based on unresolved childhood conflicts come to dominate the relationship.

Given the existence of these three levels of awareness, it will not come as a surprise that the partners who become actors in these dysfunctional 'plays' may not initially be completely cognizant (in spite of the process of projective identification) of what they are getting into. Yet before long, the participants may find themselves stuck in a vicious circle, caught up in a game that seems interminable.

We may observe how a kind of mental gridlock occurs in collusive situations as dysfunctional interaction patterns follow the same themes and are played out according to specific rules. Certain acts tend to be repeated over and over again. The participants seem to be trapped in a kind of 'parasitic' bond symptomizing arrested development (McDougall, 1985). A deconstruction of these repetitive theater pieces indicates that the parties involved are trying to get from each other what they lacked at an earlier, critical point in their development.

The cast of characters in these repetitive plays is carefully preselected. There appears to be a kind of fatal attraction between certain types of people, given their ability to complement each other in these performances. In such collusive situations, the players seem to be inextricably tied to one another. Although they may superficially act as polar opposites of each other, deep down they share a similar kind of conflict. One person finds an unconscious sounding board in the other. The roles people play in these games constantly oscillate. The more passive a position one of the parties takes, the more active the other party will be; thus if the initially passive party becomes more active, passivity will increase in the partner. It seems that an equilibrium has to be maintained, whatever the costs may be.

Soon the dysfunctional aspects of these kinds of interchanges become quite obvious. The players may become so involved in destructive fighting rituals that take a considerable amount of time and energy that there is very little left for constructive, creative work. In such instances there is no free interplay between the partners. They have become stuck in games without end.

The strikingly irrational quality to these interaction patterns is the giveaway that we are dealing with deep-seated, unresolved childhood experiences and conflicts. The players lack the ability to see their relationship objectively. They do not know how to restructure or get out of it. Resolution of these peculiar interpersonal scripts becomes particularly difficult because of the presence of irrational fears and conflicts that have deep-seated, transferential roots.

Given the fact that much of this sort of behavior is unconscious, we should not be surprised that the actors will vehemently deny that games are being played when asked about a relationship. Game-playing is a deeply suppressed part of their personality. But if we make the effort to delve a little bit deeper, we soon find out that there is a specific division of labor in these collusions. Such an exploration also reveals in each party an underlying wish that, with the help of the other, his or her own deep-rooted conflicts can be resolved.

The drama and the strain that these dysfunctional forms of interaction may cause can be substantial. Executives working under collusive conditions often end up suffering from various kinds of stress disorders— depression, insomnia, irritability, outbursts of anger, and psychosomatic complaints (i.e., stomach problems, headaches, allergies) are the most frequent. Worse, other executives may become contaminated by the collusive arrangements, leading to an enormous amount of tension in the organization which will have an effect on the success of the company. When it comes to looking for the culprit among the main parties in the plot, however, it is difficult to talk in terms of victim and victimizer; both 'actors' are addressing unconscious needs. Victim or victimizer seems a valid distinction when such a relationship is looked at from the outside, but in fact—closer investigation reveals that both parties are attracted to the plot and get some form of enjoyment from it. After all, it takes two to tango.

METHODOLOGY

The kinds of collusive interpersonal relationships I am referring to are most clearly visible within marriages. Couple therapists such as Whitaker (1958), Ackerman (1958), Dicks (1967), Minuchin (1974), Strean (1985), Sharpe (1981, 1992), Sager (1991), Lachkar (1992), Ruszczynski (1993, 1995), and particularly Willi (1984) have written extensively on destructive collusive arrangements. I have discovered in my own research on the relationship between personality, leadership style, organizational culture, strategy, and organizational structure that some of their findings are equally applicable to organizational settings—though perhaps not of the same intensity there (Kets de Vries and Miller, 1984, 1987; Kets de Vries, 1989, 1991, 1993, 1995, 2001, 2006). Consequently, concepts from couple therapy will be applied in this chapter to the study of superior-subordinate relationships in organizations.

To understand the underlying scripts that determine these collusive arrangements, we have to find out what is happening in the 'inner theater' of the executives involved. Because this inner theater organizes the way information is processed and acted upon in interpersonal situations, we have to be something of an organizational detective in our efforts to decipher 'deep' structure (Geertz, 1973, 1983; Luborsky, Crits-Christoph, Minz, and Auerbach, 1988; Luborsky, 1990; Horowitz, 1991; Kets de Vries, 2006). We have to be alert to underlying themes, hidden agendas, meanings behind metaphors used, reasons for the selection of certain words, and deeper implications of certain behaviors and activities of the individual in question.

The ability to decipher these deeper motives—to tease out the emotional, cognitive, and behavioral components of the inner scripts of executives—requires the capacity to 'listen with the third ear,' a skill I will describe in more detail in Chapter 4. Listening with the third ear implies a certain level of emotional intelligence—that is, an awareness of our own feelings, the knowledge and skill to handle those feelings, and an appreciation of emotions in other people (empathy and intuition). It also implies the ability to recognize affective contagion (projective identification processes in action) and make sense out of these elusive, transferred, nonverbal signals. Moreover, it requires the capacity to deconstruct and find the deeper meaning in the complex relational processes that take place in any human encounter.

In this chapter, I address some more prominent collusive relationships, drawing on a study of 200 senior executives operating mainly in
the information technology, pharmaceutical, and banking sectors. Much
has been said about the behavior of lower-level employees, but top
executives wield enormous power in organizations: I wanted to study
the relationship between top executives and their immediate subordinates. (Given the universality of personality patterns, however, most of
these findings would also apply to relationships among lower-level
employees.) Many of the participants in the study were CEOs of their
companies. Many had enrolled in a top executive leadership seminar at
INSEAD, the objective of which was to provide them with a better
understanding of their leadership style, help them develop their emotional intelligence, and have a better appreciation of the effect they had
on other people. An additional source of data about collusive patterns
was a number of action research projects in global companies interested
in corporate transformation (one of the most important desired outcomes
was mindset change among their executives). These interventions also
gave opportunities for personal interviews and observing some of these
executives in action. The interviews with individual participants from
both of these sources were structured around a verbalization of each
executive's life history, major relationships—personal and professional—
key events, and knotty organizational issues.

Because of the nature of the INSEAD seminar and the time spent
with the senior executives at this seminar (three periods of five days and
one of four over a year's duration), it was possible (in contrast to more
traditional interview formats) to engage in a deep analysis of each individual's motives, drives, needs, wishes, and fantasies. Since participation
in the leadership seminar was voluntary, most of the participants were
highly motivated to engage in such a process of mutual inquiry. To
control for countertransference reactions (an interviewer's transferential
biases), all discussions were facilitated by two people to enable a reality
check of what was happening during the process.

Most of these executives were the hub of a set of relationships.
During the discussions, attention was paid to the most prominent of
these relationships. It appeared that the majority of these relationships
were collusion-free. Each party's individuality seemed to be preserved.
However, these executives described a certain number of additional
relationships as characterized by various degrees of enmeshment. These
entanglements were then explored further in the discussions. It will not
come as a surprise (given the importance of the narcissistic dimension
in leadership) that more than half of the collusive arrangements were
primarily of a narcissistic nature. Next in frequency were interaction

patterns of a controlling type, to be followed by paranoid, and finally sadomasochistic enmeshments. Given the pre-eminence of narcissistic enmeshments, these controlling, paranoid, and sadomasochistic relationship patterns could, at times, be enveloped in a narcissistic collusion.

For each type of collusive arrangement seen in these executives—and discussed below—I will give an example of a 'script' and present some of the major themes in the 'play' that tied both parties together. I will also make some comments about the characterological development of the executives who participated in these enmeshed relationships. I must stress that this list of dyadic relationships is not exhaustive. I have listed only the most frequently encountered patterns. Other permutations and combinations are possible.

TYPES OF COLLUSION

The narcissistic collusion

Subordinate: I very much enjoyed your presentation about the new direction our company should be going. You were great!

Superior: You really liked the way I made my presentation? Was my position made quite clear?

Subordinate: Very much so. You really dazzled all the others with your logic. As a matter of fact, the others were nowhere; they were lagging far behind you in their thought processes; they are out of it as far as knowing where our industry is going. I'd like to ask you if I could help you in developing this new strategic marketing plan you mentioned in your presentation. It would be such a great learning experience. I'd very much like to be part of this project. I know I have a lot to learn. You can teach me a lot.

Superior: What makes you say so?

Subordinate: Everyone knows that you are the best in the business. You are the one who really sets the rules for this industry.

Superior: You really think so?

The most common form of 'play' revealed through the interviews—the above script is a good example—was the narcissistic collusion. Although there were many variations on the narcissistic theme, closer analysis revealed that the basic message remained the same. The person in the one-down position in the script would say, 'I can't function without your assistance. I can't do it on my own. You're the world to me. You're the one who knows the way. You're the only one on whom I can rely. I'll do anything for you. I'll follow you anywhere.' Individuals with a great need for admiration and applause who preferred the more dominant position were only too happy to oblige and act as a counterpart to this subservient attitude. And their follow-me attitude—'All your worries will be over if you stick with me'—was all too eagerly listened to by the subordinates in question.

The intensity, and thus the danger, of narcissistic collusion seems to depend on how well the principal actors—those in the dominant position—are able to manage their strong narcissistic disposition. As I have indicated before, we all need a solid dose of narcissism for our day-to-day functioning; an excess, however, can become troublesome (Kets de Vries and Miller, 1985; Kets de Vries, 1995). Extreme narcissists are bound to create havoc. They are too preoccupied with wanting to be superior. And as many have learned from experience, they are strongly self-centered and self-referential, tend to show an overriding need for attention and admiration, are prone to grandiose fantasies, and often possess vindictive characteristics.

As I suggested in Chapter 1, excessive narcissism can be interpreted as a compensatory strategy for early disappointment in relationships. The predominant feeling of these people appears to be that a wrong has been done to them and that the world is therefore deeply indebted to them (Millon, 1981; Kohut, 1971, 1977; Kernberg, 1975, 1985; Masterson, 1981; American Psychiatric Association, 2000). They seem to possess a great hunger for recognition and experience a chronic need for external affirmation to feel internally secure. A cohesive sense of self appears to be absent, resulting in an imbalance in the psychic structure, incoherent behavior, and serious problems centered around self-esteem regulation. Extreme narcissists are always in search of an admiring audience to support their yearning for a grandiose self-image and to combat their feelings of helplessness and lack of self-worth.

Characteristic of these people is a history of parental overstimulation, understimulation, or non-integrative, inconsistent intervention during the early period of development (Kohut, 1974; Miller, 1975; Kets de Vries, 1989). Some of them may have been (unconsciously) exploited by their caretakers for the maintenance of the caretakers' own self-esteem; they may have been forced to become narcissistic extensions of these caretakers, assisting them in their own search for admiration and greatness. The strong concentration of such caretakers on appearances and outward signs of achievement, and their disregard for their children's own personal feelings, may leave these people with a lack of an integrated sense of self; they remain confused about the life they are supposed to lead. They may end up not feeling comfortable in their own skin; many may never acquire a secure sense of inner value. The result may be an individual engaged in a lifelong compensatory struggle for self-assertion and self-expression.

When this kind of personality makeup predominates, it is not hard to predict the consequences as far as relationships with others are concerned. The outcome of this kind of dysfunctional upbringing is that the narcissist may fail to see the people around him or her as individuals in their own right, with demands of their own. In fact, it appears that the relationship between the narcissist and his or her admirers is not a relationship at all in the true sense of the word. In the same way he or she was 'used' by caretakers in the early years, the narcissistic individual considers other people as objects. They fall into the same category as a car, a horse, or a house: they may be used to show off; they are taken for granted; their only function is to act as accessories in the narcissist's pursuit of grandiosity.

It goes without saying that such a collusion will work only if the personality makeup of the two players is complementary. A requirement for the excessive narcissist, then, is a self-effacing quality in the other party—a readiness to offer continual, unconditional admiration. All attention has to be directed toward the narcissist. Nobody else is allowed to share the spotlight. Others are around to act as a positive, reflective mirror. They have to provide a lot of action in order to make the narcissistic party feel 'filled up' and able to overcome the inner emptiness he or she experiences. Those permitted to join in with the narcissist's play have to be prepared to remain in his or her shadow.

Often the person in the one-down position may suffer from a sense of inferiority and feelings of low self-esteem similar to those of the narcissist; but because of his or her past developmental history, the submissive party is used to deprecation. His or her dependency needs as a child may have been highly frustrated. He or she may have been brought up in a family where there was little love to go around. This background may have set the stage for a lifelong search for idealized figures to compensate for early emotional deprivation. Such individuals, with a predisposition toward self-subjugation, sacrifice, and self-compromisation, are often actively looking for others they can idealize as a way of boosting their own deflated sense of self-esteem. These people seem to make desperate efforts to counteract their internal anxieties and to feel safer by attaching themselves to someone who is perceived as omnipotent and omniscient. Behind these primitive idealizations may be a 'golden fantasy' of having all one's needs met unconditionally (Smith, 1977). In an indirect way, these ideal-hungry personalities are trying to obtain narcissistic supplies by searching for others onto whom they can project their fantasies. Through idealization and identification, they obtain such supplies by proxy. Willi (1982) calls these people 'complementary narcissists.' They seem to be trying to appropriate an idealized self from the partner.

Apart from complementary narcissists—people who act as a mirror image for active narcissists—there is another group of people likely to join a collusive, narcissistic arrangement. These are individuals with a dependent personality makeup (Storr, 1979; Millon, 1996). Due to excessive parental protection as developing children, these people may have failed to complete the process of separation-individuation (Mahler, Pine, and Bergman, 1975; Storr, 1979). They may have never been allowed to become completely differentiated beings, to satisfy their own wishes, and to learn to fend for themselves. Common contributing factors are maternal overanxiousness, a tendency toward sickness in the child, and/or being an only child (with the parents' concomitant and excessive fear of loss).

Other permutations are possible, but the end result in each case (mirror-hungry as well as dependent individuals) may be a personality structure characterized by excessive neediness and submissiveness. These individuals seem to lack self-confidence. It is as if they possess a negative cognitive scheme; they may never feel good enough; they may belittle their own achievements. They seem to be unable to function without the help of others. They may have a very hard time doing things independently. Instead, they allow others to take responsibility for their lives. Consequently, these people may quickly attach themselves to others who can give them direction; with such direction, they seem to be able to function quite adequately. Their dependency needs may even take them so far as to agree to things that they know are wrong. Their uncritical acceptance of the behavior and actions of the other party—unrealistic though these may be—seems to be a price they are willing to pay for closeness. Evidently, more frightening than the prospect of doing something wrong is the thought of losing the support of, and being abandoned by, the people on whom they desperately rely for direction. Thus they willingly submit themselves to others at almost any price, often making extraordinary self-sacrifices in the process.

In their intrapsychic world, it appears that these subordinates see their own happiness as completely dependent on the person they admire. Their boss always seems to be the center of their attention and conversation. This intensive relationship may even become addictive. There appears to be an unspoken wish to merge, to become one with the other person. The underlying fantasy seems to be one of total symbiosis, a longing for an earlier, happier time when there was a real or imagined perfect relationship with the primary caretaker.

This sort of possessiveness on the part of admirers, however, does not always go down well with the narcissistic target. It may be anxiety-provoking. Being idealized and idolized can be a very stifling experience. The admirers' wish to protect their boss from what they see as inappropriate influences, their self-cast role as guardian of the person admired, can be experienced as a straitjacket. Attempts to shape their idol according to what they consider to be appropriate and inappropriate behavior may (rightfully) be seen as an intrusion. Furthermore, being put on a pedestal may often be only a prelude to being knocked off it. Living up to such exaggerated expectations is highly unrealistic. When the inevitable disappointment ensues, the idealized person generally becomes at least subliminally aware of the considerable amount of aggression that has been aroused in the admirer when the 'idol' who promised so much failed to deliver.

Many leaders fail to realize the extent to which they are caught up in collusive relationships. They do not sense the dangers of narcissistic patterns of interaction and consequently are swept away by their seductive forces.

Yet some leaders on the receiving end of idealization are not flattered; feeling like prisoners of their admirers' projected glorification, they may become angry and act aggressively. Such reactions, unfortunately, are often to no avail. Their unpleasantness seems to make little difference to the idolators, who are quick to find excuses for their idol's abrasive behavior. In many instances, the person abused by the frustrated leader seems willing to take anything, and what's more, even enjoys the subsequent state of martyrdom.

The controlling collusion

Superior: Remind me of when you plan to visit the country managers in Asia?

Subordinate: I'd like to go at the beginning of February.

Superior: I don't think that's such a good idea. That's more than two months from now; that's too far off. Given our planning cycle I want to have greater clarity about the figures for the budget proposals sooner. I would like you to go next week.

Subordinate:	I'll do what I can. I'll try to make the arrangements. You do know that it's their peak season now? It may not be the best time to come and hang over them—to pester them with questions. They may need more notice.
Superior:	I don't think so. They'd better cooperate. I need these figures. And the only way to get realistic ones is to visit them personally. Remember, you need to assert your authority, otherwise they try to pull the wool over your eyes. I want these figures by the end of the month. Things have been slipping too much in Asia.
Subordinate:	I very much agree. I have been thinking along similar lines.
Superior:	And one more thing. It has come to my attention that some people in the company are flying business class—using various pretexts that they need to do so. One lame argument is that they need to be fit on arrival, as if business class is the answer. I always flew coach when I was an area manager. And I was fit enough. Our expenses for travel are far too high. You know that it is company policy to fly coach.
Subordinate:	You have a point there. I'll go and make the travel arrangements. I'll warn the country managers that I am coming.

The next most common type of collusion identified from the discussions was one that can best be described as controlling. A common script adopted by the executive in the one-down position is as follows: 'I'll remain passive. I want you to take the active role. I want you to be in control and take a leadership position.' Given the dominant partner's need for power and control, it will come as no surprise that he or she is generally ready to oblige.

The origins of the development of a controlling personality, like those of the other personality types we have seen, can usually be found in a person's early childhood. Starting with exact feeding times, unduly rigid toilet training, and very specific sleeping hours, continuing with narrowly prescribed schedules for all aspects of functioning, control is the dominant theme of family life for compulsive people. The parents of these people may be unreasonably exacting, prematurely demanding, and/or condemnatory. Any spontaneous activity may be strongly discouraged for fear of the chaos and disorder it may bring. With this sort of background baggage, the control-driven individual derives self-esteem from meeting the harsh demands of the eventually internalized parents.

The predominant feature of the inner world of compulsively inclined people is their extreme reluctance to find themselves at the mercy of events; they want to master and control everything and everyone around them. The people who flourish in controlling collusions tend to have a personality pattern characterized by rigidity, perfectionism, punctuality, orderliness, meticulousness, and frugality. Other prevalent traits are a tendency toward hair-splitting discussions, an exaggerated sense of duty, and meticulous attention to detail. Compulsive individuals can be stubborn, obstinate, inhibited, and excessively tense. They lack adaptability, are overly conscientious, and love order and discipline (Reich, 1949; Shapiro, 1965; Salzman, 1980; Millon, 1981; Kets de Vries and Perzow, 1991). As members of an organization, they may become preoccupied with hierarchy, conformity, status, and adherence to formal codes, elaborate information systems, and tightly prescribed procedures and rules.

There are several varieties of controlling collusion. In one, both parties are obsessed by dominance and submission, with one partner taking the dominant role while the other adopts a submissive position. The person in the one-up position expects total obedience. Any initiative or autonomous act on the part of the other is unwelcome. This is a world of master and servant, superiority and inferiority, suppression and subordination. The need for order is paramount, founded on both partners' underlying anxiety that without it, chaos will follow, and that things will fall apart without strict authority and control. This type of controlling collusion is animated by each partner's continuous fear that the other partner may try to reverse the situation. In fact, the partner in the one-up position frequently has only the illusion of control. In reality, he or she is manipulated by the one-down partner, who is downplaying his or her own desire for control.

In the second type of controlling collusion, the one-down partner may have a more passive-aggressive character (Dean Parsons and Wicks, 1975; Millon, 1981; Kets de Vries, 1989; American Psychiatric Association, 2000). Passive-aggressive people are ambivalent about everything and cannot make up their mind whether to be dependent or independent, active or passive. They may give vent to their underlying aggression through indecisiveness, contradictory behavior, and conflicting attitudes. Afraid of showing open disagreement, they express indirect resistance to control through procrastination, dawdling, stubbornness, intentional inefficiency, and forgetfulness, masking their negative resistance with an aura of compliance and cordiality. For passive-aggressives, this kind of behavior may be the usual pattern for dealing with people in control.

Passive-aggressive behavior patterns often originate in a child's inability to assess clearly what others expect of them. Dominated by their parents' frequently erratic and conflicting demands, the child's life is characterized by inconsistency and the absence of clear indicators for appropriate conduct. As a result, the child fails to learn what kind of behavior pays off. Another contributing factor may be a perceived lack of control over decisions when growing up. Because of the domineering style of one or both parents, the child may have no option to say no, or openly to disagree with its parents. The child's own wishes are never taken into consideration. The solution to this problem over time, is to say yes but fail to do what is asked.

In the third type of controlling collusion, the dominant actor may be partnered by someone with a dependent personality, who submits gladly to the controlling figure. This match is generally the most complementary one, causing the least amount of friction between the partners, since both play a role that suits their respective personality structures. This third combination contrasts starkly with the other two, where the central action is a power struggle, fought by both partners to decide which is to be the leader and which the follower. The drama focuses on which of the two is going to take charge. The result may be endless power play, and a less than rosy future for the organization.

Many organizations are exceedingly rigid, centralized, and administrative and offer great opportunities for acting out the controlling collusion. Formalized controls check potential abuse of power; plans are often so explicit they exclude flexibility; strategy is narrowly focused and unadaptive. The consequences of this kind of emphasis on bureaucracy tend to be predictably dysfunctional. Such rigidity in outlook is bound to have serious consequences in a world characterized by rapid change. A lack of adaptability and an obsession with details can easily spell downfall for organizations run by people engaged in controlling collusions.

The paranoid collusion

Superior: I'm very unhappy with company sales, given the number of salespeople we have. I wonder how they spend their time. Do they give their full attention to the company or are some of them spending their time doing other things? Are they playing games on the Internet? They may even be downloading pornography. I'd really like to know. Wouldn't it be nice to have a way of monitoring the time they spend on different tasks through our com-

	puter system? It would help me to catch some of the abusers. Ethics be damned, we have a business to run. Why don't you look into that possibility?
Subordinate:	I'll contact the consulting firm we've been using for systems development immediately. I think they're the right people to answer such a question.
Superior:	One more thing, what is your opinion of Ms X? You think that head office really sent her here to help us with the feasibility study for a new plant? Or is that just a pretext? Could it be that the real reason she's here is to study our operations and recommend where we'll fit in the global company restructuring plan?
Subordinate:	You may have a point here. Many of the questions she's been asking were way beyond the scope of the plant study. I'll try to keep an eye on her and, if needed, do some damage control—feed her the kind of information that will give the people at head office no reason to single us out and make us a target in their downsizing efforts.

The script for both parties involved in a paranoid collusion reads, 'There's danger lurking out there. We can't really trust anybody. We have to be on our guard. Something's out to get us. We'd better stick together.'

The interpersonal theater of executives with paranoid tendencies is dominated by the thought that the world is a very threatening place. This leaves very little room for trust. People affected by such perceptions feel that they have to be continually prepared for imminent danger (Shapiro, 1965; Meissner, 1978; Millon, 1981). They live in chronic fear of bad surprises, against which they take unnecessary precautions. Hypervigilant, they appear to be constantly scanning the environment for confirmation of their suspicions. They may be overly concerned about others' hidden motives and intentions, leading to distorted perceptions, thoughts, and memories. They may see plots to harass and humiliate them everywhere. They take everything very personally, and are easily slighted. They can be extremely litigious.

This paranoid way of thinking and behaving may create a sense of isolation, but it also compels those afflicted by it to seek validation of their perceptions from others. They have an extraordinary wish to pull others into their games. Unfortunately, such tendencies are easily supported by reality: after all, if you look for it, you can usually find some confirmation of this kind of distorted view. People do unpleasant things to each other all the time. This state of mind, however, only reinforces an already dysfunctional situation.

A major contributing factor to paranoid thinking is a suspicious attitude among a developing child's principal caretakers, who may instill the belief that the outside world is very dangerous and only family members (basically a very small group of people) can be trusted. These adults continually come up with contrived 'evidence' to support their distorted point of view. As might be expected, these childrearing practices do not help a child to develop a basic sense of trust.

In other instances, people who show paranoid traits may have grown up in homes where criticism and ridicule ruled, creating an atmosphere of persecution that made it necessary for children always to be on their guard. Individuals with this particular background have a tendency to lash out preventatively to divert the harm anticipated, rather than wait passively for real or imagined dangers.

An essential element in the functioning of the paranoid personality is the attribution of an individual's perceived negative personality characteristics to others. This projective defense mechanism becomes a powerful tool in the repertoire of paranoid executives. These delusions of persecution—which combat their sense of vulnerability—may be accompanied by illusions of grandeur. This combination of dysfunctional behavior patterns can make paranoid people very hard to live with.

Subordinates drawn into this form of collusive drama may themselves have a paranoid outlook on life and so adapt easily to a leader with paranoid tendencies. Others who are willing to play along may have frustrated dependency needs and be willing to suspend reality to be able to maintain a position of closeness to their leader. Such distorted perceptions, however, tend to have a very negative effect on sound decision making, eventually affecting the company's bottom line negatively.

Elaborate information systems and a strong emphasis on the power of information characterize organizations created by people with a paranoid outlook. Strategy making is usually reactive, conservative, overly analytical, and secretive. There is great uniformity in values and beliefs and a very narrow point of view prevails. Conflict and distrust prevent effective communication and collaboration. Suspicion means that power is centralized at the top, resulting in too little grass-roots adaptation (Kets de Vries and Miller, 1984).

The sadomasochistic collusion

Superior: Where's that report on the plant extension I asked you about yesterday?

Subordinate: Didn't you find it on your desk? I left it there this morning.

Superior: That piece of garbage? I had a quick look at it. I thought those were some preliminary notes. What about the projections I asked you about? They haven't been worked out. It's certainly not what I had in mind when I was talking to you. I am beginning to wonder if you're in the wrong job, if not the wrong company. Do you plan to produce something better?

Subordinate: I'm sorry; I guess I misunderstood. My mind must not have been completely on the job. I'm going to rework the report right away. I'll stay as long as it takes to come up with the figures.

Superior: You'd better. Otherwise this may be your last project, at least in this company.

Sadomasochistic collusion is the theater of the abuser and abused. Deconstruction of my interviews show a basic script shared by the more masochistically inclined: 'I'm worthless. I'm bad. I submit to you. I deserve to be punished for the error of my ways. My suffering is justified.'

For abrasive executives, the world is a jungle. They are compelled to behave aggressively and frighten others into submission; to survive, they have continually to be on the attack. Striking out, retaining the upper hand, and having power and control take precedence over everything else. Fortunately for them, abrasive executives can usually find masochistically inclined people who are willing to put up with their behavior. The roles of sadist and masochist are not necessarily as clearly defined as we might imagine. There is often a strong sadistic element to a masochist's facade of self-sacrifice. For example, some workplace masochists may derive a lot of pleasure from defaming their tormentors by telling others about the terrible things they have done to their detractors.

The early personal history of individuals with a sadistic disposition may be highly chaotic, with weak, depressed, masochistic mothers and explosive, inconsistent, or even sadistic fathers. Substance abuse is common in these families. Frequent moves, various types of loss, and family breakups are not unusual. The child growing up in these conditions lacks the experience of a true holding environment. Under these circumstances, it is to be expected that normal development will not take place. Hostility breeds more hostility and becomes the model for similar behavior later in life.

The lack of containment while growing up, and having to deal with what they perceive as uncontrollable forces, creates a sense of helplessness in these people. To compensate for their feelings of inferiority, sadistic individuals may develop a compelling desire for dominance and power. Showing signs of weakness or vulnerability is unacceptable. Authority figures are seen as tough, dangerous, and abusive rather than positive and benevolent. Paradoxically, while these people often reject authority figures when in a dependency position (fearful of being maltreated), in a position of authority, they tend to abuse their power.

Another possible background that can result in sadistic behavior involves parents who signal to their children that they are special and therefore exempt from the normal rules of conduct that conventional society imposes on people. They are entitled to do whatever pleases them. Anyone trying to set boundaries on their behavior (like teachers or counselors) may incur the wrath of the parents. Permission granted, the children do whatever takes their fancy. These childrearing practices can set the stage for antisocial, impulsive, and sadistic behavior.

Sadistically inclined people cannot act out their fantasies in a vacuum. They need others to participate. And, as organizational life demonstrates all too often, sadists have an uncanny ability to attract people who are willing to be victimized.

The origin of a masochistic disposition, on the other hand, seems to be based on a child's attachment needs (Bowlby, 1969, 1973). Whatever the circumstances of growing up, there is an intense wish on the part of the child to arrive at some form of interaction with the parents. Unfortunately, some parents are able to offer only painful, unfulfilling contacts. (There are some similarities here with the dependent personalities I described earlier, who had frustrated dependency needs caused by the lack of affection while growing up.) If painful contact becomes the established pattern between parent and child, the developing child will associate love and caring with receiving pain. Nevertheless, he or she will generally conclude that any attention, even if accompanied by pain, is better than neglect. Eventually, attachment through suffering seems to turn into the chosen interpersonal style of these people. They may seek out situations that recreate early experiences of receiving love through pain. Because they may perceive the gratification that comes from being abused as outweighing the pain that accompanies it, their emotional comfort will come from taking the role of victim. Martyrdom becomes the normal price of relating to others.

Critical, guilt-inducing caretakers may contribute to the development of a masochistic style of relating to others. Role reversal, where the child (age-inappropriately) is made to feel responsible for the parents, or instances of abuse, may also contribute to a masochistic orientation. Deep, unconscious guilt feelings, unresolved dependency issues, and fears of being left alone can be at the root of this form of relating. Children may internalize the reproachful quality of their parents' attitude toward them. The perception of being bad becomes a major theme in their internal theater; eventually, they take over the role of their parents and become their own worst critic. The guilt of not living up to parents' expectations may dog them throughout their lives, inducing feelings of unworthiness, guilt, rejection, and punishment. Acting out those feelings, their way of relating to others becomes masochistic.

Masochistic behavior, however self-defeating it may seem, can provide an enormous dose of 'secondary gain' by arousing the concern and interest of others (Grossman, 1986; Kernberg, 1988; Glick and Meyers, 1988; Baumeister, 1989). These people, seeing themselves as the victims of unfair suffering, may get great satisfaction and a sense of moral superiority out of the sympathy and pity others express about the way they have been abused. By enduring pain and suffering, these individuals may also hope, consciously or unconsciously, that some good will come of it. In other words, they may see tolerating abuse as accomplishing some goal that justifies suffering or averts an even more painful eventuality. These are the people who aspire to sainthood. With all the drama they create, however, they can become a burden to those around them.

Sadistically and masochistically inclined executives can be a perfect match for each other. In the interplay in this kind of collusion, the self-esteem of each party seems to be maintained by proving the other wrong. Their interactions can become extremely intense, compulsive and quarrelsome, an extremely distorted way of expressing affection.

We can encounter this kind of sado-masochistic relationship within organizations where fear rules rather than trust, affecting morale, stifling creativity, and hampering learning. In the fear-ridden organization, the quality of decision-making goes down and the most capable executives leave. Eventually, the very future of the company is endangered.

BREAKING THE VICIOUS CIRCLE

In observing these four collusions, we have seen that a certain kind of group process is created whereby the behavior of one player determines the role that the other assumes. Naturally, if the role assigned to an individual is not compatible with his or her character, that person will quit, to search for a partner or an organizational setting more suited to his or her personality. Thus we are talking not just about a person–organization fit but also about a person–relational fit.

It would be unwise to start with the assumption that there must be collusion in workplace relationships. As Bion (1959) observed, most working relationships are task-oriented and based on the rational approach of goal orientation and work sharing. Hidden agendas do not necessarily set the tone. In most interpersonal situations, the draining, stressful, adversarial processes that characterize collusive relationships and make them so exasperating are conspicuous by their absence. My interpretation of the material gleaned from my study supports Bion's view: most of the interaction patterns were not neurotic. In many of the relationships there appeared a considerable amount of transitional space; there was the kind of playful give-and-take that allowed people ample space to grow and develop.

Nevertheless, the discussions revealed a fair number of what I would term collusive relationships of different degrees of intensity. Their existence is a cause for concern, given the dysfunctional effects of collusive processes on other people in an organization. The destructive potential of corporate collusions makes it important to know how to recognize such processes—and to prevent them.

It is usually leaders who cast others in their dysfunctional theater of the absurd and who are largely responsible for initiating these collusive activities. Recognizing dysfunctional behavior patterns in an organization's leadership is an essential aspect of the diagnostic and preventive process.

The first question we should ask ourselves is whether the people at the top have the kind of personality makeup that renders them susceptible to collusive relationships. If the individuals running the organization react in strange, irrational ways that may indicate specific personality disturbances, we should be alert to the danger their conduct might pose for the organization. Symptoms of potential trouble are abrasiveness, selfishness, overambition, arrogance, excessive detachment or emotion, vindictiveness, suspicion, overcontrol, insensitivity, untrustworthiness, decision paralysis, and excessive detail orientation.

As well as these troublesome behavior patterns, narcissism has a disturbingly insidious way of working, a tendency toward one-upmanship over one's peers. Subordinates who buy into this game confirm and encourage this behavior.

How do top executives react to mistakes? How do they attribute blame? Are they likely to seek out scapegoats? Do they see conspiracies everywhere? An organizational environment will be far from healthy if leaders have created the kind of corporate climate where others are always at fault, and where they themselves never take the blame for mistakes. Because such leaders can react violently to realities that inconvenience them, they can always find partners to participate in their collusive behavior; yet others join the cabal with dire effects on future organizational functioning.

Predictably, executives who behave in such ways create organizations where only yes-men survive. Contrarian thinking is no longer permitted; disagreement with the leader's point of view is not condoned. People are not allowed to question things. Those who are prepared to participate in collusive behavior are given only a submissive role. A corporate culture evolves in which communication is restricted and lack of openness prevails. Distrust and fear soon develop. Predictably, when fear rules in an organization, the processes of organizational adaptation and learning stop.

A further cause for worry is the presence of a top executive who insists on making all the decisions and allows nobody to think for him- or herself. Having to overcontrol everything that affects the organization becomes such a person's major preoccupation. In this kind of organizational culture, empowerment is a dirty word and delegation is therefore unheard of. A top executive's refusal to plan for succession is an indication of trouble. The addiction to power and the need to hang on to control make it very hard for some executives even to think about letting go and handing over to someone else. Not surprisingly, in an organization dominated by such executives, only collusive relationships are possible—which in turn means that the best people leave.

Unpredictability should also sound alarm bells. The unpredictable behavior of an executive is bound to contribute to a climate of distrust and uncertainty in the organization. Subordinates do not know how they are supposed to act. Furthermore, because of the leader's behavior, the company may adopt a short-term, fire-fighting mentality. In such instances, priorities are unclearly set and tend to vacillate.

An additional question that should be raised when testing an organization for collusive relationships is the realism of the senior executive's outlook on the business. Strategic initiatives that bear little relation to the realities of the company's situation are a clear danger sign.

Another is low morale. Troubled companies become increasingly politicized, and infighting, gamesmanship, and silo behavior become the norm. There is a predicable lack of teamwork and good corporate citizenship; executives become turf defenders, adopting a protective, parochial outlook and no longer care about what is good for the company. A siege mentality may prevail.

I could go on. These are only some of the more obvious danger signs that can derive from collusive relationships. My observations have convinced me that these are an organizational reality. We all have some unfinished business originating from our past history. We can all find ourselves stuck in vicious circles, the victims of typecasting. The challenge is not to allow this to happen, to avoid the kinds of damaging relationships that end in organizational pathology.

What can be done to prevent such dysfunctional relationship patterns, or to nip them in the bud? How can these vicious circles be broken before they take hold? An appropriate starting point for the unraveling process would be an attempt to help executives gain a better understanding of the kind of script that they are acting out in the organization as a whole. How can we discern whether a collusive trap is set by a senior executive in the organization? How can we acquire this kind of sensitivity to what is happening?

Understanding others requires a solid dose of self-awareness, a recognition of the role of emotional processes in motivation. Thus self-knowledge is the first step in the process of disentanglement from an unhealthy situation. Emotional intelligence is a sine qua non for this (Goleman, 1995). The ability to monitor our own reactions makes it easier to understand how others may become embroiled in a collusive relationship (and the effect this can have on the organization). Executives would do well to take regular stock of their relationships to others, asking themselves whether these are continually evolving and growing or have become stuck in repetitive interplay. If executives suspect that someone is trying to draw them into a neurotic game, they should have the presence of mind to decide whether they want to participate or not—and realize the implications of participation.

Understanding one's own role in the interactive process is not easy, given the blind spots we all have about our own character. To move from a fusional state to one of true separateness can be hard work (Meltzer, 1967; Lachkar, 1992). Superior and subordinate need to be able to sort out their own subjective experiences without the kind of confusion that characterizes these collusive interaction patterns. But recognizing these patterns in oneself and others, and gathering the motivation and courage to address these failings, may require outside help. Psychotherapy, coaching, or participation in a group-dynamics seminar in which feedback about personal style is part of the process may help an individual disentangle his or her role in the process.

If we don't like a play in a theater, we can get up and leave. We can do the same if we are caught up in organizational dramas. We don't have to play along; we always have the option to quit. In organizational life, it is important to retain our sense of individuality and not be swept away by forces that stifle our ability to play and to be creative. After all, life is not a rehearsal. And mental health means having a choice.

CHAPTER 4
....

LISTENING WITH THE
THIRD EAR

We have two ears and one mouth so that we can listen twice as much as
we speak.
—Epictetus

So when you are listening to somebody, completely, attentively, then you
are listening not only to the words, but also to the feeling of what is being
conveyed, to the whole of it, not part of it.
—Jiddu Krishnamurti

It is only by closing the ears of the soul, or by listening too intently to
the clamors of the sense, that we become oblivious of their utterances.
—Alexander Crummell

What is meant by 'listening with a third ear' is that we listen attentively
not only for what a person is saying, but also the subtext of the conversation, including the tone of voice, the body language, the posture, and
the demeanor, while making mental notes about what the person might
be going through, and reflecting on how the interface affects us (Reik
1983). It implies listening not only to the intended meaning but to
everything the person we are listening to says and does.

The most important thing in communication is to hear what isn't
being said. Much of our mental life—including our thoughts, feelings,
and motives—takes place at what we might call a subterranean, unconscious level. Both neurologists and psychologists have abundantly demonstrated how unconscious processes are put into action by emotional
stimuli. Neurological studies have supplied massive evidence of unconscious processes of cognition (for example, Rizzolatti, Fogassi et al. 2001;
Stern, 2004).

What happens in interpersonal encounters is that the space between people is filled by what we evoke in one another; and as a result of those evocations, we seem always to be sending mixed messages. To put it another way, when we are communicating with each other, we not only explicitly articulate messages, but at the same time we communicate in a number of implicit ways, often with a contrary message. For example, the spoken phrase 'I am happy' conveys varying messages, depending on the speaker's body language and emotional tone. The words can be said with all the evidence of great joy, or in a joking fashion, or in a totally cynical manner. These emotional components, received intuitively, supplement the message we receive in the form of direct verbal statements. Thus the tone of a statement always contains an additional, very informative message.

But such messages are generally subtle and thus not always easy to decipher. Frequently, we know that something has happened during the exchange because we are somehow touched deep inside, but we do not really understand why. We pick up these telling cues from body language, sounds, smells, touch, or peripheral vision without being consciously aware of doing so.

Everyday conversation consists of a speaker attempting to put feelings into a listener. (This presupposes the willingness of the listener to accept these feelings, of course.) In more common language, we talk about 'putting something across,' or giving someone 'a piece of our mind.' For example, when we are in distress, we may try to convey to the other person our distress in such a way that he or she can literally *feel* it. The normal communication process consists of fairly rapidly oscillating cycles of projection and introjection: as one person communicates with words and demeanor (projection), the other receives and interprets the communication (introjection); then the listener, having understood the speaker's message, reprojects it to the original speaker, perhaps accompanied by an interpretation.

This same cycle of projection and introjection takes place in the psychotherapeutic context as well: that's what transference and countertransference are all about. In this chapter—after having explored the delicate dance between leaders and followers—I will take the theme of countertransference—that is, the feelings that a therapist has for a client—beyond the couch and apply it to the consultancy or leadership coaching setting. I highlight the theme of subliminal communication—already touched on in the previous chapter. I will explore how coaches and consultants can use themselves as instruments for gathering data—in other words, how they can use their own reactions to help them interpret what the client is trying to tell them and trying to do to them. To clarify that process, I discuss the concepts of transference and projective identification, concepts grounded in early mother–infant communication and essential to 'listening with the third ear.' In addition, I discuss various forms of alignment and misalignment between the sender and receiver of both explicit *and* implicit messages. Finally, I make a number of suggestions regarding what coaches and consultants need to pay attention to when listening to another person.

PROJECTIVE IDENTIFICATION

In the therapeutic context, *projective identification*, which I described briefly in Chapter 1, is the unwanted or unacknowledged feelings of a client that are transmitted to a coach or consultant. As I noted there, projective identification is more than mere projection. The latter is an intrapsychic dynamic, while the former takes place in the interpersonal domain; in fact, it is an extremely primitive form of relating to another person. Furthermore, in terms of the feelings experienced by the 'projector,' there is a clear difference between these two phenomena. When projective identification is at work, the sender of the communication feels at one with the other person, which is not the case with simple projection.

Projective identification turns into a self-fulfilling prophesy, whereby one person, believing something false about another, relates to that other person in such an intense way—transmitting these unacceptable feelings, impulses, or thoughts to him or her—that the other person in question alters his or her behavior to make the belief true. Thus, instead of describing these thoughts or feelings in a discussion, the projector subtly communicates the unwanted content to the receiver through actions, facial expression, body attitude, word choice, or sounds, validating an individual's projections by making the projection real (Klein 1946; Ogden 1982).

In a way, projective identification combines elements of projection and introjection (incorporating the feelings, motives, and thoughts of others). The second person is influenced by the projection and begins to behave as though he or she is in fact actually characterized by the projected thoughts or beliefs. For example, an executive who develops the delusion that he is being persecuted by his boss, begins to act in such a suspicious way that the boss begins to look for grounds on which to fire him.

Leadership coaches or consultants, experiencing these projected feelings or thoughts in themselves, may understand what the sender is experiencing, even if the sender is not consciously aware of initiating that process. Given the dyadic (and cyclical) nature of projective identification, it eventually becomes difficult to assess who first did what to whom.

As a primitive, preverbal mode of communicating and relating, projective identification finds its prototype in the mother–child interface. Infants cannot *say* how they feel; instead, they have to find ways to get their mothers to experience their emotional state, making for a deep, almost symbiotic connection between mother and child. The infant 'speaks' to the mother by evoking emotional reactions in her that, in turn, are received by the infant. The mother may also verbalize what the infant is trying to communicate, thus helping the infant on a journey of verbal concretization of psychological states.

'GOOD-ENOUGH PARENTING' AND CONTAINMENT: THE ORIGINS OF SUBLIMINAL COMMUNICATION

The mother-child relationship can be viewed as a co-constructive process whereby infant and mother impact each other on a continuous basis, regulating and aligning their modes of interaction to obtain a satisfactory equilibrium. (Schore 1994; IJzendoorn 1995; Trevarthen 1999/2000). From the moment of birth, infants communicate their feelings and other internal states through sounds, body movements, smell, and facial expressions. Caregivers generally learn how to interpret these expressions and respond to the infant to provide 'containment'— that is, to keep unwanted feelings from spiraling out of control. Therefore the relationship between the container and the contained can be viewed as a dynamic, mutually influencing process (Bion 1970).

The importance of synchronized, dyadic interactions for the developing child cannot be overstated. In fact, the child's satisfactory development rests upon what has been called a 'good enough' quality of these early caregiver-child interactions. These 'regulatory' interactions are extremely important. Unfortunately, the initial phase of the developmental process is characterized by chaos, confusion, strain, bodily tension, sleep deprivation, eating difficulties, and other problems. It generally takes some time before proper empathic resonance occurs between caregivers and their infants.

Dealing with distress signals

A key factor in good-enough care, and thus in proper alignment, is the way caregivers deal with a child's distress signals. Some mothers have a natural tendency to respond appropriately; others are out of sync. Of the latter, all but the most heartless mothers attempt to give some form of containment. Many, though, find themselves misaligned with their infant's cues.

Mothers who have a rigid attitude toward childrearing may experience the anxiety of the child but refuse (or not really know how) to respond appropriately. Although such a mother may go through a number of perfunctory movements intended to give generic comfort, she does not truly deal with the infant's distress. This failure of containment creates a state of bewilderment and disbelief in the infant, who would like the mother to feel its anxiety just as the child is feeling it. But due to her lack of appropriate response, the infant senses that what it tried to convey to the mother has lost its form or meaning.

Other misaligned mothers overreact to the anxiety of their infant. Often inexperienced at parenting, they may panic at their infant's discomfort, aggravating the problem. In such instances, the infant experiences the mother as an unsafe container, unable to tolerate anxiety and distress.

In the third type of containment, there is a high degree of resonance between mother and child. An understanding mother is able to experience the feeling of fear, fatigue, or hunger that the infant is trying to communicate, and yet retain a balanced outlook. She has the knack for feeling what the child experiences and yet still retains her mental equilibrium. This alignment, unlike containment that is either too rigid or too fragile, makes for an ongoing process of mutual influence and adaptation.

This ability of mothers to be attuned to the needs of their children continues as the young ones grow up. For example, when children are playing in the house, attentive mothers constantly listen to the sounds the children make. Mothers who are well aligned with the needs of their children have a finely tuned ability to distinguish the usual abundant noise from any sign of distress. When their 'third ear' (that organ not merely of sense but also of empathy, intuition, and understanding) hears a different sound—something out of the ordinary which may indicate danger—they immediately swing into action and go to the rescue.

We can speculate that mothers who are well attuned to their children are more sensitive to subliminal, non-explicit communication. This talent for picking up subliminal information, for deciphering projective identification as it occurs, stands them in good stead, not only with their children but in any interpersonal situation. In general, experienced mothers have an advantage in making sense of the varied communications that take place in the bi-personal field. Their capacity to listen to more than words may give them a real advantage when they take up the role of coach or consultant. Fortunately, nowadays an increasing number of men are breaking stereotype in the parental role, taking up many of the responsibilities that once used to be women's exclusive domain. As these men become better communicators with their infants, they can transfer those skills to the workplace.

Listening to what is being said, and not being said

The interchange between infants and their empathetic caregivers demonstrates the large number of responses—the various forms of empathic resonance—that can occur in an effective coach–client or consultant–client interchange. The ability to make sense of projective identification processes, an ability which we all develop to a greater or lesser extent in infancy as we learn to 'listen with the third ear,' serves as the prototype of all our future two-way communication. This listening that bypasses the ordinary senses has been part of our repertoire for a long time by the time we reach adulthood. Because of faulty mother–child communication, however, some people are not well attuned. Others, who resonated well with their primary caregivers in infancy, have been out of practice for so long that they have all but lost the skill.

SUBLIMINAL COMMUNICATION

Because remnants of the caregiver–infant dialogue will stay with us throughout life, aspects of this interactive script are revived in *any* future relationship. Scripts established in childhood color the way we disseminate or gather information, the way we convey implicit and explicit texts. While explicit texts are out in the open, we struggle to grasp and decipher implicit texts.

As we relate to other people, we are constantly processing large amounts of information. Generally that processing registers in our conscious mind only as hunches. Sometimes, especially when we are totally unaware that this information processing is taking place, we register it in another way: through acting out. Instead of trying to consciously reflect on and process the information deluging us, we act impulsively to offer our emotional response, which is often unconscious and often conflicted. But because the information flooding us has not been properly worked through, the actions that we take are sometimes destructive to self or others, and may inhibit dealing in a more constructive way with the feelings that are aroused.

While mothers have to learn to pick up subtle signals by *doing*, psychotherapists, psychiatrists, psychoanalysts, coaches, and other people in the helping professions receive training to use themselves as an instrument—to really listen. They learn to use their own unconscious minds to detect and decipher the unconscious wishes and fantasies of their patients. Using their subliminal perceptions about their patients is an important instrument in their repertoire, a way of understanding their patients more deeply. But this activity is not limited to the therapist–patient interchange. All of us use our intuition to understand people better. All of us form opinions about others with what seems on the surface to be scanty information. All of us are over-eager to verbalize our instant impressions. Consultants and coaches are no different.

Transference

Although transference has been discussed in the previous volume of this series, it may be useful to reiterate its key aspects. In any form of interpersonal exchange, one person *transfers* to the other his or her own inner experiences (Sullivan 1953). In that sense, frustrations of the past recur in the present. As mentioned in the previous volume, this concept, *transference*, is one of Freud's most important contributions to the field of psychology (Breuer and Freud 1895; Greenson 1967; Racker 1968; Luborsky and Crits-Cristoph 1998). According to Freud, transference involves a repetition of infantile prototypes that are lived out with a deep feeling of reality. Although in the past these specific behavior patterns may have been quite appropriate, for reasons of psychological or physical survival, in the present they may have become *in*appropriate. Thus, to quote Freud, transferential reactions create a 'false connection': the behavior that comes to the fore is inappropriate to the present situation. Though we rarely recognize it, *all* our interchanges revive a vast range of psychological experiences having their source in the past—experiences that are now directed to a person in the present, who becomes the recipient of the interchange. This confusion of time and place implies that all forms of interaction are inevitably both reality- and transference-based.

For example, an executive in a coaching relationship may begin to perceive the coach as if the coach were his father, transferring his feelings for the real father to the coach. Because transference is a largely unconscious process, the executive is not likely to be aware of it—and neither is the coach, initially. It is the unconscious nature of transference that makes it both so elusive and so potent. A well-trained leadership coach or consultant will gradually make sense out of what the executive is trying to 'communicate.' Astute coaches or consultants use transference data as a vital source of information. It may help them see that the script a client is following needs to change, because that client is now in a very different situation than when he or she was small. Their assignment is to help clients avoid simply repeating the past. This time, here in the present, the script needs a new twist, taking the person's present situation into consideration.

When Freud first discovered the phenomenon by which the patient inappropriately 'transfers' something from his early experiences onto the analyst, he considered it a distraction. A number of years later, however, he acknowledged that such 'false connections' could be used effectively to help patients unravel their neuroses; it could be used to help patients understand better the 'script' that motivated them. Today we are quite interested in the phenomenon of transference because of its diagnostic value as well as its therapeutic use. Transference, through a process of compulsive repetition, reveals in the here-and-now the unresolved and most crucial conflictual patterns that are still active in the patient's current life (Luborsky, Crits-Cristoph et al., 1988; Luborsky and Crits-Cristoph, 1998). If the therapist can bring the patient to make his or her own transference reactions conscious, express and acknowledge those reactions, and experience their links with current and past relationships, then transference is a powerful tool for understanding and healing, helping the patient write a new script of life.

Countertransference

In clinical training, psychotherapists pay a great deal of attention to transference. They go to great lengths to point out to their clients that certain behavior patterns, appropriate at an earlier stage of life, are no longer effective in the present. But this process works both ways. Just as patients unconsciously react to therapists, therapists unconsciously respond to their clients' transference with *countertransference* reactions.

Imagine, for example, a consultant who is trying to give advice to one of her executive clients. No matter what she says, the client's response is to repeat how useless he feels in his present situation, how stuck he feels, and how unclear it is to him what he should do. In spite of heroic efforts on the part of the consultant to help the executive see things in perspective—see that things are not so bad—he sings the same refrain, apparently ignoring her words. What's more, he shows increasing contempt for the consultant's advice. The consultant, meanwhile, feels increasingly useless, since none of her interventions seem to work, and begins to feel irritated and angry. As the sessions continue, she has to make a great effort to keep herself from erupting in anger.

The projection by the executive and the introjection of his feelings into the consultant are very clear. Depending on the degree to which the consultant is a prisoner of this interchange, it may take some time for her to realize what is happening. While the exchange is taking place, she may be too perturbed by the interaction to function properly. Indeed, if she is at her wit's end, she may even 'act out' and express her irritation. But it is also possible that she will *not* 'act out' her feelings in a knee-jerk manner. She may take a more reflective pose, engaging in vicarious introspection, trying to understand what the client is 'doing' to her, and also asking why she herself feels impelled to be so active. Listening now with the third ear, she may ask herself a number of other questions. Why does she feel such a great need to reassure her client? Why is she feeling useless, irritated, and increasingly angry? As she tries to metabolize these feelings, she may realize that people like her client remind her of an older sister who made it a habit, in childhood, of telling her how useless she was. Thinking back, the consultant may recall how these incidents made her feel not only helpless but also angry. Usually, these situations would end up in a big fight, after which the child-consultant would run for reassurance to her mother.

The consultant, having gone through this reflective process, has entered another, more subterranean level in the exchange. Recognizing how the client had made her feel useless, and why she had become so irritated, she sees that she has to do something different to really be helpful to the client. With this awareness she will no longer become caught up in the kind of folie à deux that might eventually have ended in an angry outburst on her part. It is clear that if she had stuck to her own script, the relationship with her client would probably have been doomed.

This example shows us that one of the compound tasks of leadership coaches and consultants is to decipher what the client is trying to enact and how the consultant is tempted to *re*act, and then help them both not to act out the usual scripts (the client's and the consultant's), but to create a new, healthier outcome. Leadership coaches and consultants should not acquiesce under pressure (in spite of the fact that certain lines in a client's script may reverberate with their own script) and buy into the client's script. What is needed in these situations is a re-enactment, but a re-enactment with a twist. The outcome must be different.

Like transference, countertransference includes all of the conscious and unconscious responses aroused during the interpersonal exchange by the activities of the client (Epstein and Feiner, 1979; Searles, 1979; Hedges, 1987; Marshall and Marshall, 1988; Wolstein, 1988; Gabbard, 1999; Hinshelwood, 1999; Goldstein and Goldberg, 2004; Maroda, 2004). And, like transference, it needs to be dealt with. Countertransference *responsiveness* is the consultant's ability to hear and deal with the client's infantile past, taking his or her own past into consideration. As the previous example illustrated, countertransference reactions, if not recognized for what they are and responded to, can create serious problems in the interpersonal interface.

Initially, however, countertransference was viewed as a subject to avoid. The unconscious conflict aroused in the psychoanalyst was something to learn from when it occurred but to be gotten rid of as soon as possible. Freud viewed countertransference as an impediment to the psychoanalytic process. He felt that it distracted the psychoanalyst from doing his or her therapeutic work effectively (Freud 1915).

Since the time of Freud, views of countertransference have fallen generally into two camps: one that advocates a rather narrow definition of the term (the impediment position); the other that advocates a broader definition. Over time (as with the concept of transference), the broader view has become the more dominant one (Balint and Balint, 1939; Heimann, 1950; Winnicott, 1975; Langs and Searles, 1980; Casement, 1985; Bollas, 1987; Ferenczi, 1988). Presently, countertransference is no longer seen as a bothersome impediment to clinical work; rather, it is seen as an additional source of data about the client, and as an opportunity to obtain greater insight into the emotions and reactions that occur when two people interact with each other.

While countertransference is undeniably a source of data, it is not necessarily a source of relevant evidence. What the data are and what they can contribute has to be sorted out in the interchange. Complicating that sorting-out process is the fact that the leadership coach or consultant needs to operate on two alternating levels: he or she has to be an objective observer of another person's ideas and emotions while also being a subjective receiver. Those coaches and consultants who are skilled and astute handle the two levels deftly, using their subjective emotional life actively and directly in the dyadic interface.

THE ACTION TRAP: 'I ACT; THEREFORE I AM'

It is clear from this discussion that the emotional interface is always a two-way street. The client is always sending subliminal messages (transference), and the coach or consultant is always reacting (countertransference). Thus there is always a struggle to make meaning and sense out of what takes place in an encounter, and both parties are constantly tempted to act out perceived meanings rather than verbalize or mentalize them.

In the course of this struggle, every leadership coach and consultant inevitably falls into the action trap at some point. This is especially likely to happen when strong fantasy material emerges during an encounter, prompting a mutual resistance to feeling and working with emotional data. When coaches and consultants do not promptly recognize what is going on, do not quickly enough make sense out of the subliminal messages that they are receiving, they may succumb to 'flight into action'—that is, they may react immediately to information given by the client, without being aware of this acting out. After all, no matter how impeccably trained a leadership coach or consultant is, he or she is still a human being and still has emotions—and probably a number of issues which have not yet been resolved. If leadership coaches and consultants unconsciously accept a role ascribed to them by a client, they may respond by placing their own unacceptable feelings onto the client without realizing that they are doing so.

To illustrate, one particular client reminded a consultant of her daughter, who had been responsible for much trouble while still at home. During the daughter's adolescence, various family members had gotten caught up in a vicious cycle of escalating destructive communication. Given this association, the consultant found it a challenge to keep her cool, maintain sufficient distance, and not to get trapped in parallel behavior.

In another example, a client was perceived by an executive coach as spoiled, self-centered, and a manipulative bastard. While that may have been a valid assessment, a much more important issue is why this person evoked such a strong reaction in the coach. Did this client strongly resemble some detested individual from the coach's past—perhaps a father who split from his wife, left her and the children without any financial support, and was never seen again?

What is important in such situations is that leadership coaches and consultants recognize these feelings in themselves and do something about them—or rather, refrain from doing something about them. They need to keep themselves from falling into the action trap. When they recognize such feelings in themselves, they need to be extremely careful what they say, keeping themselves in the present rather than descending back into the past. For example, the coach in the previous example, looking at her client through a filter of distaste and disapproval, needs to be doubly sure that she is not missing something because of her biases.

Danger signs

Leadership coaches and consultants, knowing that countertransference reactions can misdirect them and derail their attempts to read another person, need to be vigilant in watching for warning signs. The most common sign that countertransference reactions are taking over is a stalemate in the coaching or consulting relationship, a feeling that the intervention is not going anywhere. Another giveaway that the client is doing something to the coach of which the leadership coach is only subliminally aware is when that coach cannot get a specific incident with the client out of his or her head; fragments of some previous interchange linger on. Coaches and consultants often talk about unwittingly bringing clinical situations home, and some even find a particular client's material invading their dreams.

Additional warning signs that countertransference problems are in play include using pejorative language to or about the client; being subliminally aware of becoming annoyed (as in the previous case example), overprotective, manipulative, flattered, envious, anxious, fearful, disappointed, or even sexually interested; experiencing a sense of abandonment or hopelessness and depression about the client; fearing engulfment—that is, having a sense that the client is violating boundaries; and, as noted earlier, feeling impelled to do something 'active.' All these warning signs alert leadership coaches and consultants that they may be in the thrall of a countertransference reaction.

Part of the training to become a psychotherapist or psychoanalyst (or any other individual in the helping professions) is learning first to detect signs of unconscious countertransference reactions and then to bring these to conscious awareness, to refrain from acting upon them unthinkingly. If clients transfer images of parents or other people close to them onto their therapists, coaches, or consultants, and regress to childlike or otherwise inappropriate behavioral patterns, the recipients of these forms of communication need to be able to respond without falling into a countertransference reaction. Such reactions, when they do happen, can seriously distort the communication process.

If a client makes unreasonable demands or declares romantic love, well-trained leadership coaches and consultants let these words pass through them. Providing containment, maintaining an attitude of calmness, equanimity, and caring concern even when they feel themselves reacting out of countertransference, coaches and consultants are able to serve as unobtrusive mirrors, permitting their clients to acquire glimpses of themselves without having the coaches' own needs get in the way.

Unfortunately, many people never bother to try to understand why they feel the way they do, or to objectively understand the source of their feelings. Indeed, they remember nothing of their internal conflicts but only *express* them—and that indirectly, through action. They prefer action to facing conflicts head-on.

Choosing reflection over action

If leadership coaches and consultants want to avoid falling into the action trap, they need to take a reflective attitude toward the messages projected by clients. It is a constant challenge for coaches and consultants to identify and decipher the painful and intolerable emotions of their clients— emotions that are likely contributing to problem behavior in those clients—while simultaneously sorting out their own countertransference reactions and providing a 'holding environment.' Leadership coaches and consultants need to guard themselves against precipitate and premature action—saying something unconsidered—simply to reduce their own anxiety, and instead learn to engage in a consistent and constructive exploration of affect and behavior (of self as well as client), no matter how intense those feeling may be, or how disturbing they are to self-esteem.

In the hands of reflective coaches and consultants, countertransference reactions are useful tools, helping to reveal the unconscious wishes and fantasies that clients are projecting onto their helpers. In this sense, countertransference reactions fuel their work. That's not the only benefit, however. While well-studied countertransference reactions certainly improve coaches' understanding of their clients, those reactions also guide coaches in their own journey of self-discovery.

While there is no way to overcome totally the problem of countertransference (since all of us form opinions of others), coaches and consultants can learn to use it productively rather than allow it to affect the therapeutic relationship unconsciously. Leadership coaches and consultants who are able to recognize what they are feeling, and can decipher how those feelings relate to what the client is doing to them, keep their own unconscious processes 'inside the equation,' thereby preserving the bi-personal frame.

As reflective practitioners, coaches and consultants learn to listen to their clients at two levels. While not ignoring the content of what the client is saying, they must ask themselves questions, such as: How do I feel listening to the client? What is the client doing to me? Am I truly engaged? Do I feel comfortable? Am I bored? Do I feel uneasy? Do I feel in control? Do I feel confused? Am I getting irritated, angry? Do I feel seduced? What do I find disturbing in my relationship with this client? In addition to these in-the-moment assessments, coaches and consultants need to assess how their feelings change over the course of their dealings with the client, evaluating their own emotions and behavior in light of what's happening with their client's behavior and with the therapeutic relationship as it progresses.

Acquiring a reflective stance is not easy, however. Reflection demands a high level of self-awareness on the part of coaches and consultants—an understanding of their own thoughts and feelings—as well as a sound grasp of the psychological basis of their work. It all comes down to maintaining a questioning attitude toward one's own feelings and motives.

ALIGNMENT

As we saw in the mother–child discussion, alignment is the ability to be in sync with another person's feelings and thoughts. That ability to feel and experience what is going on within another person is a prerequisite of reflective coaching or consulting; ironically, it is also a by-product of such coaching. For leadership coaches and consultants the challenge is to use their own unconscious as a receptive organ—that third ear I spoke of earlier—directed toward the transmitting unconscious of the client. As was noted, coaches and consultants need to listen attentively not only to the explicit text but also to the implicit one. In order to decipher the underlying text of a conversation, they need to observe the client's overall body language, posture, demeanor, and other factors.

In addition, they need to keep in mind the fact that their own affects, thoughts, associations, and actions are reflections of elicited or awakened conflicts within themselves. Processing those conflicts and reactions is a difficult task, because the accumulation of data from both transference and countertransference is massive. Moreover, data from one area need to be used to make conjectures about the other. In listening simultaneously to both the client and themselves, leadership coaches and consultants are in fact attending to communication in three modalities—cognition, affect, and action—as both parties in the therapeutic relationship stir associations and conflict in the other. The good news is that the conflicts and inappropriate feelings that are stirred up in coaches and consultants—if properly assessed—supplement information garnered by their eyes and ears. Their challenge is to systematically explore their visceral response to the other person, assessing the appropriateness of their gut feelings as they explore their unconscious.

'Strike when the iron is cold'

Skilled, aware coaches and consultants do not confront their client with their projections in an abrasive manner, nor do they scold him or her for thinking or acting inappropriately. Instead, they realize the power of resistance, and rather than tackling conflicted issues head-on they reframe them. They also know the importance of timing: they 'strike when the iron is cold'—that is, when their client is prepared to hear what they have to say. Coaches and consultants who pay attention to transference and countertransference reactions know how to create the right circumstances for their client to gain awareness and insight into the specifics of the situation. They help their client to recognize his or her projected fantasies. Furthermore, they keep in mind (while working with their client) that their own countertransference reactions will not go away, and that they cannot simply ignore their experience of the other.

Humans are both feeling and thinking beings. If we ignore our feelings, we psychologically blind ourselves to important information about the world; and if we ignore our ability to use logic, we do the same thing. If we do not use both faculties together—feeling and thinking—we are not able to integrate our inner and outer worlds.

Going for gold

Understanding and analyzing our own developmental history—exploring our inner world—helps us, as coaches and consultants, to moderate our affects and responses. We need to accept that our emotional reactions will not just go away, but we also need to recognize and process those reactions rather than simply acting on them. If we come to know ourselves better and understand our own weaknesses, vulnerabilities, limitations, and secrets, then our emotional responses to people and to our surroundings can be valuable tools in helping us interpret the world.

In short, an understanding of transference and countertransference is essential to effectiveness as a leadership coach or consultant. As coaches and consultants we should always keep in mind that there are (1) things we can know about the client, (2) things we may be able to know if we listen with the third ear, (3) things we will never know, and (4) things that we do not want to know for one reason or another. Being aware of these agendas in the bi-personal field helps coaches and consultants explore their client's wishes and fears, especially those which are not completely conscious and thus contribute to conflict and anxiety. Possessing this kind of awareness, coaches and consultants are more likely to view their client's emotional demands in perspective, thereby avoiding an 'acting out' agenda. While mere action can enslave us, reflection—the ability to allow ideas to float in our mind without the need for immediate understanding or action—goes a long way toward helping us better understand this complex, subterranean interpersonal domain. As a French proverb goes, 'In water one sees one's own face, but in wine one beholds the heart of another.'

LEADERSHIP AND PERSONALITY

INTRODUCTION

Part 2 extends the clinical orientation of my work on leadership, taking many of the themes of Part 1, including leader-follower relationships, and how leaders dramatize their 'inner theater,' and fleshing them out with case observations of organizational and political leaders. I identify a range of character types and leadership archetypes, and examine the ways they operate within organizations—for good and bad—offering suggestions about how we can deal with them as superiors, subordinates, colleagues, leadership coaches, or consultants.

However, to start with, in Chapter 5, I ask readers to join me on a flight of fantasy, imagining Vladimir Putin as CEO of a company—Russia Inc.—and reviewing his former presidency by the criteria I would apply to analyzing a CEO's successful (or otherwise) performance as head of an organization. Applying the criteria of what effective CEOs do, how good was Putin at his job? What legacy has he left behind? Looking at Putin in a historic context, he emerged on a wave of national and international optimism about the future of the Russian Federation, and his two terms in office promised much. However, Russia's performance has been only mediocre, economic results only average and the new regime, with the dubious legality of some of its actions and the rise in bureaucracy and criminality, has proved to have many similarities with the old Soviet era. While Putin seemed reliable and trustworthy when he took office in 2000, he departed as president with a very different image: that of an unpredictable and dangerous man. I couldn't put Putin directly on my couch and sadly have not had an opportunity to interview him, but there is much to be learned from material in the public domain, not least his autobiography. This chapter can be read as a template for many of the perennial issues concerning leadership—in particular the leader, or CEO, life-cycle—that will be developed further in Part 3.

In Chapter 6 you might recognize someone you work with—or even some aspect of yourself. Did you know you were rubbing shoulders with Sisyphus, Nobel Prize winners, Faust, the Count of Monte Cristo— and even the occasional troll—on a daily basis? These are the names we can give to a number of psychological complexes, less familiar than others we have all heard of, like the inferiority or Oedipus complexes. In this chapter I examine the way people laboring under a variety of complexes function in the workplace, the roots of their behavior in their earliest formative experiences, and how the influence of complexes can be lessened with help, through counseling and psychotherapeutic intervention.

Over the last 30 years, I have studied the behavior of executives from all over the world in a specially designed, lengthy leadership workshop at INSEAD. This workshop is intended to go deep below the superficialities that characterize much leadership education. It creates a safe transitional space—using the life case study as a major vehicle— where individuals are encouraged to unpeel the various layers of their personality. In the workshop, executives' behavior and character issues are put under a microscope with the purpose of looking at what works and what they can do differently. During the year in the workshop they are given personality tests and a number of other multi-party feedback survey instruments. They are regularly put into smaller groups to explore difficult organizational and personal issues.

These workshops show that executives tend toward a specific behavior pattern that can be highly effective at one stage in their career but quite dysfunctional at another. The group work often reveals behavioral inflexibility as people struggle to adapt to new organizational situations. I have also observed that team complementarity is vital to an organization: all is well if an individual's weaknesses are counterbalanced by others' strengths. The opposite is also very true. These findings have been confirmed repeatedly during organizational interventions with groups of executives undertaking a high-performance team building exercise.

Taking executive role constellations (teams) as a point of departure—moving away from an emphasis on complexes in Chapter 6—I have listed eight distinct leadership archetypes. These categories are derived from the cumulative observations of the workshops for which I am responsible, and discussions with colleagues in the organizational behavior and strategy fields. Although 'roles people play' is a well-trodden field, my archetypes have the unique advantage of having been drawn from real life, not laboratories, and are the result of extended study of real executives in real situations. However, as organizational life does not permit the same extensive and deep analysis that is possible in a more psychotherapeutic context, I needed to find a way to enable the observation of an individual's behavior and actions in the workplace as an easy tool for assessing personality and organizational 'fit.' As the next step in this journey, I constructed the Leadership Archetype Questionnaire (LAQ), a diagnostic multi-party feedback instrument for individuals and organizational stakeholders to use to identify leadership style. The LAQ consists of 48 questions, carefully constructed to elicit indicators of an individual's personal style and to supply 360-degree feedback. Chapter 7 presents how the LAQ came about and provides guidance on how to mix-and-match, manage, and work with people with very different character types and skills. Leadership and personality are indivisible. The crucial factor is achieving best fit and to do this, we have to know what we are like and where we should be. At its most effective, leadership is a set of creative complementarities. To quote Benjamin Franklin, 'We must all hang together, or assuredly, we shall all hang separately.'

VLADIMIR PUTIN, CEO OF RUSSIA, INC.: THE LEGACY AND THE FUTURE[1]

It has become fashionable to speak of change and liberalization in Russia under President Dmitry Medvedev. May 7 marked his one-year anniversary in office. He has recently granted an interview with an opposition newspaper, allowed a few human rights activists to criticize Russia's regime, and even started a blog. There is also a new administration in Washington that wants a fresh start with foreign powers.

However, Mr. Medvedev's gestures have not been matched by policy. It is more appropriate to think of Russia as living under Vladimir Putin's ninth year in power.

—*Garry Kasparov*

A few years ago, a friend showed me a *matryoshka*, a present from Moscow. The main figure was Vladimir Putin. Handsome, blue-eyed, dressed in a dark executive-style suit, he stood on a solid brick wall, carrying the Russian flag, and an imperial eagle adorned his chest. Inside him was Boris Yeltsin, florid-faced, wearing an electric blue suit and a mayoral sash, like the representative of a less-than-affluent provincial town. Inside Yeltsin was Mikhail Gorbachev, holding a hammer (labeled *Perestroika*) with which he had just smashed the Berlin Wall. Tucked under his arm was a red Soviet flag; the birthmark on his head was generously if randomly rendered. Inside Gorbachev (and without the

[1] Much of this material can be found in the article by Kets de Vries, M.F.R. and Shekshnia, S. 'Putin, CEO of Russia Inc.: The Legacy and the Future,' *Organizational Dynamics*, 2008, 37 (3), 236–253. I am very grateful for the help and contributions of Stanislav Shekshnia.

slightest reference to any intervening leader) was Stalin. He looked like an avuncular Sean Connery. In one hand was a pair of cufflinks, in the other a lit pipe. His bare arms emerged from the sleeves of his uniform, reassuringly strong and hairy. Inside Stalin, looking for all the world like a prosperous lawyer, was Lenin.

These figures, and the ways some of them were represented, intrigued me, as the images they presented diverged so much from the impressions we have received from history and television. Why was Stalin so cuddly? Why was Gorbachev painted as such a hard-liner? And why was Putin, the cold-eyed, furtive bungler who seemed to yearn for the certainties of the Soviet era, dressed for the boardroom? Was that eagle rising like a phoenix from the pit at Yekaterinburg?

What were these representations telling us about the way their leaders are viewed by contemporary Russians? Did the painter of the *matryoshka* mean to suggest that Vladimir Putin was leading his country forward into a brave new future that would eclipse the glory of the past? Was he building solid foundations on the last century's tragedies and conflicts? It made me wonder what sort of job Vladimir Putin would really have done as the CEO he looked like on the *matryoshka*, heading his company—Russia Inc.

Not only does Vladimir Putin dress like the head of a modern global company, wearing business suits and expensive though unobtrusive ties, but he also acts like a CEO: always taut and vigorous, active and terse, he speaks in simple terms that a broad public will be able to understand; from time to time, he 'mingles with the people,' flies in fighter jets and helicopters, and bares his muscular chest for photographers during his summer vacations, demonstrating his strength and healthy life. Such outer similarities led me to evaluate his results and performance before he stepped down as Russia's president in May 2008. In this chapter, I examine Putin's years as president through the same questions that one asks in evaluating the work of other CEOs: how effective was President Putin on the job? Which particular qualities did his style of leadership demonstrate? How well did he prepare his 'company' for the future, and what could we expect of him after he moves on? To a degree, the results of this line of questioning were unexpected, but then again, they were also more or less predictable. Just as with corporate CEOs, the actions taken by the President and his leadership style in general are determined not only by the needs of the organization he heads, but also by the scripts in his inner theater. His time in office as president, and his successes, did not change him that much, but only served to strengthen certain distinctive features of his behavior. The example of Putin, whose story is well-known, is not only interesting in itself, but significant in illustrating my ideas about effective contemporary leadership.

Many CEOs, on attaining the top job, go through a three-stage 'life cycle': distinct periods of entry, consolidation, and decline. The period of entry is typically characterized by a high degree of uncertainty as fledgling leaders struggle to understand what their new position entails, deal with the legacy of their predecessors, and search for themes that will take the organization forward. Once their power is consolidated, the environment in which they operate understood, and the key themes identified, new CEOs concentrate on pursuing these themes to make their mark on the organization. In most instances, it is during this period of consolidation that they reach their highest performance and build a solid foundation for the organization's future. In the final stage, the period of decline, CEOs begin to lose their interest in doing new things (though they typically retain their interest in preserving their power base), often becoming myopic, complacent, and stuck in their ways. They may even engage in paranoid thinking, fearful (frequently with good reason) that others are trying to get rid of them. Leaders in this end stage can become real threats to the companies they have led successfully for many years.

Effective business leaders manage to shorten the entry period with careful preparation, and the period of decline through a timely exit. They make the most of period two, the phase of consolidation. But no one is capable of running a complex modern corporation indefinitely. In today's fast-changing world, tenure of seven to eight years is close to optimal for well-prepared, highly capable, and resilient CEOs.[2] That corresponds to two four-year terms (since extended to six years), which the Russian constitution allowed Vladimir Putin to serve as President. How well did he do? And what sort of legacy did he leave his hand-picked successor, Dmitry Medvedev?

EIGHT YEARS AT THE HELM: EXPECTATIONS AND RESULTS

From the moment that Putin was unexpectedly appointed president of the Russian Federation in 2000, both the Russians and the international community were captivated by him. As happens so often with political and business leaders, people projected their own fantasies onto Putin, and onto his past, present, and especially future course of action. Effective CEOs use this tendency (either consciously or unconsciously) to

[2] See Chapter 9 for a detailed discussion of the CEO life cycle.

rally their followers behind their vision and to use their creative energy to achieve extraordinary results. Let's see how Mr Putin fared.

When Putin became Russia's president, the Russian economy had not yet recovered from the financial crisis of 1998. The first result that Russian citizens expected from their new leader was an improved standard of living. But people also looked at the new president with hopes of finding what they had lost with the collapse of the Soviet Union and the socialist system. When they looked back on Boris Yeltsin's time in office, many saw a period of humiliation, headed by a man whose responsibilities could not keep him from the bottle: Russia had lost much of its former influence in the world, in Eastern Europe, and in the former Soviet republics; massive inflation had destroyed people's savings. A murky privatization process, a powerful oligarchy, ever-increasing corruption, and a demoralizing war in Chechnya: there were more than enough points for irritation. Russians' hopes were reborn when a young, athletic, energetic, and sober Putin assumed the top job: Russians wanted a better life, but they also wanted a more meaningful life—and they thought that perhaps Putin might usher one in (Sakwa, 2004; Baker and Glasser, 2007).

Russia Inc.'s potential 'partners,' i.e., the leaders of most Western countries, wanted some clarity and consistency in Russia's attitudes and policies regarding the West, to enable the establishment of fruitful working relationships. They wanted Putin to reaffirm that Russia had chosen the route of democracy and market economy, definitively leaving behind its imperialistic and military ambitions in the former republics of the USSR and in the countries of Eastern Europe. They wanted Russia to support this new world view not only by reforming the army but by bringing home all Russian troops that had been stationed abroad. Western leaders hoped that Putin would prove a reliable, constructive partner in promoting democracy and security in the contemporary world.

How has the CEO lived up to his key stakeholders' expectations?

When Putin took over the top job, the Russian economy, which had been struggling for almost a decade, rebounded, posting stronger growth than most developed economies in the world. Between 1999 (the year before he became president) and 2007, Russia's GDP increased by 69 percent and in purchasing power parity terms reached a $1 billion threshold. Never in their history were Russians as rich as in 2008. Russia's

GDP per capita surpassed USSR levels and the Russian population has been enjoying the dividends of Putin's economic policy through a higher disposable income (aided by the introduction of the 13 percent flat income tax) and much expended opportunities to spend it on consumer goods, leisure, and foreign travel. From a consumer point of view, the underdog Russia has become one of the most dynamic markets in Europe, its domestic consumption growing in double digit numbers over a period of five years.

The majority of the Russian population credits Vladimir Putin and his policies with a spectacular economic turnaround. However, the real picture is far more complex. Yes, Russia Inc. grew fast during Putin's tenure, but it has one of the slowest growth rates compared to the other former Soviet republics, only three of which grew more slowly than Russia. According to some experts, the Russian economy would have actually contracted under Putin—as the 2008–2009 financial crisis dramatically demonstrated—if energy prices had remained at their 1999 levels. Three other hydro carbonate-rich ex-Soviet republics—Azerbaijan, Turkmenistan, and Kazakhstand—grew by 270, 190, and 120 percent correspondingly. If we compare the results of Russia Inc.'s CEO with those of the CEOs of real companies in Russia, his growth statistics look very modest.

While the personal income of Russians almost tripled in nominal terms during Putin's rule as president, double-digit inflation was eating away at a significant chunk of that gain. More importantly, the benefits of economic recovery were being distributed rather unequally—the rich (individuals, cities, regions) were getting richer while the poor remained poor, a real recipe for future unrest. With Putin as president, Russia passed the United States' level of inequality in national income distribution. To summarize, the economic results of Putin's tenure were merely average.

One might suggest that Putin is a visionary strategist who built a foundation for future growth, undertaking profound structural reforms that will benefit Russia's citizens in the future. But a sober analysis shows that this is not the case. In 1999, Putin came to power at a very favorable moment. Ironically, because of the debt crisis, the financial system was in much better shape than it had been, as bad debt had been dealt with. The structure of the Russian economy did not change, however. Its dependence on raw-materials exports increased (oil and gas representing three-quarters of its exports), its manufacturing sector shrank, and its services contributed just about 50 percent of the GDP, compared to 70–80 percent in developed economies. Finally, the number of new start-ups—a key indicator of economic growth—remained low compared to both Eastern and Western Europe. No world-class Russian company emerged. Imports grew much faster than manufacturing. The break-up of Yukos, Russia's largest oil company, and the imprisonment of its boss Mikhail Khodorkovsky, had an ominous after-effect, as it demonstrated the absence of a functioning legal system, and that property rights count for very little, given the possibility of arbitrary bureaucratic decisions. It deterred foreign investors and entrepreneurs (Kets de Vries, Sheksnia, Korotov, and Florent-Treacy, 2004).

A handful of giant industrial financial groups controlled between 60 and 70 percent of the Russian economy. A new feature of the Russian economic landscape was the emergence of state-owned or controlled giant companies such as Gazprom and Rosneft, which spread their activities into dozens of non-related industries through aggressive M&A activities, often involving brutal arm-twisting of the acquisition targets. Moreover, these state controlled companies were anything but exemplary in spending money on their core business and boosting productivity. In tandem, the number of bureaucrats increased dramatically. In contrast to the 1990s, polls during Putin's time showed that more than half of young Russians wanted to work in the government, not engage in entrepreneurial ventures.

Furthermore, the corruption that began to multiply under Yeltsin increased dramatically over the period of Putin's rule, making Russia the murkiest economy in Europe, and ranking with countries like Nigeria and Kenya near the top of the world corruption scale. And corruption become even more entrenched, with a negative effect on investments. By all accounts, Russian economy under Putin's presidency lost some of the important achievements of the initial market reforms of the early 1990s and with them, its relative competitiveness in the world market. As a result, it has slipped in virtually all international rankings such as 'ease of doing business,' 'effectiveness of governance,' 'rule of law,' and other matters.

However, Vladimir Putin changed Russia's mood. Both opinion polls and experts confirm that self-confidence returned to Russia and its population during his presidency. After the chaotic Yeltsin years, the Russians welcomed Putin's nationalistic rhetoric, his strong stand in dealings with foreign partners, his longing for the old Soviet Union, and his determination to bring back Russia's greatness. His tough language resonated with the majority of Russians, who feel that under Putin they became not only better off, but also safer and happier. At the same time, crime statistics demonstrate that Russia remains one of the most dangerous places in the world.

By the same token, it is hard to say that the results of Putin's inter-action with his foreign partners were very satisfactory. Initially, Putin, an ex-master spy recruiter, who speaks fluent German and some English, seemed quickly to establish close and informal relationships with many foreign leaders, such as Gerhard Schröder, Angela Merkel of Germany, George Bush, Tony Blair, and others. However, for the most part, these relationships failed to bring any tangible results to Russia and its part-ners, because, although charming and persuasive in a tête-à-tête, Putin resorted to a black-and-white, rather suspicious world view and a uni-lateral decision-making style when setting and implementing Russia's foreign policy. Furthermore, his brutal suppression of the opposition, the squeezing of independent media, the fickleness of the delivery of gas and oil to the rest of Europe, and the overkill response to the conflict in Georgia, made international investors, politicians, and the media increasingly apprehensive. In the end, Putin's Russia was not perceived by the international community as a reliable trustworthy partner, but as an unpredictable and at times dangerous country, which played by its own rules and tried to get its own way in whatever manner it could (Jack, 2005).

Given his positive qualities—his energy, apparent personal humility, social and listening skills—and the favorable timing of his taking office, why did Putin fail to fulfill the relatively simple expectations of his stakeholders? The answer is simple: he did not do what effective CEOs do.

WHAT DO EFFECTIVE CEOS DO?

Briefly, effective CEOs:

- articulate an attractive vision for the future;
- set challenging but reachable goals;
- strive for alignment between vision, strategy, and behavior;
- demonstrate decisiveness and courage in difficult situations;
- study the competition and develop strategies for staying ahead;
- create a complementary constellation of collaborators who share the organization's vision and values;
- strive to energize and inspire their followers;
- build trust ('walk the talk');
- listen to their people;
- create learning and development opportunities;

- create transparent, client-centric organizations;
- combine operational autonomy with personal accountability for their subordinates;
- give people a sense of ownership in their work;
- encourage innovation and entrepreneurship;
- embrace change;
- put the interests of the organization before their own self-interest;
- and work to create an organization that will thrive beyond their tenure.

If this algorithm for effective leadership is so clear, why do only a few people manage to become effective leaders? The answer is that effective leadership is more than the possession of a set of qualities or skills. It is more than a one-person show. 'Heroic' leaders very soon prove to have clay feet. In contrast, truly effective leaders know their strengths and weaknesses. Effective leaders know how to build alliances. Effective leaders know how to select good people and get the best out of them.

Furthermore, effective political leadership depends on a successful 'marriage' between personality and historical moment, and on the successful enactment of many out-of awareness processes on a public stage. Most importantly, a leader's style is influenced by his or her 'inner theater,' the unique life-script that all of us act out. If we want to know why Putin did not do for Russia Inc. what successful business leaders do for their corporations, if we want to understand his past actions (and non-actions) as well as his future behavior, we need to look beyond the directly observable and try to reconstruct the inner world of this person, his system of values and his motivations. It will help us to understand better the reasons for certain behavior patterns.

The quiet president

'Do not underestimate the determination of a quiet man,' said Iain Duncan Smith, the 'quiet man' of British Conservative politics, who tried to turn the soubriquet with which he had been burdened into a positive attribute of leadership. To little effect: he soon effaced himself entirely as one of a series of short-lived leaders of the post-Thatcher party. But his aphorism holds a certain grain of truth. It characterizes the style of Vladimir Putin, the quiet man who stalked his way to the top job under the cover of a strategic unobtrusiveness. Winston Churchill once described Russia as 'a riddle wrapped in a mystery inside an enigma.' The same could be said of Vladimir Putin. To characterize a leader, psychologists, psychoanalysts or psychiatrists need to interview him for hours. I did not have this opportunity. To some extent, however, as a public persona, the Russian president lifts the curtain of his 'inner theater,' which gives us the possibility of addressing this theme. For example, in 2000 a book entitled *First Person* was published, drawing on 24 hours of interviews that three Russian journalists conducted with Putin (Putin, Gevorkyan, Timakova, and Kolesnikov, 2000). This is how Putin sums up his life at the beginning of the book:

> In fact, I have had a very simple life. Everything is an open book. I finished school and went to university. I graduated from university and went to the KGB. I finished the KGB and went back to university. After university, I went to work for [Mayor Anatoly] Sobchak [in St. Petersburg]. From Sobchak, to Moscow and to the General Department. Then to the Presidential Administration. From there, to the FSB [Russia's internal security services]. Then I was appointed Prime Minister. Now I'm Acting President. That's it! (p. xiv)

All of this indicates an almost incredible degree of restraint and secrecy. Putin's comments about his family and career suggest that his gift for dullness might be an inherited survival strategy. He describes his background as 'very ordinary' but mentions with pride that his grandfather, a cook, 'was transferred to one of Stalin's dachas [and] worked there for a long time.' He adds that 'for some reason they let [my grandfather] be. Few people who spent much time around Stalin came through unscathed, but my grandfather was one of them' (p. 3). Subsequently, Putin introduces the salient quality that may have enabled his grandfather to survive: 'My grandfather kept pretty quiet about his past life. My parents didn't talk much about the past, either' (p. 3). This 'very ordinary' family survived for generations in a deadly environment, apparently using reticence and dullness as a safety net.

Putin was born in St. Petersburg (Leningrad at that time) on October 7, 1952, six months before the death of Stalin. We can surmise that as his parents' only surviving child (two older brothers died before he was born), he was subject to a certain amount of overprotection and/or tremendous pressure to live up to idealized memories of those lost children. Some children cope with overprotectiveness by presenting a bland exterior that gives them a degree of distance, allowing them to maintain their individuality and making it more difficult for the caretakers to get a handle on them. Others, seeing themselves as replacement children, suffer from survivor guilt and feel driven to live up to parental expectations. Overprotection and pressure may lead to feelings of claustrophobia and a desire for more individual freedom in developing children. In Putin's case, this might account for the polarity between conforming and rebelling, order and disorder, that runs like a red thread through his life. It is clear, however, that whatever rebellious streaks he had were suppressed as time went on: conformity and the need for order gained the upper hand.

Initially, Putin was not a model student. A considerable part of his early education seems to have taken place on the street where he hung out with a group of 'hooligans' (his own expression). Perhaps what saved him from becoming a hooligan himself was sport. He took up judo, which he continued to practice even when president. To some extent, judo can be seen as a metaphor for much of Putin's later way of dealing with others. One of the main lessons of judo is never to tackle a person head on, but to get into a position where you can make them defeat themselves with their own weight. This could sum up Putin's approach in life: working at not appearing to be a threat to others.

As a youngster, Putin also loved spy novels and spy games. He said later that he was drawn to the KGB by movies and books describing the heroic feats of Soviet agents. To Putin, being a spy seemed to be the way to 'put things right' in what seemed to him a highly chaotic, unpredictable world. It would let him remain invisible while providing him with the ideal setting to make an impact, to create order.

The invisible man

After his graduation from the law school of St. Petersburg University, the KGB invited Putin to join. After a stint in counterintelligence, he was offered a spot in foreign intelligence. The KGB assigned Putin to Dresden, where his duties included economic intelligence and the recruitment of spies. His work was successful, but not exceptional. His stint in Dresden, however, gave him some idea about the way people operate in the West. The turbulent ending of his tour of duty, in the whirlwind of German reunification, must have reinforced his belief in the need for an ordered, planned world.

In the 1990s, after the downfall of the Soviet Union, Putin left the KGB. He described that move as the 'toughest decision of my life.' He became a deputy to Anatoly Sobchak, the flamboyant mayor of St. Petersburg. Being Sobchak's right-hand man was his first high-level political post. In 1996, after Sobchak's political defeat in the mayoral elections, Putin moved to Moscow. Anatoly Chubais, the architect of

Russian privatization, had noticed him and introduced him to Boris Yeltsin. In 1998, he was appointed deputy head of the presidential administration. Even in this very senior position, Putin managed to keep a low profile, never appearing as a threat to others. Under Yeltsin, he used his charm, loyalty, KGB training, discipline, and common sense in a series of jobs that included running the federal security service, the FSB.

In the drunken, faltering Yeltsin, Putin found yet another man in need of a strong, reliable, loyal deputy, and he made himself indispensable. Beset by corruption scandals, health problems, and the threat of impeachment, Yeltsin used his young lieutenant as a guarantee of a safe exit from political life. This background does not suggest that Putin is a natural leader. Rather it paints him as a bureaucrat, more efficient at executing orders than giving them.

But his bland exterior does not mean that Putin is unemotional. Clinical experience has shown that many very emotionally restrained people use detachment to defend themselves against strong emotions, fearing that if they let go the process will become uncontrollable. (This may also explain why Putin, who led a nation of accomplished drinkers, avoids strong drink.)

A hunger for control

Putin's desire for control dovetailed with the needs of Russian society following the wild Yeltsin years. The strengthening of control ended the chaotic policy-drift of the Yeltsin years and slowed down capital flight. But in most areas reforms fell far short of what they needed to be to create a more efficient market order.

The shortcomings of Putin's style of government were quite serious. Putin preferred policies that enhanced state—or better, presidential—control over the economy and the political sphere. Under his watchful eye, the growing influence of the intelligence services permeated all levels and agencies of the government. As Putin consolidated his power, he left very little room for organized action or the press by anyone who would dare to challenge him.

Laughter can be seen as a subtle form of communication. Reading between the lines, jokes become important signifiers of behavior. As a rule, jokes about Putin share themes like the consolidation of Kremlin authority, attempts to get rid of opposition and silence independent mass media, and domination of other authorities. One joke popular in Moscow during his presidency told that Putin dreamed Stalin came to see him in his study in the Kremlin. Putin asked Stalin's advice about how to run the country. Stalin said: 'The first thing you do is round up all democrats and send them to Gulag. Second, have the Kremlin walls painted green.' 'But why green, Iosiff Vissarionovich?' asked Putin. Stalin replied: 'Aha! I knew you wouldn't have a problem with the first thing!'

Putin seemed to understand the importance of organizational architecture and talent to the successful implementation of his plans. However, when he chose his team of 'top executives,' he placed his bets not on the talent of the candidates, but on their loyalty. It is clear that he did not trust the emerging generation of Western-educated Russians who could have been ideal bridge spanners. Instead, he found his political base among representatives of the military and security services, known as the *siloviki*. According to one Russian estimate, over 75 percent of Putin's top 500 Russian government officials had worked for the KGB or other special services in the past. This estimate suggests that people with nationalistic, xenophobic views gradually increased their hold on power in Putin's Kremlin.

Paranoia and societal regression

Caution, vigilance, and the ability to sense danger on time are healthy qualities that any leader will find useful. However, in some cases, vigilance can develop into paranoia, an inadequate response to potential danger. Paranoia has been called the 'disease of kings,' because people who spend their lives wielding power are very much prey to it. Given Putin's position of power and his history with the KGB, we can assume that he is no stranger to suspiciousness. Of course he faced very real dangers as president, from Russia's geography alone. In addition to the problems in Chechnya, Ukraine was hopping from one political crisis to another. Georgia, Moldova, and Azerbaijan, with their pro-Western leanings, were also serious causes for worry. Moreover, the erratic leaders of countries like Belarus and North Korea would give any neighbor a serious headache, as would a number of unstable autocrats running the republics of central Asia. As if that were not enough, Russia's relationship with Japan had been strained for years because of a number of disputed islands, and China's increasing success made that country more of a perceived threat to Russia's Far East. Finally, Russia's relationship with the West was the chilliest it had been in years. Dangers—perceived or real—were everywhere.

Unfortunately, when paranoid thinking takes root, leaders are prone to faulty reality-testing. These problems are aggravated when leaders question the trustworthiness of their advisors, and start to listen for—and find—hidden meanings in even the most innocent remarks. The balance between vigilance and paranoia is extremely delicate. Once the pendulum has swung toward paranoia, suspiciousness spreads like the plague, becoming the habitual mode of thinking of the whole inner circle.

To contain the spread of paranoia, effective leaders ground their behavior in sound political practices that limit and test danger, and they rely on trusted associates—people who can speak their mind—to help them stay safe and sane. Did Putin have such associates, people unafraid to tell the truth? It seems unlikely, given that so many in his inner circle had connections with the former KGB, which is not the most open organization in the world. Many of these people seemed to prefer secrecy to transparency, as their handling of the Moscow theater siege, the loss of the crew of the submarine *Kursk*, as well as the tragic outcome of the siege in Beslan, demonstrated. Keeping people in the dark—a key weakness of the paranoid style—is not an effective way to create either a high-performance business organization or a smoothly functioning society.

A controlling and paranoid disposition produces a distinctive style of leadership and draws in its wake distinctive responses. When paranoid thinking takes over and control becomes tighter, there is a danger of societal regression. As control is pulled from the general public and hoarded at the top, the 'little' people feel increasingly powerless. In that mindset, they are vulnerable to delusional ideation—ideas completely detached from reality—and authoritarianism. Under paranoid leadership and especially during stressful times, a rigid, bipolar view of the world is common, with the world split into camps of friends and enemies. Conspiracies and enemies abound. Leaders will encourage this kind of approach, since the shared search for enemies results in a strong conviction of the righteousness of a common cause and energizes new struggles. A variant of the well-known fight or flight response, it is also a way of coping with emerging anxiety, channeling it outward.

The need for heroes

Another way to cope with anxiety is to 'contain' it. Leaders who are effective at containment radiate certainty and conviction, thus creating meaning for their followers and offering a holding environment that creates a modicum of security. Anxious followers, grateful for the security, project a sense of grandiosity on their leaders: a powerful leader implies that they might become powerful themselves.

Putin's portrait is to be found in most officials' offices; pop songs extol his discipline; he has cafés, ice-creams, and tomatoes named after him. He is the hero of a textbook for schoolchildren, in which he is depicted as a non-smoking fighter pilot who loves his family. His face appears on T-shirts, carpets, and *matryoshkas*, the famous Russian nesting dolls.

To any student of history, personality cults are a worrisome sign. From the days of the czars to the days of Lenin and Stalin, personality cults have not served Russians well. Of course, Putin did not slide into the kind of behavior of which his most notorious predecessors, Stalin and Lenin, were capable. Russia today is much more pluralistic than it has ever been in the past. However, that doesn't mean that we should lessen our vigilance. After all, authoritarian rule, even in its most modern forms, is not capable of managing an object as complex as Russia Inc.

SUCCESSION AND LEGACY

Organizational wisdom states that there is one task no CEO should neglect: the preparation of a successor. To many scholars of organizations, the acid test of anyone's effective leadership is the performance of his or her successor. Putin faced a huge challenge when considering who would take over from him: he not only needed to find the right person, but he had to set the precedent of transferring power in Russia after his constitutional term expired. He had two traditions working against him: Russian leaders tend to hang on to power until they are carried out in a coffin, and they favor an '*après moi le déluge*' perspective on developing successors.

On the evening of the Russian presidential election day, March 2, 2008, two short, casually dressed men—Vladimir Putin and Dmitry Medvedev, the winning candidate, walked (like prize fighters, dressed in leather jackets) down from the Kremlin to the Red Square to address a crowd of their young supporters, who listened to performances by a succession of the country's rock stars. As usual, as they climbed the podium, the crowd roared: 'Putin, Putin, Putin.' Medvedev, however, spoke first—he thanked the people for voting in the election, he thanked them for their support, and vowed to continue Vladimir Putin's course. In his turn a smiling Putin expressed his deep belief that the right course would continue to make Russia a great place to live. The first Russian TV channel transmitted that scene to the millions of Russian households. The spiritual succession had taken place; the formal one followed two months later, in May.

Both the way in which Vladimir Putin managed his succession and the actual choice he made provide some important insights into his leadership style and his future actions. The succession was carried out in full accordance with the law, but it largely ignored its spirit, depriving Russian people of their constitutional right to choose their President. The succession process was opaque, undemocratic, focused on the outgoing leader, and supported by a massive marketing campaign. With all the advantages that came with control of the mass media, combined with Putin's genuine popularity, the logical tactic would have been to ignore the opposition. Instead, it was dealt with in an extremely heavy-handed way. Apparently, the Kremlin was unable to relinquish total control. No chances were taken to assure that Medvedev would be elected.

Among Dmitry Medvedev's qualities, one sticks out—unquestionable personal loyalty to Vladimir Putin. And in the spirit of the Kremlin tradition, Putin kept people in suspense about who would succeed him and what he would do after his second term expired. This approach fueled all kinds of speculations rather than creating an opportunity for a national debate about what kind of leadership the country would need for its next phase in development. To his credit, however, Putin always firmly rejected all suggestions that he should run as president for the third term. But he has made it quite clear that he intends to stay in power. When the mechanism for doing so—becoming prime minister—became apparent, Putin joined the United Russia Party electoral ticket. Given the power of his position, it gave him a huge advantage, making for an absolute parliamentary majority that approved its 'choice' for the presidential candidate Medvedev.

The succession process can be compared to a horse race behind closed doors, with two publicly known pretenders, Dmitry Medvedev and another Vice-Prime Minister Sergey Ivanov, together with many unknowns, struggling for Putin's blessing. As a good power broker, Putin waited until the very last moment to announce his choice. Civil society was completely excluded from this exercise—no debates were aired, no programs compared, no candidates assessed publically. The official campaign did not offer much more to the voters: Medvedev stayed away from televised debates, and made no program statements except those expressing his support for Putin's course. The mass media portrayed him as Putin's closest collaborator, a busy minister with no time for campaigning—a Russian patriot. And this strategy turned out to be extremely effective. In a matter of two months Medvedev's popularity surpassed that of Putin and he won a landslide victory in the first round of the elections. So Putin got what he wanted—a trusted man to succeed him elected in full accordance with the democratic procedure. Russia Inc. got another unknown as its new CEO.

Dmitry Medvedev, who like Putin grew up in St. Petersburg and graduated from the same law school, spent almost all his working life beside his predecessor, as his legal counselor, deputy, head of presidential administration and later Vice-Prime Minister. Like Putin, before becoming president, Medvedev was more of a bureaucrat than a visionary leader. Having no personal leadership experience, he must have learned leadership by observing his senior colleague. Similarities are abundant, which may suggest that Vladimir Putin, like many outgoing business executives, was subconsciously trying to replicate himself and 'prolong' his days in office.

Taking into account Vladimir Putin's extreme vigilance, his deeply-ingrained fear of disorder, and Russian tradition of forgetting or even ostracizing former leaders, one can see his handling of his succession as both a personal survival strategy and an attempt to protect his legacy. It may, however, turn out to be as ineffective as many similar strategies of business executives have proved to be.

Judging by his good mood and public comments, President Putin was more than satisfied with his two terms in the top job. He considered economic prosperity, stability and the re-emergence of Russian national self-consciousness as his major achievements and legacy. He did not recognize, however, that his leadership failed to bring about profound changes to the Russian economy and society to ensure true and lasting prosperity, stability, and self-esteem. Today Russia—as the financial crisis of 2008–2009 has demonstrated—was (and is) ill-prepared to deal with the challenges of the twenty-first century as it still stands on the foundation built in the previous centuries. Russia's public institutions, law and law enforcement, governance, ideology, and ethics require a comprehensive overhaul if Russia is to compete with other developing and emerging nations. Without such dramatic change, the recent vision articulated by Putin of making 'Russia the most attractive country to live in' will remain pure demagogy. To orchestrate such a profound change, Russia needs a very different type of leadership.

One of the characteristics of CEOs who do well at succeeding s trong and long-standing predecessors is that they are different from them. Not surprisingly, Putin's initial popularity was based on his contrast with Boris Yeltsin. To be effective, Putin's successor—or the incoming leadership team—needs not only a different agenda, but also a different style.

Many effective successors are 'inside-outsiders' who combine a deep knowledge of the organization they will be responsible for with an independent, almost external perspective on it. In many instances, successful newcomers have particular expertise in whatever interventions need to be taken. Exceptional leaders like Jack Welch of General Electric (an inside-outsider working outside the core business) and Louis Gerstner of IBM (an outsider) are good illustrations from the business world. Three previous Russian leaders were highly effective at implementing large-scale country transformations: Peter the Great, Catherine the Great, and Josef Stalin. They all possessed this combination of an insider's deep knowledge and an outsider's marginality. Peter the Great spent many of his formative years in the foreign settlement in Moscow, built ships, and traveled abroad. Catherine the Great, who was born a German princess, moved to Russia at the age of 15 to marry the heir to the throne and spent 17 years becoming acquainted with a bewildering new culture before becoming an absolute monarch. Stalin came from Georgia, which although part of the Russian empire was a distinctively different country.

Peter the Great had a deep knowledge of industry, navigation, and the military—areas in which the country made great leaps forward during his reign. Catherine the Great was an astute student of government, diplomacy, philosophy, and literature, giving her the grounding she needed as Russia created a new administrative system, made significant territorial acquisitions, became a heavyweight in European politics, and laid the foundation for great scientific and artistic breakthroughs. Stalin was a student of theology, a discipline that prepared him for life as a professional revolutionary preaching the benefits of Marxist ideology and helped him create a mighty military–industrial complex and lead the Soviet Union into the nuclear age (though at a high cost in human suffering). However, given stalin's extreme psychopathology, his is not exactly a role model to emulate.

THE LEADERSHIP STYLE RUSSIA NEEDS

What qualities will Dmitry Medvedev and people who work with him need to demonstrate to take Russia Inc. to a higher level of national and global performance?

Viewed from within the context of Russian culture, Dmitry Medvedev will need to have an authoritative (though not authoritarian) style of leadership. He will need to be resourceful and charismatic, because Russians like leaders who are larger than life. The country needs an innovator and creator who takes an entrepreneurial attitude to his job. For inspiration and role models, Medvedev can look to successful Russian entrepreneurs who built successful businesses by formulating specific challenging goals, energizing their constituencies with an achievable vision, designing and maintaining flexible, high-performing organizations and networks, and courageously destroying outdated structures. Moreover, in contrast with many government officials, these new Russian entrepreneurs put the long-term interests of their businesses above their personal concerns.

The new CEO of Russia Inc. should take innovative approaches to many issues and adopt entrepreneurial decisiveness when dealing with them. The impasse in Chechnya, for example, cannot be resolved within the existing paradigm, nor can Russia's problems with the military, the educational system, or health care. Each of these areas requires the fresh approach of an outsider, although one who understands how the system works.

Although Putin missed many opportunities to turn Russia around, those opportunities are still there to be exploited by a new leader. One of them is the European Union. Instead of sounding off about the search for a national idea, Russia needs to do what other Eastern European countries have already done, namely to request membership or another form of association with this organization. A message like 'Linking Russia to Europe' could suggest a powerful vision for the new presidency. It would resonate well with a significant part of the Russian population, although perhaps not with the existing national and regional political elites. Even if the EU rejected any formal association, Russia would benefit from the application, since as an applicant it could use the EU's strengths to help bring Russia's economy, legal and administrative systems, pension and social security systems, and legislation more in tune with the twenty-first century. Needless to say, even the formulation of this type of conception would require a great deal of foresight and courage.

Great visions remain empty slogans if they are not supported by the leader's personal commitment and behavior. Acting from behind the scenes will not ignite the Russian population: the new president should get closer to the people, roll up his sleeves, and get his hands dirty in building a new Russia, as Peter the Great did 300 years ago and as many Russian entrepreneurs are doing now.

The new CEO of Russia Inc. should not come to the job with plans for personal enrichment, but with a vision of making the country more internationally competitive and helping it become a better place to live and work, preparing it for long-term growth. And one of the major tasks will be to root out corruption. Over the past 15 years Russia has produced many wealthy individuals whose fortunes will last for many generations to come. For many of them, the time has come to give something back to society. These people should set an example of non-corrupt political leadership and help instill a new, more entrepreneurial culture in the government.

This will be a daunting task. The late general and politician Alexander Lebed once said, 'Russia is like a dinosaur. A lot of time is needed for change to reach the tail from the head.' The task of creating a turnaround in that country will surely be monumental, as Lebed suggested. The question is, will Dmitry Medvedev be up to the task? If he tries to act in a traditional Kremlinesque way, playing people off against each other, promoting loyalists, destroying foes, and creating Potemkin villages (something that appears elaborate and impressive but in actual fact lacks substance), the answer is a firm 'no.' But it can be done, with the help of a broad coalition of people who have a genuine interest in making Russia a better place to live, and possess the skills and experience to manage large-scale change projects. Russian business represents a natural source of such people for the new political leadership to draw upon and to learn from.

WHAT WILL HAPPEN NEXT?

Winston Churchill once allegedly said that Kremlin power struggles are like bullfrogs fighting under the carpet: you hear a lot of growling but don't know who won until one of them emerges. But although the outcome of the power struggle in the Kremlin is impossible to predict, there are three likely scenarios, some combination of which will most likely shape Russia's future during Medvedev's.

The first scenario has been discussed in great detail in Russian and Western press—Vladimir Putin being a powerful prime minister and Dmitry Medvedev his marionette, stepping down at some point to clear a way for Putin's re-election. Some of Putin's comments—he referred to the prime minister's job as a 'chief executive power'—have been interpreted as indications of a plan of this kind. And yet this would be one of the worst things Putin could do to Russia's future and his own legacy. With Medvedev as nominal and Putin as de facto head of state, Russia Inc. would have a CEO who had already entered the third and final stage—decline—of his life cycle at the helm. There are signs that Putin has already made this transition. He appears to be increasingly internally focused; his tolerance of criticism has diminished; he talks more about the glorious past of Russia and his achievements, and less about Russia's real and problematic future; at times he looks like a new Russian bureaucrat rather than a global CEO. If these trends were to persist, this *modus operandi* would have a devastating effect on Russia's

development. The outdated structure of its economy would be preserved, corruption would increase even more, the bureaucratization of
the government would accelerate, and innovation in all areas would stall.
Sooner rather than later, serious economic troubles would result, even
if energy prices stayed high. And if energy prices went down, Russia
would suffer a severe crisis.

But apart from these developments, an emotionally and psychologically ailing (albeit physically healthy) leader without an exciting vision
for the future would deeply traumatize the collective psyche of the
Russian population, especially its younger members. Traditional skepti-
cism about reform and deep mistrust of the government would soon be
back, straining the creative energy of the population and pushing the
most industrious individuals to leave the country.

Remaining in power behind the scenes would have deeply negative
consequences for Putin himself. It would significantly reduce his credibility if he tried to impose his agenda without political legitimacy. He
would guarantee a negative legacy: he would be remembered as yet
another KGB man who seized power, played the democracy tune when
it suited him, and abandoned it when it was no longer useful. Whatever
modest contributions he made to stabilize the nation during his terms
in power would soon be forgotten, while the corruption of power and
the stagnation of Russia, Inc. would be long remembered.

There is a second scenario, even though it may sound overly pessimistic—the Russian *siloviki*, whose most electable man, Sergey Ivanov,
was passed over as Putin's successor, might consolidate their power,
remove or isolate Putin, and dictate their agenda of further strengthening
the state, including its security branches, increasing its role in business,
supporting enemies of Russia's presumed international foes, and promoting the ideology of Russia's unique way of running the government.
Such developments would throw Russia decades back and have a devastating effect on its economic competiveness and international standing.
Under this scenario, Putin would probably go down in the Russian
memory as another sympathetic political martyr, who could not,
however, protect his achievements.

The third scenario is the most plausible. Under it, Dmitry Medvedev
will become a fully-fledged CEO of Russia, Inc. He will chart a new
course for the country, which will include creation of a rule of law,
modernization of Russian government institutions, separation of business and politics, modernization of the Russian economy, overhaul of
its social security and health systems on the basis of market logic—very
important things that Medvedev has already spoken about. He will
concentrate on creating a transparent, efficient system of government,

leaving most of its implementation to private initiative. The President will make Russia a truly attractive place for long-term foreign investment by enhancing its legal framework, especially law enforcement.

Rather than talking about past greatness, and rewriting the history books (as is presently taking place) he will help Russians to come to terms with the country's not-so-glorious past (including the gulag system) and focus on building their future. The president will consolidate the Russian people around human values of peace, development, creating a better future for their children, and living normal lives.

The new president needs to make Russia a predictable international player and win new friends in all parts of the world. He will need to normalize Russia's relationships with Ukraine and other former Soviet republics, making them equal partners and true friends. The president needs to negotiate with Western countries to stop a stone-age entry visa practice, ending the humiliation for Russians traveling abroad and foreigners coming to Russia.

So far Dmitry Medvedev has not demonstrated the qualities he will need to enact such a scenario. However, we should not underestimate the power of the office in Russia. Who would really have thought in 1999 that a little known acting president named Vladimir Putin would become such a central figure in the first decade of the twenty-first century? The outgoing CEO of Russia, Inc. has a great opportunity to assure his legacy by facilitating his successor's entry into the job. Putin can help Medvedev in many ways, but he will be most helpful if he leaves him alone to create his own power base and decide on the future course for Russia. Although this advice may be counterintuitive to the over-controlling and super-vigilant Putin, the true legacy of leadership is to leave a successful successor. What should not happen is described in the following joke.

> Vladimir Putin and Dmitry Medvedev wake up in the Kremlin in 2023 with a vicious hangover. Putin says to Medvedev, 'Who of us is president and which of us is prime minister today?' 'I don't remember,' Medvedev replies. 'I could be prime minister today.' 'Then go fetch some beer,' says Putin.

CHAPTER 6

'COMPLEX' EXECUTIVES I HAVE 'MET' IN COACHING AND CONSULTING[1]

The feeling of inferiority rules the mental life and can be clearly recognized in the sense of incompleteness and un-fulfillment, and in the uninterrupted struggle both of individuals and humanity.

—*Alfred Adler*

I was a personality before I became a person. I am simple, complex, generous, selfish, unattractive, beautiful, lazy and driven.

—*Barbra Streisand*

I have an inferiority complex, but not a very good one!

—*Anonymous*

During the course of their career, organizational consultants, leadership coaches, psychotherapists, psychiatrists, and psychoanalysts often meet people who present a bewildering array of responses and behaviors. Psychologically trained professionals often resort to traditional psychiatric classification schemes such as personality types, discussed in Chapter 7, to make sense of such people (Millon, 1996; American Psychiatric Association, 2000). The boundaries of these schemes can be quite narrow, however (although the concept of 'co-morbidity' suggests that other disorders typically accompany the most important one). One helpful way of going beyond narrow boundaries in the classification of conduct is to take a closer look at the concept of the psychological 'complex.'

[1] Most of the material in this chapter has previously appeared in published form in the following: Kets de Vries, M.F.R. (2007). "'Complex' Executives I have 'Met' in Coaching and Consulting," *Organizational Dynamics*, 36 (4), 377–391.

In everyday language, people use the word 'complex' to refer to just about any psychological or emotional difficulty. But applied correctly, the term 'complex' is more precise than that. It creates a common reference point; in effect, it maps a person's psychological make-up. (The term 'complex'—originally 'feeling-toned complex of ideas'—was first introduced into the language in 1989 by the Austrian psychiatrist Theodor Ziehen.) Ascribing the label 'complex' to an individual's experience implies that we have identified several clinically recognizable features, symptoms, or characteristics that occur simultaneously in that person. Basically, a 'complex' refers to a cluster of related thoughts, feelings, memories, desires, and behavior patterns—many of them not under conscious control and often detectable only indirectly—which, taken together, explain someone's otherwise mysterious conduct (Jacobi, 1971).

The content of a complex can be as varied as the human experience. For example, people can have complexes about intimacy and love, order, power, status, honor, intelligence, achievement, recognition, fame, sexuality, money, food, health, and so on. Given its effect on an individual, each complex will determine how that person reacts in specific circumstances. Although we talk about someone 'having a complex,' it is really the other way around: it is the complex that 'has' the person.

Because of the unconscious origin of most complexes, these combinations of thoughts, feelings and desires can put false ideas into our heads, resulting in irrational, distorted conceptions about ourselves, other people and situations. For example, we may jump to conclusions, interpreting events in one particular way without supporting evidence. We may engage in all-or-nothing, black-or-white thinking. Typically, this means perceiving everything negatively. We may feel helpless in certain situations, believing we have no control over the events in our lives. We may make a catastrophe out of nothing, expecting a larger (actual) catastrophe to strike at any moment. We may be preoccupied with rules about how we or others should act. We may always need to be right. And so the list goes on. Because of these distortions, many complexes are highly detrimental to our sense of self-esteem and influence the way we deal with others. The themes central to the complex tell us that we are incompetent, unlovable or unattractive, creating specific intrapersonal and interpersonal problems.

As might be expected, the origin of a complex is to be found in childhood experiences, particularly the nature and quality of the parent-child interface. Even parents who are kind, loving and mean well are not perfect: life dictates that parents are not always immediately available, and a certain dose of frustration is one of the inevitabilities of growing up. But delays in receiving food, attention, and comfort when children really want or need them result in frustration, disappointment, and feelings of anger or sadness that may contribute to the formation of a complex.

Conversely, overprotective parents can also sow the seeds of a complex in their children. If they indulge and reward their children so lavishly that they develop unrealistic expectations of how the world should treat them, those children may have trouble dealing with reality as adults. Having received the message that their abilities and possibilities are unlimited, and that they are in some way superior to other people, they may experience self-esteem problems when the world tells them they are actually—ordinary. They may carry burdensome feelings of self-doubt or exaggerated self-confidence (or some of each, depending on how their unique complex develops), based on their childhood experiences.

The tendency of some parents to stereotype their children also contributes to complexes in adulthood. Parents who unwittingly transmit the message that a child is temperamental, unattractive, lazy, stubborn, or a klutz, have no idea how powerful that message is. In adulthood, most children of such parents find it difficult to relinquish the attributes given to them by the parents who, in a child's eyes, are all-powerful and all-knowing. This can be seen in family business situations, in particular.

Not all complexes result from parental messages, however. Some arise from incidents outside the home—exceptionally easy successes, guilty episodes that result in shameful memories, episodes of rejection or adulation, or any other major life event or transition. These experiences become part of the template that dictates how people perceive and deal with the world at large.

Complexes are not always negative, or at least not exclusively so. Take, for example, the father complex that might develop in the absence (or non-availability) of an early male caregiver. The search for a caring father, continued into adulthood, can produce a respectful attitude toward people in positions of authority, which in turn can facilitate constructive working relationships in organizations. However, a negative father complex can lead to ambivalence and distrust of older males, a continual need to question authority, and can hamper work (and career progression) in hierarchical organizations.

A 'COMPLEX' HISTORY

Probably the most widely known complex is the inferiority complex, described in the first decade of the twentieth century by Alfred Adler, one of the early disciples of Sigmund Freud. According to Adler, the cause of this complex is a perception of weakness or defect in some part of the body (Adler, 1956; Hoffman, 1994). However, this complex is really rooted in the young child's original experience of weakness, helplessness, and dependency. The primary indication of this complex (of which the person is usually unaware) is a persistent feeling of inadequacy or a tendency toward self-diminishment. Someone under the sway of this complex may feel a strong urge to overcompensate for it, resulting in either spectacular achievements or deviant, destructive behavior. For example, a youngster who is ridiculed at school because of his poor athletic performance may compensate for this sense of inadequacy as an adult by making a great effort to acquire the power to control others.

Before Adler identified the concept of the inferiority complex, Freud had already introduced the notion of the 'Oedipus complex' into the psychological literature (Freud, 1899). Freud believed all children experience the triadic Oedipus complex when growing up and saw the complex as a universal template for human development. The name is taken from the Greek myth of Oedipus, a man who unknowingly kills his father and marries his mother. The Oedipus complex is defined as a male child's unconscious desire for the exclusive love of his mother. This desire is accompanied by jealousy and rivalry toward the father and the unconscious wish for the father's death. Resolution of the Oedipus complex is believed to occur through identification with the parent of the same sex and through the renunciation of sexual interest in the parent of the opposite sex. The corresponding situation for a girl—desire for her father and antipathy toward her mother—is often described as the 'Electra complex' or, perhaps more accurately, the 'Persephone complex,' after another Greek myth illustrating conflict between child and parent.

The term 'complex' was further popularized by Carl Jung, who suggested that all human beings possess a number of common psychological predispositions, or 'archetypes' (Jung, 1971a, 1971b). These predispositions are capable of influencing thought and conduct, especially in dysfunctional directions. Thus Jung, in contrast to Freud, saw complexes as organizing structures that are derived from the collective unconscious. According to Jung, several complexes occur simultaneously in most people, vary from person to person, and have at their core an archetypal theme with the same name as the complex (the death complex, for example, grows out of the death archetype). It is almost as if Jung were describing autonomous, split-off parts of the psyche—in other words, separate personalities.

We can conclude from this short overview that any body of suppressed tendencies and experiences showing activity independent of the conscious mind can be considered a complex. In that respect, we can find many similarities between a complex and a personality or character type. However, there is greater definitional clarity using the notion of personality types. The boundaries are more muddled for complexes, but the net that captures them is wider.

COMMON WORKPLACE COMPLEXES

Let us now turn to a number of common workplace complexes I regularly encounter in my leadership coaching and consulting work, or can see described in literature or the business press. In listing them, I am building on Sigmund Freud's work 'Some Character Types Met with in Psychoanalytic Work' (Freud, 1953). In that study he offers a number of brilliant insights into the behavior not only of his patients but also of well-known figures from literature, such as Lady Macbeth and Richard III.

The God complex

Individuals who are said to have a God (or messianic) complex act in an arrogant, haughty manner suggestive of divine authority. It will come as no surprise that this complex is quite similar to the narcissistic personality.

Some of the major movers and shakers within the world of politics, business, and finance seem to be driven by the God complex. An exemplar can be found in the special class of nouveau riche Wall Street wheeler-dealers that Thomas Wolfe describes in his novel *The Bonfire of the Vanities*—men and women who came of age in the 1980s (Wolfe, 1988). The protagonist of that novel, Sherman McCoy, insulated by his newly acquired wealth, embodies the God complex. Sitting in the bucket seat of his expensive Mercedes sports car with his classy mistress by his side, he subjects the reader to a self-congratulatory stream of consciousness. But McCoy loses his mental equilibrium when his mistress, taking a turn at the wheel, accidentally drives over a young black man in the Bronx. Fearful of the dangers a white man faces in a hostile black neighborhood, McCoy flees the scene for the guilty safety of the mistress's turf and his Park Avenue home. Prosecutors, politicians, the press, the police, the clergy and assorted hustlers close in on him as he tries to deal with the unraveling of his upper-crust life.

People suffering from the God complex have such a tenuous grip on reality that they indulge in fantasies of omnipotence and omniscience. Their grandiose sense of self-importance prompts them to act pompously, arrogantly, and disdainfully. Attention-seekers who like to be in the limelight, they exaggerate their achievements and talents, convincing even themselves with their fantasies of unlimited success and fame. Needing a constant supply of narcissistic fuel, these individuals require sustained admiration, attention, and affirmation. To that end, they tend to surround themselves with sycophants who encourage their self-centered, self-indulgent behavior.

Such people are not particularly responsive to the needs of others. They lack empathy, and seem unable or unwilling to identify with, acknowledge, or accept the feelings, needs, preferences, priorities, and choices of people they interact with. They shamelessly take others for granted and are 'interpersonally exploitative,' meaning that they have a knack for using others for their own ends. They expect special favors from others without giving any thought to reciprocation.

Another characteristic of people driven by the God complex is their strong sense of entitlement. They believe that the world owes them, big time, and that they deserve what they want when they want it. They seem to maintain their sense of self-worth by rigidly insisting that they are above the hoi polloi. Believing that rules are for others, not for them, they demand automatic and full compliance with their expectations of priority treatment. Full of themselves, they try to associate only with other special or high-status people (or institutions).

However, the mental equilibrium of people with the God complex is delicate. They tend to be extremely envious of others. With that comparative mindset, they are quick to see themselves as wronged and respond with paranoia when they do not get what they want. When frustrated, contradicted, or confronted by people whom they consider inferior to themselves, they sometimes explode in bouts of rage.

Given their narcissistic predisposition, people under the influence of the God complex prefer the world of illusion to the tedium and demands of real accomplishments, although they discuss their triumphs with anyone who will listen. Yet when an outsider takes a closer look, many of their touted accomplishments turn out to be devoid of much substance.

Because the God complex makes them competitive, ambitious and self-assured, these people often find themselves in positions of leadership. Unfortunately, in an organizational setting, their self-centered behavior may give rise to serious problems. Surrounded as they often are by syco-phants, they may lose touch with reality, making decisions on inadequate information (having long since 'killed' all bringers of bad news). They may even resort to unethical behavior. Predictably, the organizations they lead may have difficulty keeping competent people. Principled men and women, who refuse to toe the line, will leave. For that reason, many organizations led by people with the God complex have ended up in reorganization or bankruptcy.

The God complex, like all complexes, has its origins in early conflicts in interpersonal relationships. The roots are typically found in parental under- or overstimulation. In the case of the former, the parents are unable to give their children the attention they need. Consequently, those children escape into their own world and remain stuck at a developmental stage in which their sense of self remains grandiose and unrealistic. The child remains psychologically dependent on approval from others for his or her sense of self-esteem. In the case of overstimulation, the parents' indulgence of their children's moods and demands freezes those youngsters in a state of childlike grandiosity, making them think of themselves as enduringly special. Their resulting need for special treatment—what I term self-deceptive narcissism in Chapter 1—becomes an obsession that remains with them in adulthood.

For a good real-life illustration of the God complex, we can take Dennis Kozlowski, the former CEO of Tyco, a conglomerate with business interests that include electronic components, health care, fire safety, security, and fluid control. The fortieth birthday party Kozlowski gave for his wife, a bash with a $2 million price tag, is indicative of what happens when the God complex is in full swing. Tyco footed about half the bill for this party in Sardinia, which featured an ice sculpture of Michelangelo's David that dispensed vodka from its penis and a birthday cake in the shape of a woman's breast with sparklers mounted on top. The formidable cost also extended to flying in the singer Jimmy Buffett and his group for entertainment.

This sort of plundering of company resources was not Kozlowski's only indulgence. He was also accused of avoiding more than one million dollars in sales tax on six pieces of art, including works by Monet and Renoir that he purchased for $13.1 million in 2001. He had bought the art for his Manhattan apartment but claimed the pieces were being sent to Tyco's New Hampshire headquarters, in order to elude New York sales tax. Clearly Kozlowski thought the world's rules did not apply to him. Eventually, he was accused of plundering Tyco to the tune of $600 million—facing up to 25 years in prison.

The Sisyphus complex

Sisyphus, the mythical King of Corinth, was lauded as a clever but devious man who killed travelers and guests in violation of the laws of hospitality. He was condemned by the gods after first deceiving Hades,

Lord of the Underworld, and then locking him up. With Hades unable to guide humans into the Underworld, a crisis developed: no human could die. As punishment for his trickery, Sisyphus was sentenced to roll a huge rock up a steep hill for eternity. Before it reached the summit, the rock always fell back, and Sisyphus had to start the whole meaning-less process all over again.

In psychological terms, Sisyphus was doomed to a life of nonpro-ductivity, performing a specific task over and over again, but never achieving completion. Worse, he was cursed with the knowledge that, because he could never reach the top of the hill, his work was wasted. In other words, the purpose in his life was to accomplish exactly nothing. The gods seem to have reasoned that there is no sentence more terrible than meaningless and hopeless work (Camus, 1991).

In organizations, we regularly encounter people who suffer from the Sisyphus complex. Needing to be constantly busy, these individuals keep on pushing the organization's 'rocks' without ever asking them-selves why they are doing what they are doing. Successful as these people may be at accomplishing certain tasks, they never feel a sense of satisfac-tion. They rush on to new goals and new challenges—goals that often have no inherent meaning or objective—rather than questioning why they are running or what they are running toward. Like T. S. Eliot's J. Alfred Prufrock, who 'measured out my life with coffee spoons,' they grow restless the moment a task is completed.

Although the drivenness of the Sisyphus complex can result in posi-tive career repercussions, Sisyphean workers are in danger of losing their sense of balance and perspective in the pursuit of immediate goals. Because reflection is not part of their mental makeup, they are unable to develop and pursue a long-term strategic orientation. They are so focused on immediate results that they are unable to engage in the exploration necessary to the development of tomorrow's business. In addition, their sense of focus is often underdeveloped, creating difficul-ties when companies are faced with market discontinuities.

Furthermore, when people with the Sisyphus complex are in a senior position, their behavior can become contagious. In their mindless pursuit of the next challenge, they may create an overcompetitive culture that encourages people to work hard rather than smart; a culture where people are concerned only with short-term wins, losing the broader perspective; a culture that ignores ethical and social considerations. Only people who themselves favor the Sisyphean mindset can survive in such a culture. The result is an organization full of insecure, tough-minded, workaholic overachievers. They will also create corporate cultures with scant regard for family values.

Many executives in Japanese companies appear to follow the Sisyphean template. Every year a substantial number of Japanese executives die from overwork—enough to engender a term for the phenomenon: *karoshi*. There is so much concern about *karoshi* in Japan that families have sued companies for their failure to intervene in an employee's self-destructive behavior.

People with a Sisyphean orientation generally experience personal distress as well as work dissatisfaction, as the extreme nature of *karoshi* suggests: unable to stop to smell the roses, these people feel directionless and unfulfilled unless they are pursuing yet another challenge, then another, and another. They confuse ends and means, stunting their life. They compose endless lists of 'shoulds' at home, as well as at the office, and they tackle those lists at the expense of their own wants and desires. But since time is limited, not everything gets done. So, obsessed as they are with getting things done at work, they neglect their personal life; and as their personal life suffers, they respond to that new discomfort by working even harder at trying to get more things done at work—and the vicious cycle created by the Sisyphus complex accelerates. Their addictive behavior, and their tendency to define themselves by what they do rather than what they are, drives them on from challenge to challenge, as life passes them by. At its most intense, such behavior drives up stress levels, divorce rates, and early death on retirement.

This kind of behavior is often rooted in a family of origin that values control over most other virtues. Children who try to please parents who emphasize discipline, order, reliability, loyalty, integrity, and perseverance tend to become extremely self-disciplined, restrained, and self-critical. Children who feel valued only because of their achievements never feel appreciated as human beings; they value themselves only on the basis of other people's approval of their accomplishments. Thus their goal in life is to try ever harder to please first their parents, then later people in positions of authority. Because their parents judged them harshly when they failed to live up to parental standards, as adults they are harsh in their judgment of themselves.

John Pearson[2], vice-president of communications at a global media company, was prey to the Sisyphus complex. John's long work hours, his intensity, and his devotion to his job were infamous. He seemed to need very little sleep. The organization was his life; he had no outside hobbies, and did not seem to miss them, nor did he believe in socializing or taking vacations. Thriving on multiple deadline pressures, he loved to work on many projects and tasks at the same time. Although multi-tasking creates the illusion of effectiveness, the reality is quite different.

[2] Name disguised.

Although John appeared to be productive at work, there were some problems with his performance. He had poor relationships with people who did not share his work addiction: he would push them to see things his way, and then push them even harder. And because he had no time or energy for family life and friends, his marriage suffered. One day his wife declared that she could not stand living with him any longer and demanded a divorce. This declaration came totally out of the blue for John, who had been so driven at work that his interpersonal radar had not been functioning properly. Wanting to save his marriage, John agreed to see a family counselor. After a number of difficult sessions, the family therapy with his wife started to have an effect on him. He made a serious effort to spend time with his wife and children, and found that he enjoyed it immensely. He even began to include social activities in his weekly agenda.

But getting away from his Sisyphean behavior was far from easy for John. In fact, it represented yet another uphill struggle. To use his own words:

> I'm embarrassed at how my mind loses focus when I'm with people I care about. Even if I don't turn the subject of conversation around to my work, I'm thinking about it while I talk to someone. I realize that I need to rediscover how to do nothing; learn how to relax; relearn that rest isn't a waste of time. Activity isn't necessarily productivity. But I also realize that this preoccupation with business is an attempt on my part to control an outcome that's mostly beyond my control. I'm becoming aware of the fact that there's a difference between commitment and compulsion, between passion and obsession. Lately, however, I feel less dependent on the approval of others. I've come to realize that I've been working extremely hard without enjoying what I've been doing. It was like being on automatic pilot. So now I'm working on overcoming feeling guilty when relaxing. For example, I no longer look at my e-mail during the weekend, and I answer calls only from family and friends on my mobile phone during that time. I realize that my challenge is to work smarter rather than longer and to resist technology's seductive call to stay forever connected.

The Nobel Prize complex

A certain amount of anxiety is typical for anybody who is subject to public scrutiny and under pressure to perform well. But people who suffer from the Nobel Prize complex feel more than that baseline anxiety. These people, having been successful at lower levels of the organization, put so much pressure on themselves to attain Nobel prizeworthy goals as they climb the career ladder that by the time they reach a senior position they are obsessed with the fear of failing. Wanting to excel but expecting to fail, they fear making mistakes. And meeting one goal, or two, or ten, never feels good enough. They set such unattainable, unrealistic standards for themselves that even Superman could not attain them. The inevitable 'failures' that result fuel self-defeating thoughts and behavior.

While these people are the authors of their own misery, they rarely see it that way. They believe that their perfectionistic self-expectations are merely mirrors of the expectations that others have of them, a belief that adds to the pressure. They assume that, because of their perceived (distorted) deficiencies, they will be judged harshly, perhaps even ridiculed. Fearing that they will be rejected and humiliated if they let others see their flaws, they isolate themselves behind their public façade, where their driven search for perfection leads to loneliness and paralysis of action (Kets de Vries, 2001, 2006).

People under the sway of the Nobel Prize complex engage in all-or-nothing thinking. Even if they have a string of successes under their belt, they believe that they are worthless if those accomplishments are not perfect—and what accomplishment ever is? Having completely lost their sense of perspective, they do not see that the blacks and whites of life are highlighted and thrown into relief by shades of gray. And they apply that all-or-nothing approach to others as well as to themselves: while they see their own flaws to the exclusion of their virtues, in others they see only the good. They believe that others achieve success with a minimum of effort, few errors, little emotional stress, and maximum self-confidence. Because they have attained a position of leadership despite their own 'worthlessness' and others' worth, they feel that they are impostors—a personality type I have discussed in Chapters 4 and 5 of Volume I of this series. And they fear that others, seeing that disparity of worth, will resent their successes. So the pressure on people with Nobel Prize complex comes from all directions. Not only do they find it difficult to cope with criticism when they do not reach perfection, they also fear the envy of others if they are successful.

The consequence of this psychological muddle is that people with this complex become paralyzed in the workplace. They overanalyze decisions; they procrastinate; they keep their options open as long as possible; they hesitate to give direction. When people in a senior position in an organization adopt the analysis/paralysis approach to work, it will spell disastrous consequences for the entire organization. Inevitably, failure to act will bring about exactly the personal failure that these people have been fearing.

Whatever these people do, they are damned, because the Nobel Prize complex sets a vicious cycle into motion. First, they set excessively high goals for themselves. Second, they fail to meet these goals—because, after all, the goals were impossible to begin with. Third, they perceive their predictable failures as serious setbacks and, obsessing about those setbacks, find themselves reducing their productivity and effectiveness even further. Fourth, they blame themselves for their ineffectiveness, contributing to self-esteem problems, anxiety, decision paralysis, and sometimes depression. As I noted earlier, even if they succeed initially they eventually fail, because their success makes them anxious: they fear that the green-eyed monster of envy will strike.

Looking for origins of the Nobel Prize complex, we generally discover that these people are conflicted about authority and independence, about being able to 'do their own thing,' and about doing better than their parents. Typically they grew up in a household where at least one parent was competitive. Fledgling Nobel Prize seekers try to emulate their parents, internalizing their competitive behavior and high standards. But this striving becomes a minefield, because while they want to do better than their parents, they fear that if they are too successful their parents will become envious, and will reject or humiliate them. To deal with the ambivalence of both wanting and fearing success, they often underplay their accomplishments. But donning an invisibility cloak works only until they become so successful that their accomplishments are noted.

As a good example of the Nobel Prize complex, consider Susan Larosse,[3] a senior executive working for a precision machinery company. From all appearances, her career progressed seamlessly until she was appointed country manager for China. Most of her previous jobs had been in staff positions, where her advice had always been highly valued. In her new position, however, Susan felt exposed, vulnerable, and unsupported. It was no longer sound advice that was expected from her, but shrewd action. Furthermore, she was in a horse race for the position of CEO of the organization worldwide and under close scrutiny. While there had been many people she could talk to in her previous positions, in her present role she was increasingly isolated. Her growing sense of vulnerability made it difficult for her to make decisions, and her sluggishness began to get her into trouble. One of the senior officers at the head office approached her, asking why it took her so long to take certain decisions. Susan did not know what to say, except to tell him that she needed time to understand the Chinese marketplace.

[3] Name disguised.

A friend helped Susan get in touch with an executive coach to help her explore the issues she was struggling with. In these conversations, the leadership coach helped her distinguish between reasonable and unreasonable demands. He reminded her that she was in a transition, on-boarding phase and needed to be realistic about the time needed to be comfortable in her new position. He suggested that in every new position there are inevitable false steps, helping her understand that she was not alone in her dilemma. He explained to her that she needed to be less harsh on herself—less inclined to dwell on mistakes and more inclined to praise herself for her accomplishments. He helped her understand that mistakes are opportunities to learn and grow, not signs of diminished personal worth. He also helped her understand that although envy is an inescapable part of human life, her company was not the kind of place where people seethed with resentment when colleagues were successful.

As time went on, the executive coach helped Susan experiment with making decisions as she softened her all-or-nothing stance, accepting that life had far richer categories than simply 'winners' and 'losers.' He convinced her that her feelings of anxiety were largely a result of emphasizing winning over enjoying the game. Putting his suggestions into action, she found that she achieved better results when she relaxed a bit and tried less hard. The coach also taught her how to be better at prioritizing and encouraged her to delegate more. To Susan, practicing these new insights brought a great sense of relief and led to a greater effectiveness in her work.

The Monte Cristo complex

The Monte Cristo complex is named after the eponymous hero of Alexandre Dumas's book *The Count of Monte Cristo.* Set in the Napoleonic era, this novel tells the story of Edmond Dantès, a man sentenced to spend the rest of his days in the Château d'If (an infamous island prison) for a crime he did not commit. Betrayed by three jealous acquaintances, he is dragged off to prison on the eve of his marriage to the beautiful Mercédès. In prison he meets another prisoner, the Abbé Faria, who has begun digging a way out. He learns that the Abbé knows of an enormous treasure hidden on the island of Monte Cristo. After escaping from the fortress, and finding Faria's treasure, Dantès reappears some years later, having reinvented himself as the enigmatic and fabulously wealthy Count of Monte Cristo, with a complicated plan to take revenge on his former enemies (Dumas, 2004).

People who choose to deal with the hurts of childhood through vindictiveness and spite—and it is a choice, albeit usually an unconscious one—suffer from this complex. Although we all occasionally feel a desire to get even, for people who suffer from the Monte Cristo complex, revenge is more than a fleeting temptation: it is a way of life. Getting even is all that matters. It becomes more important than wealth or power.

People in the grip of the Monte Cristo complex have a great need to dominate others. Aggressive, irritable, and sometimes violent, they are masters of vindictive retaliation when opposed, and often believe themselves to be immune to the consequences of their vindictive actions. With their elephantine memory, they rarely forget perceived hurts and insults, which fester like an infectious disease of the mind. Like the Count of Monte Cristo, these individuals live for the 'day of reckoning,' a time when they will prove their superiority, put their enemies to shame and show the world how they have been wronged. And their enemies are many: believing that threats abound in this dog-eat-dog world, emulators of the Count of Monte Cristo have a vision of life as a battle and refuse to be seduced by traditional morality or their own softer feelings.

Although the Monte Cristo complex can be triggered by major life events (as it was for the Count himself), its origin can generally be found in childhood. Typically, children learn vengeance in their family environment, as they are exposed to parental or sibling antagonism, vindictiveness, and harassment. Children who grow up in such conditions always have to be on guard. They learn first hand about the survival of the fittest. Over time, out of self-defense, they begin to model themselves after their aggressive parents or siblings, first in the schoolyard and then in the corporate and political environment.

Well-known examples of the Monte Cristo complex in the political world include Adolf Hitler, Slobodan Milosevic, and Saddam Hussein. In the corporate world we find an exemplar in Larry Ellison of Oracle. Ellison's uninterrupted leadership, coupled with the fact that he still owns a considerable amount of Oracle's stock, has given him a tight grip on one of the most powerful companies of this century (Wilson, 2003).

By turns brilliant and intolerant, inspiring and frightening, persistent and ruthless, energetic and detached, Ellison is one of the most intriguing business leaders of a major twenty-first-century corporation. Although he has great innovative and business skills, his leadership style and interpersonal manner leave much to be desired. Former employees tell horror stories about his arbitrary behavior. Even people who thought they were getting along well with Ellison have ended up being fired or being made to feel so uncomfortable that they chose to leave on their own account. Typically the reason given for these firings was something vague—Ellison had gotten tired of them or felt threatened. A saying from Genghis Khan, 'It's not enough that I succeed; everyone else must fail,' has been so often used with reference to Ellison that many people think it originated with him. Indeed, Ellison is often called a modern-day Genghis Khan, because he has elevated ruthlessness in business to a carefully cultivated art form. Unable to tolerate executives who dare to stand up to him, he has systematically purged Oracle's senior ranks.

While Ellison does not hesitate to fire employees, he has always seen voluntary departures from the organization as high treason. Seeking vengeance, he plays a central role in unseating former employees who he feels have spurned him. For example, after former Oracle executive Craig Conway shifted allegiance to PeopleSoft, Ellison and Oracle launched a hostile takeover attempt of the new firm that resulted in the firing of Conway.

Likewise, there was no love lost between Ellison and Thomas Siebel when the latter left Oracle to start his own company. When Siebel was at Oracle, he came up with the idea of customer relationship management software, but Ellison refused to support it. Siebel eventually left and went on to found Siebel Systems. Initially, that new venture was a great success. In fact, Siebel received the Entrepreneur of the Year award from Stanford's Center for Entrepreneurial Studies in 2001, noting in his speech that he ran his company in a very different way than 'the average Silicon Valley company' was run, which many listeners took to mean that he ran Siebel Systems in a more ethical and professional manner than Larry Ellison ran Oracle. Given Ellison's vindictive, competitive streak, such a provocative comment was a suicidal flourish on Siebel's part. Not long after that speech, Oracle entered the customer relationship management software market with a competitive product. Siebel Systems growth stopped as Oracle ate into its market, and Siebel's share price dropped steeply. Eventually Oracle took over Siebel Systems, offering a considerable amount of money, but a far cry from Siebel's valuation a number of years earlier.

The Troll complex

There are two meanings of the word 'troll' that play into the troll complex. In Scandinavian folklore, trolls are mythical creatures that dwell in caves and hills. Ranging from fiendish giants to human-like beings, they are often portrayed as ugly, obnoxious creatures bent on mischief. Today's Internet trolls, on the other hand, 'fish' for prey by 'trolling'—that is, by drawing bait behind them. These trolls often post specious arguments or personal attacks to a discussion forum for no other purpose than to annoy someone or disrupt a discussion. These trolls are trying to 'bait' other users into responding. They have no interest in making a real contribution to learning; they want to sow discord.

These two types of troll merge in the workplace in the form of the troll complex. People suffering from the troll complex are found in every organization. You can recognize them by their sour, negative outlook on life. Always whining and complaining, they expect the worst even when things are going well. They display irritable moodiness and unaccommodating, fault-finding pessimism. Resistant to authority, they react to requests from above with procrastination, forgetfulness, stubbornness, intentional inefficiency, and lame excuses. These passive–aggressive skills make them masters of organizational sabotage. Envious and resentful of authority figures and others they perceive as more fortunate, they see themselves as victims who never had a lucky break. Busy complaining that they are misunderstood, unappreciated, and victimized, they have little time or energy for constructive action.

People suffering from the troll complex have a repertoire of defensive reactions. For example, they are extremely talented at displacing their anger away from more powerful targets to safer ones—people who are less likely to reject them or retaliate. In addition, because they are incapable of accepting blame for their own shortcomings, they externalize anything that bothers them. Although these people tend to be articulate when describing their discomfort, they rarely explore what is wrong or seek a solution to their difficulties.

Unfortunately, people who believe that they are misunderstood and unappreciated generally receive confirmation of their outlook from the negative responses of others, irritated by their defeatist attitude. Thus they are caught up in a self-fulfilling prophecy. Because of their obnoxious behavior—and out of self-protection—other people avoid or minimize contact with them. As a result, troll-like people become socially isolated.

The origin of this kind of behavior can be found in endless power struggles between children and parents. Because the comparative helplessness of children makes it impossible for them to win, they adopt the face-saving technique of passive resistance as tactic of choice. Parental overcontrol, neglect, or favoring one sibling over another all contribute to the development of a life strategy of passive resistance, silent protest, and grudging obedience.

Trolls are most likely to be found in work settings where there are relatively few consequences for nonproductive behavior—in other words, organizations that are not performance-driven. For an example, let's look at Peter Behr,[4] a senior researcher in a large government agency. A survey of Peter's career trajectory suggests that he had reached a plateau. His superiors' feedback on his performance made it clear that more senior positions were unlikely to be open to him.

Although Peter was intellectually capable of producing brilliant research, he tended to waste his time in heated discussions with other executives in the organization, often becoming worked up about trivial issues. He had a talent for making any meeting unproductive, creating stalemates, and nitpicking every option presented. He was abusive about his subordinates, and complained constantly about the incompetence and unfairness of his bosses. In his many run-ins with people at all levels of the organization, he never acknowledged that his own behavior was contributing to the situation. Conversations initiated by people from the human resource department about his attitude problem produced no results: Peter always found ammunition with which to blame others. Finally, out of sheer fatigue, his colleagues—including the superiors who had the clout to enforce change—let him be. They felt that it was just too much trouble to try to help Peter out of the hole he had dug himself into, and firing him was too much of a legal hassle.

The Faust complex

One of the most durable legends in Western folklore is the story of Faust, the scholar, astrologer, and magician who sold his soul to the devil in exchange for greater knowledge and power. Although honored by the students who came from afar to learn from him, and revered by the townspeople to whose ills he ministered, Faust felt a strong sense of futility. In his quest for advanced knowledge and meaning, Faust summoned the devil (Mephistopheles), who offered Faust eternal youth, riches, knowledge, and magical power in exchange for his soul. Faust agreed to this pact and signed away his soul. Some versions of the story have it that Faust met his tragic end when the devil came to claim his soul, while other versions say that he repented and was redeemed (Goethe, 1994).

The various versions of this legend make it clear that Faust was bored. (Another way of framing the legend of Faust can be found in Chapter 8 of this book.) He had seen everything and learned everything, and nothing he knew or had experienced could get him out of his funk.

[4] Name disguised.

He needed new challenges that would make him feel alive and new ways to amuse himself. It was fortunate that he found a person like Mephistopheles willing to help him out, even though the price was high. Not too high for Faust, though: apparently he thought it better to experience life to its fullest than merely to go through the motions.

Faust is not alone in trying to overcome boredom. Many people—and, more to the point, many executives—suffer from a similar problem. Nearly all of us have episodes of boredom, regardless of who we are or what we do. Contrary to popular belief, boredom is not a result of having nothing to do; as the Faust legend tells us, boredom is what happens when none of the possible things we can do appeals to us. Boredom is very subjective: what is mind-numbing to one person can be riveting to another.

In the workplace, all of us—sometimes or often—face the challenge of dealing with assignments or situations that are repetitive and lack external stimulation. We may find ourselves bored by specific assignments, specific people, or an entire job. We may even be bored within ourselves, finding nothing to interest us. When boredom becomes a chronic, debilitating condition, however, we call it the Faust complex. Like Faust, such people have a hard time keeping themselves interested or entertained. After short periods of excitement when they encounter something new, every experience ends up seeming dull, repetitive, or tedious.

All of us need constant sensory stimulation to stay alert. When exposed to tedious situations, most of us cope with the help of fantasy and play. In our private, inner world we nurture fantasies about love, sex, success, happiness, material wealth, and revenge. As we deal with a tedious chore, we are stimulated by those fantasies, along with images of the past and anticipation of future events. People with the Faust complex, however, seem to lack this rich kaleidoscope of inner imagery. Instead of being self-sufficient, they need the continuous stimuli of others to make them feel alive. Their fantasy life is stunted because of a paucity of inner emotional experiences. Never having been able to stockpile adequate resources to cope with repetitive or otherwise tedious situations, they experience boredom as a cancerous growth that undermines the quality of their lives.

Organizations can be adversely affected by leaders suffering from the Faust complex. Such leaders often contribute to an organizational culture lacking in vitality and creativity. Alternatively, they turn to sensation-seeking to alleviate their feelings of boredom, creating an external environment that is varied and stimulating. This is not necessarily a bad thing: but when sensation-seeking leads to substance abuse, gambling, ethical trespassing, and other attempts at living on the brink, it is sure to have a disastrous effect on the organization.

The origin of the Faust complex can often be found in a one-sided parent-child interaction pattern whereby the parent takes all the initiative to stimulate the child while the child, a passive recipient of these efforts, is not expected to show any initiative. Unfortunately, by taking over the so-called transitional space where the child experiments with the free interplay of fantasy and reality, the parent deprives the child of the inner resources needed for self-stimulation. Without a satisfying inner fantasy life, the child needs to surround him- or herself with others for adequate stimulation, a pattern that turns into a lifelong struggle with boredom.

A good example of a person under the sway of the Faust complex is Paul Hearst,[5] who was the CEO of a luxury goods company. Years earlier, after completing his MBA, he had dreamed of becoming the CEO of a large corporation before the age of 45, and he surpassed that goal impressively. His golden touch in developing the luxury goods market meant that he was asked to take over the helm of the company at the age of 40. But now, having successfully built up the cosmetics business, Paul felt as if he were on automatic pilot. Boredom, an affliction to which he had been prone all his life, was once more raising its ugly head. He had accomplished what he set out to do, but it gave him only a temporary high. Occasionally he wondered whether he been too successful, too soon. What else was there to strive for? His life felt meaningless. He had tried to deal with his boredom by experimenting with drugs, and he had even become entangled in a sordid affair, but all to no avail.

In an effort to rediscover a sense of meaning, he undertook a dramatic European expansion program with the help of a consulting firm. As the company's debt skyrocketed, he realized that his attempt to bring excitement into his life was endangering the financial stability of the company. The situation was salvageable, fortunately, but Paul knew it was not something to be repeated. He had to find other ways to maintain a sense of freshness and excitement.

An opportunity to do something about his state of mind arose in the form of a leadership seminar, in which one of the primary objectives was executive and organizational renewal. The seminar created the kind of transitional space that allowed Paul to explore his inner world and future challenges. In a safe forum where he could share and learn from others, he began to experiment with fantasy, imagining other worlds he might conquer. The deep exchanges he had with the other participants

[5] Name disguised.

helped him to understand himself and envision an alternative future. A discussion he had about poverty with a CEO from Africa touched him particularly deeply. That conversation made him realize that he could use his considerable management talent to get a children's hospital off the ground in one of the African countries. It would provide him with a great opportunity to use his formidable energy to do something that was as meaningful as it was dramatically new. Paul's desire to engage in valuable action turned out to be a powerful antidote to boredom.

COPING WITH COMPLEXES

So how can people find out if they have a complex? What are some of the indicators? And if they have an identifiable complex, how can they deal with it?

While the specifics of each complex are different, we can watch for behavior patterns that all complexes share. For example, one way of recognizing that people are influenced by a complex is their absolute determination that things have to be done in a certain way. Guided by an invisible, unconscious force, they try to inflict their way of doing things on others. When asked why, they cannot give a rational explanation; they state dogmatically that that is the way it is done. Their perspective is simply skewed. For example, some people look at any situation through rose-colored glasses, in spite of negative data (and with no attempt to argue those data away). Others predict a doomsday scenario in the face of optimistic evidence.

Another marker indicating that we are dealing with a complex is excessive emotional reactions to certain situations. Because complexes are deeply rooted in childhood, events in the present can trigger recollection of important early incidents, causing the passion associated with those earlier events (in other words, transference reactions) to flow into the present. For example, someone with the Monte Cristo complex, hearing a colleague's minor criticism about some technicality, might interpret a suggestion for improvement as an assault on his or her very being—and respond accordingly. Others will perceive that sort of passionate reaction as inappropriate, of course, because they do not share the same history. In addition, people in the grip of a complex will become very insistent or passionate about certain issues or projects, an enthusiastic reaction that goes well beyond the merits of the case. They do not permit the usual give-and-take of normal discussions about those issues; indeed, because of their emotion, they are no longer open to reason.

The good news is that if a complex is hampering effective action, distorting perception, complicating relationships, and interfering with our goals—if, in short, it is causing unnecessary pain and discomfort—we can change. We can learn to lessen significantly the influence a complex has on our lives. We will not be able to obliterate it (complexes are too deep for that), but we can take back the power of choice and keep unconscious forces from completely running our life.

The first thing we have to do in coping with a complex is to identify it. However, that is easier said than done. Just as fish do not find the wetness of their surroundings remarkable because water is all they know, we do not always notice an emotional muddle even when we are bang in the middle of it. To arrive at a level of awareness, we generally need the help of others—perhaps a friend, a family member, a therapist, a psychoanalyst, a psychiatrist, or a leadership coach. These people may point out to us the driven nature of our behavior and show us where and how we have abandoned reason. If we pay attention to these observations, they can set in motion a process of self-exploration that will help us become more aware of the unconscious forces that dominate our being. That process will improve our emotional intelligence, provide greater insight into our motivations, and help us understand what our specific complex is trying to accomplish.

That sort of understanding is critical to any personal change process, but it is only the beginning. Change takes time and effort. Being human, we will resist some of the observations from those helping us work towards change—after all, they are questioning our habitual modes of being and relating—and we have to work through that resistance. Only when we understand the dysfunctionality of our complex can we 'manage' it. If our resistances are particularly strong, we may need an emotional jolt (such as the jolt Paul Hearst felt when the Faust complex brought his company to the brink of financial ruin) to set this reflective process in motion. As we work through our resistances and make the unconscious conscious, we take decision-making control back into our own hands. By suffering our complexes consciously, we can restore to awareness the experiences on which the complexes were built, deal with those experiences reflectively and rationally, and reduce their effect on us.

We cannot expect miracles, however. There will always be a part of us that holds on to our complex, because after all these years it is part of our identity as a person. That continuity will be seeded in us, but we can change our perceptions by growing new branches. Even as those branches leaf and flourish, we will feel a sense of sadness, for the dead wood we leave behind us is a part of ourselves.

CHAPTER 7
....

LEADERSHIP ARCHETYPES: A NEW ORGANIZATIONAL CONSTELLATION[1]

Nearly all men can stand adversity, but if you want to test a man's character, give him power.

—*Abraham Lincoln*

You can easily judge the character of a man by how he treats those who can do nothing for him.

—*James D. Miles*

People do not seem to realize that their opinion of the world is also a confession of character.

—*Ralph Waldo Emerson*

There was once a general who faced a formidable battle. He had three regiments, led by three colonels, each with a very different character structure. The first colonel was entrepreneurial and self-confident. The second was conscientious and highly efficient, if lacking in imagination. The third was abrasive and confrontational but always seemed to achieve the impossible. The night before the battle, the general visited his three colonels in turn. First, he told the entrepreneurial colonel briefly that he needed him to take the lead in planning the morning's attack. Then he sat his second colonel down and gave him a detailed battle plan. To the

[1] Material in this chapter has previously appeared in published form in the following: Kets de Vries, M.F.R. 'Decoding the team conundrum: the eight roles executives play,' *Organizational Dynamics*, 2007, 36, (1), 28–44, and Kets de Vries, M.F.R. *The Leadership Archetype Questionnaire: Facilitator's Guide*, INSEAD, 2007.

third, he confided that the battle was already lost, that they had no chance. The colonel disagreed violently—the general was wrong, and the colonel's regiment would wipe the enemy off the field. At dawn the next day, the three regiments attacked, each was victorious and the battle was won.

There is no one 'Great Man' in this anecdote. Instead, we find four highly effective leaders. Our general was an astute judge of character. He understood how each of his men would think and act and he knew what buttons to press to get them to do so. He knew that their personality make-up would determine how they led their troops and faced the enemy. He knew how to leverage each member of his team to maximum advantage. He knew how to build an effective team.

An example from a business context illustrates the importance of understanding the roles people can play in a team. Mary Johanssen was an HR manager in an international cosmetics company when she was spotted by Harry Oller, VP Europe for the company. 'She gave a superb presentation about how they'd dealt with new hire integration in a South African subsidiary. I said to my colleague, "Great strategic insights! She seems to be the ideal person to sort out Poland." We were having major problems with a new acquisition there.' It was a big leap in terms of promotion but Mary was given the job of introducing and implementing a new cascading excellence program within the Polish subsidiary. 'It was a disaster,' Oller remembers. 'A load of money spent on consultancy and implementation studies; rudimentary, half-hearted efforts at running an inappropriate program; and a workforce that had no clearer idea at the end of 12 months what they were doing or why.' What had dazzled Oller were Johanssen's strategic and communication skills. She was at sea, however, in a more operational role. Apparently, the script in her inner theater was not aligned with the new role assigned to her. Characterologically or otherwise, she seemed ill-suited for the task at hand. She didn't have the right mindset for an operational position.

LAYING THE GHOST OF THE GREAT MAN TO REST

Although the ghost of the Great Man or 'Heroic' Leader—the stereotypical all powerful, undisputed leader who controls an organization and determines its success or failure—still haunts leadership studies, most now recognize that successful organizations are the product of distributive, collective, and complementary leadership. It is clear that an individualistic notion of leadership is inadequate, given the increased complexity and fluidity of the work environment. In spite of the obstinate survival of Great Man or Woman theories, a more collective view of leadership is required, where lateral relationship building plays an essential role. However, this implies that all the roles played by senior executives in a leadership role constellation need to be considered. We need insight into the qualities and skills leaders must have to be successful, to be able to respond to different situations and contexts, and also to understand the leader's role in relation to the other people he or she works with. Executives need more than a fixed set of generic leadership qualities or competencies to function at senior levels. Leaders need to realize that they cannot do it alone.

Effective organizations are characterized by a distributive, collective form of leadership. At every level of the organization, leaders are successful because they know how to enlist the help of the right people. This finding suggests that in order to assess leadership potential in an organization, we need to clarify the various roles leaders must take on to be effective in different contexts. We have to devise leadership role configurations that contribute to lesser or greater organizational effectiveness. And to be able to engage in a leadership design like this, we need to have a modicum of understanding of the interconnections between leadership behavior and character—as the general in our story realized. We need to know the qualities or competences leaders must have to be effective, and the roles they must play.

Senior management in vanguard organizations realize that they need to structure a group of carefully selected individuals in such a way that it becomes a highly effective team that delivers much more than the sum of its parts. The first step is to identify each individual's personality make-up (or character) and leadership style, and then match their strengths and competences to particular roles and challenges. This sort of creative team configuration can energize and enhance the workplace. On the other hand, a mismatch can bring misery to all concerned, and cause considerable damage. Organizational designers have to appreciate that the roles executives play in organizations complement each other. They also need to understand how these roles evolve. They need to have a modicum of understanding of character development and remember that character is the foundation on which leadership qualities (or competencies) and roles are based.

A QUESTION OF CHARACTER

'Character' means the deeply ingrained patterns of behavior that define an individual. The word derives from the Greek word, meaning engraving. And it is our character, sometimes referred to as our personality, which distinguishes us from others. It is the stamp impressed on us by nature and nurture that defines who we really are. It determines the final direction and outcome of our motivational needs, temperament, and traits. Character contains values, beliefs, and attitudes. It is a composite of habits we choose and develop, but which gradually come to drive us. There's a saying that warns, 'Watch your thoughts; they become your words. Watch your words; they become your actions. Watch your actions; they become your habits. Watch your habits; they become your character. Watch your character; it will become your destiny.' And that's not always good: as August Strindberg put it, 'Man with a so-called character is often a simple piece of mechanism; he has often only one point of view for the extremely complicated relationships of life.'

Some students of psychology distinguish character from personality, maintaining that personality defines visible, superficial behavior, while character refers to the deep, underlying structures that make a person distinctive. In general conversation, character can also have moral connotations: we talk about someone having a 'good' or 'bad' character. There is ample opportunity for confusion: here, character and personality are used interchangeably to signify the same thing.

Character, or personality, is central to the way people perceive themselves and to the way they present themselves in a public setting. It determines motivation and ambition and dictates the way a person relates to his or her internal and external world. It colors the nature and quality of our relationships with others and the way we pursue our goals in life. Character also affects an individual's moral compass—that amalgam of moral, ethical, and motivational principles that guides us through life. And character determines leadership style. Heraclites said rightly that character is destiny.

Personality traits are the most conspicuous features of an individual's character. Temperament and early experiences (including where we are in the birth order) influence the development of emerging psychological structures and functions, in the process creating personality traits—salient, stable ways of functioning that are of long duration and characterize an individual's inner theater, the template of scripts that influence behavior and action. And although the genesis of behavior, emotions, attitudes, and defensive structures can be traced to infancy, traits tend to become more prominent in adolescence or early adulthood. These traits persist throughout life and affect every aspect of day-to-day behavior.

Observations about leadership style need to acknowledge the concept of character because it has a great influence on an individual's leadership style and how this style is perceived by others. Character traits also affect leadership competences (whether personal, cognitive, or social), and the roles an individual will play in an organizational setting.

Leadership roles

In the first volume in this series, I wrote that effective leaders have two roles—a charismatic one and an architectural one. In the charismatic role, leaders envision a better future and empower and energize their subordinates. In the architectural role, leaders address issues related to organizational design and control and reward systems. Both are necessary for effective leadership. As an architect, the leader has to design organizations, to implement the structures and policies that allow him or her to carry out the envisioning, empowering, and energizing duties of charismatic elements of leadership. Neither role is sufficient without the other (although one role is often more dominant than the other, depending on the situation). These two roles have to be aligned. But it is a rare leader who can fulfill both roles equally well. Usually, alignment is only achieved within an executive role constellation that enables the different members to take on the required roles. (See Figure 7.1 for an overview of the Leadership Cycle.)

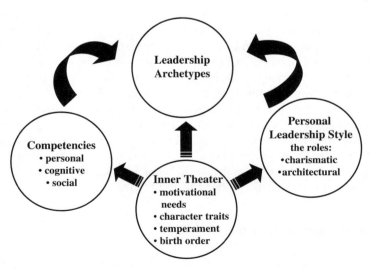

Figure 7.1 The leadership cycle

Building below the surface: the development of character

From a conceptual point of view, we can discern a number of specific patterns in the evolution of character traits or behavioral dispositions (Millon 1996). One is the pleasure–pain axis, which assumes that all of our motivation is ultimately aimed in one of these directions. People will move toward situations that are attractive and positively reinforcing, while they move away from situations that are negatively experienced. Another is the active–passive axis. A vast range of behavior depends on whether a person takes the initiative in shaping the events in his or her life, or whether behavior is determined in response to events. In other words, does an individual feel in control of his or her destiny, or does he or she feel controlled? A third axis is subject–object, or self–other, which parallels Carl Jung's distinction between introverts and extroverts (Jung, 1923). Is emotional energy directed toward the self or toward others? Although these three axes form the basic behavioral matrix, many different permutations and combinations can evolve to determine a person's unique imprint on the external world.

Certain personality or character traits cause interpersonal problems, or 'personality disorders' (American Psychiatric Association, 1994; Kets de Vries and Perzow, 1991; Carver and Scheier, 2001; Pervin and Oliver, 2001; John, Robins, and Pervin, 2008). Individuals with personality disorders have a tendency to blame others for their problems, as these traits have become an intrinsic part of their personality. Everyone recognizes stinginess, generosity, vindictiveness, arrogance, and independence. They pervade a wide range of personal and social situations. If these traits become rigid and self-defeating, however, they can impair social and professional functioning. When they do, they are said to have become egosyntonic, meaning that the individual is unaware of what others see as dysfunctional behavior. If that is the case, a person may be suffering from a character or personality disorder, enduring inflexible behavior patterns severe enough to cause internal distress and significantly impair day-to-day functioning. Personality disorders will have an effect on leadership style and this darker side of a leader's behavior can contribute to organizational decline and failure.

How to describe people

Character is made up of a constellation of character traits, which can be used in a number of ways to describe people:

Dimensional traits   Describing a person's character in terms of dimensional traits is popular with personality theorists as it allows a great deal of flexibility. Using a set of traits means that inclusivity is always possible, however bizarre a person's behavior may be. The problem with trait approach (a conundrum that also affects the assessment of leadership traits and competences) is that there are almost as many traits as studies of traits. These studies draw on nearly all the adjectives found in the dictionary describing positive or negative human attributes, leading to clutter and inconclusive results.

Configurations of traits   The other way of describing people is to construct configurations of traits. Comparable to the notion of complexes, personality theorists recognize that certain constellations of traits, character or personality types recur on a regular basis. It can be seen as the quintessence of a specific behavior pattern, a model with which other people can be compared. Identifying combinations of traits is a more finite process than compiling data on dimensional traits; it simplifies a highly complex world and provides some closure, enabling clinicians to make quick assessments about the best intervention strategy.

This approach to classifying people has not been without its critics, however. Some maintain that labeling is demeaning. They argue that it is too simplified a way of looking at people, and ignores the richness of personality. It is also more difficult to classify strange, infrequent or hybrid conditions that may not fit the established categories. These are valid criticisms, but the notion of character or personality type can nevertheless be helpful, even if categories are more fixed and inflexible than traits.

Whatever approach is taken, any sensitive researcher of personality, psychiatrist, psychoanalyst, psychotherapist, or leadership coach realizes that people are far too complex to be summarized in a simple personality description, and the various taxonomies provide only provisional answers. Archetypes are only the start of the descriptive process. Descriptions will be modified as more evidence becomes available. Nobody can be understood completely through either abstract configurations or dimensions of individual differences.

From character to leadership style

So, in order to understand people's leadership styles we need to know something about character or character traits. This is an urgent requirement if we want to help people change some of their behavior patterns.

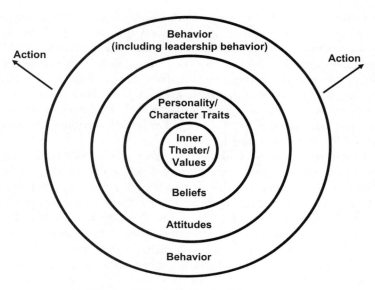

Figure 7.2   The leadership onion

Understanding character is a priority in analyzing leadership behavior. We have to remember that people are multi-layered, like onions.

In each individual we can find layers of the self. At the core of the leadership onion is a person's inner theater—his or her character or character traits; in the next layers we find the values, beliefs, and attitudes that have evolved over time to shape behavior; the outer skin is the individual's actions in response to environmental pressures (see Figure 7.2).

To go from the surface of the onion to the core can be an exciting but difficult journey. To understand a person, we need to make sense of his or her inner theater, the various scripts or behavioral dispositions that determine the person's character and their character traits. Peeling this onion can be difficult, however. Many people are hard to decipher. But only by deciphering the scripts playing in a person's inner theater, will we truly understand why people behave and act the way they do. We need to remember that underlying any leader's behavior—whatever a person's particular leadership style may be—are character configurations or traits. We need to make sense of a person in a holistic way. If personal change and transformation are issues, piecemeal approaches will have only a limited benefit. Both surface manifestations and the inner core need to be dealt with. Consideration of all layers of the onion will make any change effort much more powerful.

The question is, how can we get a sense of this inner theater? Are there ways to make behavior more transparent? How can someone be encouraged to open up? Psychotherapy uses techniques of intervention to understand better a person's functioning, including out-of-awareness behavior; personality tests can tap the deepest layers of an individual's personality. Although complete insight into what a person is all about will be the exception rather than the rule, a start can be made. The safest method is to move from the surface of the onion, and then go deeper, by peeling layer after layer of the onion away.

Sometimes the underlying dimensions are quite clear from the outer layer, but in other instances this will not be the case. Further exploration will be needed to unpeel these underlying layers. Unfortunately, in many instances, we may not have the time or resources to embark on such an inner journey; and even if we did, the person under the microscope may not be prepared to undertake such an in-depth exploration. Often the timing might not be right. Looking into the self might be too anxiety-provoking. But even if deep understanding is not possible, the person will probably be prepared to receive feedback about the outer layers.

Most leadership questionnaires have focused on the outer layer of the onion. This is unsurprising, given the strength of human resistance. They have not been designed to address the intricate matrix of connections expressed in leadership behavior. However, people who want to work on problem behavior need to understand the continuity between their past and their present, between normality and abnormality. They have to understand where they come from, they need to make sense of their personal history, in order to change or reaffirm identity. They need to recognize their preferred defensive patterns, and how they deal with emotions; they need to understand their perception of themselves and how they perceive others. Merely dealing with surface phenomena can have a Band-Aid effect: problems are only temporarily suppressed, to pop up some time later.

TESTING, TESTING

So if an understanding of individual character is essential to identifying leadership strengths, what tools do we have to help us? Because deciding 'She's good,' as Harry Oller learned to his company's cost, is not enough. The question is, 'Good at what?' There are a number of so-called diagnostic tests around, of debatable value. Learning that someone is abrasive and could be a character in the film *Sunset Boulevard* might make you feel better about your perception of her as an individual, but will be of limited help in deciding how best to use her in your organization. It is not enough merely to slap a label on someone. Until we understand a person's inner theater—the dramas and major scripts that play within all of us from birth—we will not understand the person's behavior. But how do we dig deeper than this and how deep, feasibly, can we go?

Outside a psychotherapeutic context, the answer is probably, 'Not far.' But we can observe behavior and action patterns, and compare these with individual self-perceptions. Most of us are motivated by a natural curiosity about how we come across to others and whether their perceptions of us are consistent with our own. We want feedback about our effectiveness; we want to know how we can change, if change is needed, either for the better or simply to adapt to changing circumstances. Feedback can have a behavioral impact and will have action implications. The process is rather like peeling an onion: as the outer, superficial layers come away, our core life experiences are steadily revealed.

THE ASSESSMENT OF LEADERSHIP BEHAVIOR

There are, of course, a number of conscientious leadership questionnaires that are worlds away from the enneagrams and compatibility tests that litter the life-coaching circuit. Most try to identify certain recurring behavior patterns considered more or less effective in a leadership context. In the most popular of these tests executives are classified as being people- or task-oriented (Fiedler, 1967; Blake and Mouton, 1985; Bass, 1981). In the people (consideration) orientation, leaders are concerned about the human needs of their employees. Such people are assumed to be more effective in creating teams, in helping employees with their problems, and providing psychological support. In the task (structure) orientation, such leaders believe that they get results by consistently focusing on the task to be done.

Another common approach found in leadership questionnaires is to assess whether leaders have an autocratic or democratic leadership style (Tannenbaum and Schmidt, 1958; McGregor, 1960; Likert, 1961; Bass, 1981). In the autocratic (directive) style, the leader tells employees what needs to be done and how to do it, without soliciting the advice of the followers. In the democratic or participative style, the leader includes the employees in the decision making process. However, the leader is still responsible for the decisions that are made.

As I discussed in Chapter 1, a relatively recent distinction has been made between transactional and transformational leadership. The transactional leader works through creating structures that make it clear what is required of subordinates, and the rewards that will accrue through following orders. Transformational leaders, in contrast, seek to transform organizations, including the tacit promise to transform followers in the process. Supposedly, the result of transforming leadership is a relationship of mutual stimulation and elevation that converts followers into leaders. Thus while the first kind of leadership is more short-term oriented, focused on tactical issues, transformational leadership transcends daily affairs and helps release human potential (Burns, 1978; Bass, 1985; House and Shamir, 1993; Bass and Avolo, 1994). And in spite of the differences both styles of leadership will be needed to be more effective in an organizational setting.

Many variations on these basic themes can be identified, some more realistic than others. Classifying leaders in this way, however, frequently creates extremely simplistic two-by-two matrices, presenting a number of leadership styles. But in spite of their oversimplified nature, these approaches have some merit, as their insight can point a person in the right direction. They can also help identify people configurations that will be more or less effective in an organizational setting.

Deeper insights can come from a more clinical approach. Henry Mintzberg was a pioneer in this area. He identified ten essential executive roles: figurehead, liaison, leader, monitor, disseminator, spokesman, entrepreneur, disturbance handler, resource allocator, and negotiator (Mintzberg, 1973). Mintzberg suggested that effective executives need to play a variety of these roles at different times and to different degrees, depending on the level and function of management. Meredith Belbin looked similarly at the construction of teams, concluding that balanced teams, made up of people with complementary behaviors, were more effective than randomly assembled teams (Belbin, 1996, 2003).

A whole consulting industry has grown out of studies like these, using a plethora of tests based on various configurations. At times, unfortunately, the literature describing the merits of these tests is reminiscent of the sales pitch of a used-car dealer: a lot of promises but in the end it's the same old same old. And as you would if you were closing the deal on your second-hand car, you want the answers to different questions: Just how solid is it? Have these tests been developed while observing real individuals or are we dealing with the results of laboratory studies? Are these tests valid, reliable, honest, and authentic? Or do they just look superficially appealing?

IDENTIFYING LEADERSHIP ARCHETYPES

At the danger of sounding like a used-car salesman myself, I want to introduce a new approach, and a new tool, for assessing leadership behavior: the Leadership Archetype Questionnaire. In doing so, I look at leadership somewhat differently from others. My work is based on observational studies of *real* leaders at the strategic apex of their organizations. My aim is to help executives see and understand the continuity between their behaviors in the workplace—the outer layer of the onion—and the inner core of their deep-seated character traits. Leaders' attitudes and interactions with people are the result of a complex confluence of their inner theater (including relationships with authority figures early in life), significant life experiences, examples set by other executives, and formal leadership training. Sometimes, the antecedents of specific leadership behavior are quite clear; at other times the connections are more tenuous. I use the term archetype to signify the complex interface between outer and inner reality as far as it concerns the acting out of a specific leadership style. The word archetype is derived from the Latin *archetypum* and the Greek *arkhetupon* (*arkh* as in chief and *tupos* as in stamp).

My research has shown that there are a number of recurring patterns of behavior that influence an individual's effectiveness within an organization. Over time, I formulated these patterns into a number of leadership archetypes, templates for interpreting observations and behavior. The eight leadership archetypes I identified are: *strategist, change-catalyst, transactor, builder, innovator, processor, coach,* and *communicator*.

It is, of course, impossible to include all existing character types and their behavioral consequences in a study of this sort. People in positions of leadership are a self-selected group. The identification of these eight leadership archetypes is a direct consequence of their prominence in a leadership context. For example, I came across very few people with self-defeating, dependent, depressive, or detached personalities—ways of behaving that makes the attainment of a leadership position quite difficult (Millon, 1996).

A leadership archetype characterizes the way in which leaders deal with people and situations in an organizational context. The Leadership Archetype Questionnaire (LAQ), was devised to help executives identify their predominant leadership archetypes, understand their behavior more clearly and identify organizational situations in which a particular leadership style could be most effective. It should also be noted—given the importance of behavioral adaptability—that effective leaders tend to score high on a number of these archetypes. Some of them will be able to switch focus depending on the circumstances. A lack of fit, however, between a set of leadership archetypes and the context in which executives operate will be a main cause of organizational dysfunctionality and executive failure. The LAQ helps executives analyze themselves and those they work with, identify specific leadership styles, and then think about what it's like to work with people demonstrating certain dominant behaviors. What are the best roles they can play in the team—how to align individual strengths with team roles? What's the best way to manage them? What's the best procedure if you work for them? How do you get the best out of them? Who else will they work well with? What combinations of styles should you avoid? What kind of leadership archetype configuration is needed for future organizational success? By applying this sort of analysis you can avoid toxic combinations and construct A-teams. Additionally, you can map the feedback from various constituents (how the other team members view them) and see where perceptions differ and where they overlap. We'll look at that later. First of all, what are the archetypes?

THE ARCHETYPES

The strategist: leadership as a game of chess

> *Strategists* are good at dealing with developments in the organization's environment. They provide vision, strategic direction, and outside-the-box thinking to create new organizational forms and generate future growth.
>
> • Excellent at abstract, imaginative thinking
> • Long-term orientation
> • Ability to see the big picture and plan accordingly
> • Great conceptualizers/presenting all the options
> • Talented at simplifying highly complex situations
> • Capacity to think globally
> • Ability to think laterally: groundbreakers
> • Great interest in undertaking new things/solving unorthodox, difficult problems
> • Champion unconventional thinking
> • Agile in response to change
> • Excellent at aligning vision with strategy
>
> *Works best in turbulent times, when changes in the environment require new directions.*

In times of crisis a strategist can provide the vision, confidence, and strength to motivate a disorientated and demoralized workforce. President Franklin D. Roosevelt did it for a nation when, in the grip of the Depression, he told Americans, 'The only thing we have to fear is fear itself.' The confidence he inspired won him an unprecedented four consecutive terms, as the US moved from the crisis of the Great Depression to the conflict of World War II. We see that President Barack Obama is trying to do the same thing, with his rallying cry, 'Yes, we can!'

In the workplace, a strategist may know the right direction to take, thus making for many admiring people, but may not be so good at convincing them to follow. Although strategists usually have a very high IQ at times, they may be lacking in EQ—emotional intelligence. Despite their talent for aligning vision with strategy, they are not always good at taking the next step—aligning strategy with values and behavior—as this would entail the sort of awkward human interventions they are reluctant to deal with. To compensate for this deficiency, strategists often join forces with coaches.

In one European retailing chain, where the managing director was involved in time-consuming and complex negotiations to fight off a takeover bid, he began to rely on his affable, rather older head of sales—whose preferred end-of-day position was a comfortable seat at the bar in the company's leisure suite—to keep people up to date with what was happening. This informal arrangement, which grew out of one specific situation, worked so well that the head of sales was also brought in to facilitate communications and people issues during a limited downsizing operation the following year.

Working for strategists

- Do not reject out-of-hand what appear to be bizarre suggestions.
- Be aware of the fact that strategists are not very good at aligning strategy with the behavior needed to implement action plans. Take on a complementary role to help them do this.
- Do not expect strategists to give you specific objectives or instructions. In dialogue with a strategist, assume responsibility for implementing these objectives or instructions.
- Realize that strategists' abstract ways of thinking can contribute to communication problems. Help them to 'translate' their ideas into more understandable language to be able to reach a broader constituency.
- Do not expect strategists to monitor your work in detail. Remember, they are much more interested in the broad outlines.
- Do not expect a strategist to compliment you on work well done. Strategists tend not to be the cheerleader type.
- Accept that strategists are not always the best people managers. Be prepared to give them a hand in rectifying this problem.

- Talk with strategists on a regular basis. Seek their advice. It will give you a sense of where they are at with their ideas and may give you new ideas. Remember, strategists like to present their ideas to others.
- Provide them with market and product studies to confirm or question their vision.

Managing strategists

- Recognize and encourage their creativity. Do not expect them to be detail oriented.
- Spend a considerable amount of time listening to them. Help them shape their ideas, and try to make them more operational.
- Protect them from the executives in the organization who like to use a 'cookie-cutter' approach to people management. Expect them to be different. Be responsive to their needs. There is always the danger that their talent will be destroyed by overly bureaucratic practices. Too much structure may cause them to leave.
- Be patient with strategists. Because of their visionary thinking, concrete results are not always immediately forthcoming.

THE CHANGE-CATALYST: LEADERSHIP AS A TURNAROUND ACTIVITY

Change-catalysts love messy situations. They are masters at re-engineering and creating new organizational 'blueprints.'

- Skilled at recognizing opportunities for organizational transformation
- Great capacity for identifying and selling the need for change
- Prepared to take on risky, independent assignments
- Good at turning abstract concepts into practical action
- Always looking for new, challenging assignments
- Possessing a great sense of urgency
- Ability to make difficult decisions: tough mindedness
- Very talented at implementation
- Setting high standards and monitoring performance
- Ability to align vision, strategy *and* behavior
- Aptitude in selecting executive talent to get a task done

Works best in situations of culture integration after a merger or acquisition, or when spearheading a re-engineering or turnaround project.

Rudy Giuliani was used to tough assignments. As mayor of New York, he cut crime by two-thirds, and made the city a model for crime management all round the world. However, his aggressiveness and turbulent private life polarized opinions about him. Then, on September 11, 2001, Giuliani was one of thousands who fled for their lives during the terrorist attacks on the World Trade Center and people saw another side to him. On the day of the attacks, with President George W. Bush kept off the ground in Air Force 1 for his own safety, Giuliani became 'America's mayor,' broadcasting calm and informative bulletins, comfort and reassurance. He convened police and fire chiefs and kept them with him throughout the day, coordinating the rescue services; he brought together leading local and national government figures for strategy meetings; and he went on to the streets to see and be seen. In the following days he insisted that the city stayed open for business as usual and he attended the funerals of more than 200 emergency service workers who died in the attacks. 'Tomorrow,' he said, 'New York is going to be here. And we're going to rebuild, and we're going to be stronger than we were before.'

If change-catalysts thrive on crises and difficult decision-making, the flip side is that they get easily bored with the status quo. They might revert to rocking the boat in order to liven things up, or lose patience and leave the organization.

Simon Levinson,[2] in his early fifties, has the energy of someone half his age and has made a career of turning round failing overseas markets for a number of multi-media companies. The longest he has remained in one company is five years. His wife recognizes key signals: 'The three-year point is classic. First the restlessness starts—he can't carry on doing this job for the next n years—then he starts discovering things to feel resentful about, lack of support, slow responses. Then the calls start to come from the headhunters and there are weeks of anticipation and uncertainty before I find out whether I've got to start learning another language, or whether I'm going to be faced with an extended period of depression and sulking.'

Simon's energy could be channeled if he worked with a team that included a coach, processor, and/or communicator archetype. The different perspectives offered by these individuals could help him to take a longer-term focus, and guide him in projects that would keep his interest after the initial turnaround effort.

---

[2] All executives' names and positions disguised.

Working for change-catalysts

- Change-catalysts have a short-term orientation, and can act hastily without fully understanding the implications of their actions. Be prepared to help them slow down, and help them see the consequences of their quick decisions.
- Because of their sense of urgency, change-catalysts can be insensitive and thoughtless.
- Beware of the dangers of a culture of fear and abuse establishing itself around a change-catalyst. Help them see the consequences of their actions and be prepared to take on a buffering role.
- Be prepared for action. Change-catalysts do not indulge in lengthy planning exercises.
- As change-catalysts are quickly bored with stasis, there is always the danger that they will initiate a transformation program for the wrong reasons. Be ready to point that out, or try to stop them when that is the case.

Managing change-catalysts

- Use them as trouble-shooters, to clean up messy situations in the organization.
- When they present ideas for a change program, ensure they articulate the reasoning behind it, to avoid change for change's sake.
- Do not stifle their enthusiasm. Be open to their propositions and reframe what they plan to do in a constructive, positive way.
- Be sure to set boundaries whenever you give change-catalysts something to do. In their enthusiasm they may take certain projects too far, making it difficult to exert control.
- Try to develop their reflective side, to prevent them from becoming stereotyped as change agents and to enable them to take the next step on the career ladder.
- Point out to them that organizational change is more than structural change. Help them develop their emotional intelligence to take better care of the people involved in their transformation programs.

THE TRANSACTOR: LEADERSHIP AS DEAL-MAKING

Transactors are great deal makers. Skilled at identifying and tackling new opportunities, they thrive on negotiations.

- A preference for novelty, adventure, and exploration
- Thriving on new challenges
- Less interested in day-to-day management
- Great salesmen/negotiators
- Embracing change
- Enthusiasm/dynamism
- Proactive mode
- Short-term focus
- Great adaptive capacity
- Creative networking to attain goals
- Great risk tolerance
- Powerful drive to accumulate wealth
- Good reader of people

Works best when negotiating acquisitions or other deals.

Tom Maral's negotiation skills—acquiring or making licensing deals (particularly in the pharmaceutical industry)—led to a meteoric rise and made him a very young partner in the investment bank where he worked. He and his deputy made a particularly effective team. His deputy was detail oriented, good at dealing with people, and knew how to select and keep the right people to make a deal work.

By the time he was in his early thirties, Tom had become restless at the bank and was looking for another challenge. It didn't take him very long to find a group of investors happy to support his idea to set up a private equity firm, specializing in the pharmaceutical industry. But Tom was a disaster as his own boss. Although he closed a number of very promising deals, everything fell apart. Day-to-day managerial responsibilities bored him, and he constantly put off or changed decisions and meetings. This led to poor relations with a number of scientist-entrepreneurs, whose cooperation was essential to making the business model a success. After a few years of struggle, the investors had had enough and severed their association with him. Tom found himself looking for a new job.

Transactors' dynamism and judgment skills are often counter-balanced by impatience with structures and procedures. Although they are excellent at wealth generation, left to act too much on their own, they can create havoc within an organization. They need strategists, processors, and coaches to redress the balance.

Working for transactors

- Be prepared for action. Do not expect long meetings and consensus-building sessions.
- Transactors will mostly make the decisions themselves and expect you to carry them out.
- Be prepared to take on a complementary role. Transactors are not interested in the details of day-to-day management and this may create problems. Help to make this part of the executive equation work.
- Do not wait for a transactor to come to you. Proactive themselves, they expect you to take the initiative, whether it's about a promotion, a salary increase or a new idea. Transactors want to know that you are where the action is. Be direct when recommending action. Transactors like people to be straight and to the point. They have no patience with long-winded explanations.
- Maintain their interest in what you're saying: transactors are easily bored.
- Be prepared to be a sounding board in order to curb their enthusiasm (and bring them back to reality) as they can be overoptimistic at times, taking people along on wild goose chases. Be wary of their entering into a transaction just for the sake of it.
- Expect surprises. Some transactors will use Machiavellian tactics to get what they want. Engage in regular dialogue with them in order to understand what is really going on.
- Some transactors may have a volatile temperament. When they explode, take it in your stride. Their memories are rather short. They do not bear grudges.

Managing transactors

- Recognize their low threshold of boredom. To get the best out of them and keep them fulfilled, give them transaction opportunities on a regular basis.

- Be realistic about their short-term focus. Help them see the longer term consequences of their actions.
- Be realistic about their lack of interest in day-to-day management, while making it clear that you expect a basic level of administrative diligence. Suggest help, when needed.
- When transactors have a temper tantrum draw their attention to it. Explain the effect poor mood-management can have on their subordinates and other people in the organization.
- Tell them to be straight with you. Explain that you want transparency from your people. Make it clear, however, that you won't tolerate manipulative people in the organization. Explain that it is one thing to enjoy complex negotiations (with all the political ramifications); it is another thing to try to manage your boss.
- Remember that financial incentives can be a great driver for transactors. Keep this in mind when designing reward structures.

THE BUILDER: LEADERSHIP AS AN ENTREPRENEURIAL ACTIVITY

Builders dream of creating something and have the talent and determination to make their dream come true.

- Great need to be independent/to be in control
- Enormous amount of energy, drive, dynamism and enterprise
- Single mindedness/very focused/very decisive
- Enormous perseverance: great capacity to deal with setbacks
- Ability to live with a great deal of insecurity/ambiguous situations
- Capacity to thrive under pressure
- Long-term focus
- High achievement orientation
- High but calculated risk taking propensity
- Good at creative adaptation/creativity
- Strong motivation to create something
- Great talent for getting buy-in from others/to obtain resources
- A moderate dose of social skills
- Difficulties in dealing with authority

Works best setting up 'skunk works' or other ventures inside or outside the organization.

After having worked in a large mobile phone company for a number of years, the politics and slow decision-making process began to get to Niels Johansen. Despite his remarkable career in the organization, in which he was singled out for the fast track, it no longer held any charm for him. Niels decided to quit and embarked on a doctorate in industrial engineering at a prestigious engineering school (a decision he considered some kind of career 'moratorium'). He was a star student and after graduation applied for and received a prestigious scholarship for a year's postdoctoral fellowship at Stanford. His plan was to use that year to look around for interesting opportunities in the telecommunication industry. But he knew in his heart of hearts, coming from a family of entrepreneurs, that he wanted to start his own business. At Stanford, he was approached by a Swedish information technology firm interested in his research on the mobile phone industry. Niels initially hesitated to take up their offer, but it turned out to be hard to refuse. The Swedish company was badly in need of some form of technology transfer. Given his expertise in that industry, he was asked to start up a venture in Palo Alto. He would be in charge of a select group of the best and the brightest from the Swedish operation, to help him get the venture off the ground. It was explained that the start-up was a 'skunk work,' a venture working outside the usual rules of the organization. The idea was that this kind of set-up would facilitate the acquisition of a new technology for the next generation of mobile phones. Niels would be reporting directly to the president to shield him from the usual 'noise' existing in large organizations. Although it would be a risky start-up, Niels felt it was a great opportunity. And even if it didn't work out, the learning experience, given his desire to start on his own, would be invaluable.

Builders tend to be strongly controlling and have little regard for others' authority. They live with the illusion (and this may have been true once) that nobody can do things as well as they do. Given their great need for control and ambivalence toward authority they have great difficulties with empowerment and delegation. Although their leadership can be inspirational, at times, poor communication and a culture of fear can make some of these people lose touch with reality, and contribute to dysfunctional decision-making. Difficult as it may be for them, they need help of more organizationally oriented types—the processors—to bring their organizations to the next phase.

Working for builders

- Point out how their independent leadership style can create bottlenecks in the decision-making process. Help them adopt a more professional way of doing things. If necessary, find a more process-oriented person to help them.
- Use benchmarking to persuade them to adapt a more professional way of doing things. Show them examples of how other organizations manage the work flow.
- Help builders understand the need for involving other people in decision-making processes, explaining the advantages of delegation.
- Assist them in the setting of priorities. Analyze together where they can add their greatest value.
- Be prepared to challenge 'groupthink' in the organizations or units for which they are responsible. Be ready to play the role of the devil's advocate or sparring partner (although this can be career endangering, it can be worth the risk). Point out the perils of creating a false reality, and making decisions based on wrong assumptions.
- Do not expect many compliments from builders. Accept that they are not very skilled in creating a culture of positive feedback. Realize that they can be extremely result oriented.

Managing builders

- Listen to them. They like to be heard. Make sure that they realize that their projects have your full attention. Explain that there is a place for them in the organization.
- Realize their need to be independent and in control but help them understand the benefits of involving other people in their decision making. Urge them not to do everything by themselves. Explore together the advantages of delegation.
- Do not overload them with demands for information.
- When they are overly optimistic about their projections, pay attention, compliment them about their ideas, but help them arrive at a more realistic perspective.

THE INNOVATOR: LEADERSHIP AS CREATIVE IDEA GENERATION

Innovators are focused on the new. They possess a great capacity to solve extremely difficult problems.

- Great drive to pursue their ideas
- Creative and imaginative
- Always on the lookout for future possibilities: new projects, new activities, and new procedures
- Never satisfied in developing their ideas/difficulties with closure
- Tolerance for and enjoyment of complex problem solving
- Stretch goals at whatever needs to be accomplished
- Enormous perseverance/focused
- Long term orientation in the pursuit of their ideas
- Not political/quite naïve about organizational politics
- Ineffective communicators
- Financial gains are secondary
- At times appear eccentric

Works best as idea generators within an organization.

Innovators are constantly generating new ways of doing things, whether they are inventors or inventive implementers, devising new ways to position products or services. A prominent, somewhat controversial example is Madonna, who is constantly reinventing her image and style and segues seemingly effortlessly between acting, singing, writing, and celebrity wife-and-motherhood, depending upon which of her talents is in the ascendant or particularly in demand.

UK inventor James Dyson spent nearly ten years developing the bagless, dual cyclone vacuum cleaner that has made him a household name. He nearly bankrupted himself with the hefty cost of annual patent renewals before he saw a penny in sales. Now worldwide sales have exceeded £3 billion, and 'dyson' has joined 'hoover' as a transitive English verb. The sole shareholder of his company, Dyson has a personal fortune of £700 million. Dyson's inventiveness is matched by shrewd marketing and planning. In 2005 he rode out adverse publicity when he moved his manufacturing out of the UK to Malaysia, to save costs and allow expansion. Research and development remained in Britain and within a year Dyson was employing more people in the UK than before he moved the manufacturing off shore.

The downside of innovators is a tendency to introversion and insularity. The subtleties of organizational political life may escape them but if teamed with people who complement their talent with more highly developed social skills, they can be a powerful leadership force.

Working for innovators

- Realize that innovators don't like managing people, so don't expect too much direction or feedback. Be prepared to be a self-starter.
- As they are open to ideas, play the role of sparring partner to help them focus on the projects most likely to benefit the organization.
- Help them to be aware of the financial implications of the projects in which they are engaged. Innovators are inclined to ignore the financial dimension. Bring a touch of reality to their projects.
- Be aware of innovators' tendency to 'tinker' with the projects they are working on. Accept that they will never be satisfied and help them to achieve closure.

Managing innovators

- Channel their energy by encouraging them to pursue unorthodox ideas.
- Protect innovators from other (more process oriented) executives in the organization who may have a negative response to their eccentricities.
- Do not put innovators in executive positions. If you want them to provide inspiration to a team of people, create a partnership with a processor archetype to ensure that the organizational processes and procedures are observed.
- Be prepared to steer them towards projects that will bring greatest benefit to the organization. Help them to achieve closure.
- Use their enthusiasm in a constructive way. Channel it, so that it inspires other people in the organization by allowing them to communicate the exciting projects they are working on.

THE PROCESSOR: LEADERSHIP AS AN EXERCISE IN EFFICIENCY

Processors like an organization to be a smoothly running, well-oiled machine. They are very effective at setting up the structures and systems needed to support an organization's objectives.

- Systemic outlook
- Extremely effective at turning abstract concepts into practical action
- Good at implementing process-based actions
- Effective at providing structure/processes/boundaries
- Dislike for unstructured situations
- Adherence to rules and procedures
- Possessing a great commitment to the organization
- Good corporate citizens/loyal and cooperative
- Great self-discipline, very reliable, efficient, and conscientious
- Remaining cool-headed in situations of stress
- Positive attitude toward authority
- Excellent at time management

Works best when creating order out of disorder.

Processors are adaptable and collaborative, and complement most other leadership styles. They are important in any executive role constellation, and they are not the kind of people who will get an organization into trouble. Deeply loyal, they are not afraid of difficult decisions, even if there is a personal cost involved.

When Gerald Ford became US President in 1974, his major task was to restore confidence in the presidency, which his predecessor, Richard Nixon, had brought into disrepute. Maintaining that 'the difficult decisions always come to this desk,' within a month of taking office he issued a formal pardon to Nixon, sparing the former President the humiliation of a highly public trial. Ford then faced out national uproar and a congressional enquiry into allegations that the pardon had been part of a pre-arranged deal before Nixon's resignation. Ford judged that the pardon was 'the right thing to do,' in order to re-establish the authority of the White House, and, as Ford's successor Jimmy Carter put it, 'heal our land.' Watergate cast a long shadow over Ford's achievements, however, and cost him re-election in 1976, although his work to reunite the country was later recognized by the Presidential Medal of Freedom awarded to him by Bill Clinton.

Sometimes a respect for order, systems and rules can shade into stubbornness and inflexibility, so that a processor can be slow to respond to new opportunities or even hinder them. But generally processors are good team players, and know how to make things work.

Kiera Rhodes was director of international development at a leading educational institute when she was asked to undertake an urgent downsizing study: the institute had to pare down a workforce that was already stretched. Kiera knew that the answer was to eliminate an entire area of operation, either within the faculty offerings or an administrative function. One candidate was the chemistry department. Following a nationwide trend, chemistry was attracting fewer student applicants. However, the department's field of research was cutting-edge and internationally recognized. The institute could not afford to lose that acclaim and intellectual capital to a competing body. Another candidate immediately became apparent: the department of international development. Although a small department, its overheads and expenses were disproportionate to its size and returns remained stable—but low. Kiera's final recommendation was to make herself, and her department, redundant.

Working for processors

- Explain to them the importance of complementing with strategists, transactors, and builders. Make the importance of their balancing role clear to them.
- Understand that processors may stifle others' creative abilities. Be ready to point this out to them.
- Serve as a buffer between the people who work for you and the processor. Try to elicit creative responses from them without interference from your superior.
- Help processors recognize new opportunities. Encourage them to be more adventurous and decisive. Present the case for taking action.
- Accept that, if you are to work successfully for a processor, you will have to function according to the established rules and procedures. Deviating too far from these rules will cause irritation and possibly damage your career.
- Appreciate that when you work for processors, you are more likely to be rewarded for conformity than for innovation.

Managing processors

- Reward them for what they are good at: taking care of detail, but also help them see the larger picture. Explain that cost-cutting and creating greater efficiencies can only go so far to benefit the organization. Impress upon them that the major gains are in strategic innovation.
- Demonstrate how they can help other people in the organization for whom detail orientation is not a priority.
- Prevent them from instituting a stifling set of structures, rules, and procedures. Explore with them the adverse consequences of doing so, on personal issues for example.
- Support them in making decisions quickly. Help them overcome their need for excessive information before they are ready to make a decision.
- Calm them down when they are distressed by others who fail to observe rules and regulations to the letter. Remind them that we live in an imperfect world.

THE COACH: LEADERSHIP AS PEOPLE DEVELOPMENT

Coaches create high-performance teams and high-performance cultures.

- Empathic/high EQ
- Good listeners
- Inspire trust
- Affinity with people/cooperative
- Excellent at handling difficult interpersonal and group situations
- Talent for creating high performance cultures and teams
- Great developers of people/giving constructive feedback
- Excellent at giving career guidance
- Great motivators
- Good communicators
- Have a positive outlook
- Good delegators
- Preference for participatory management

Works best when instituting culture change projects. Particularly effective in networking, knowledge-based, highly complex organizations.

Adrien Fribourg had worked for some time as an interim manager, taking short-term appointments troubleshooting in a succession of high-tech companies, when his agency called with a proposition. A small software developer, with one outstanding product, had just rid itself of its founder-CEO but was floundering. They wanted someone for the long term, who would give the company a new style of leadership, something different from the very directive, hierarchical style favored by the departing CEO. Adrien hesitated. His life worked out very nicely as it was. With his children independent and out of the house, and homes in France and Italy, short-term, intensive missions suited him well—and they were lucrative. However, there was something very appealing about the company profile. The single product excelled in the market and for the time being at least its position looked unassailable; there was clearly no shortage of creative thinking in the organization, although it was largely frustrated; and the people were all high caliber. Unfortunately, they were also disaffected and the company had high exit rates.

Adrien took the job. During his first two weeks, he rarely saw the inside of his office as he systematically met every individual working in the company, the suppliers, and major clients. For three days he traveled with members of the sales team. Towards the end of his first month he called all the employees together. First of all, he summarized the situation as he saw it and announced that, over the next two months, he would be formulating a plan to bring in new financing and kick-starting some project innovation that had been lying dormant. Then he said that during that period his door would be open to anyone to come and present ideas: and after that, his door—and everyone else's—would be gone. The internal partitions that divided the company premises (the top two floors of a converted warehouse) into small, somber offices would be removed.

Adrien had identified likely leaders for development teams and immediately put them to work on some of the slumbering projects. He assembled a special unit to look at second and third generation developments from the alpha product, bringing in client representatives as advisors. The sales team recruited new members and were given specialized training. Adrien's office was also in the new open-plan workspace and he was careful to maintain a presence there, overcoming some initial wariness from employees. Eventually, he was obliged to relocate to an interior 'pod,' to establish a degree of privacy and confidentiality—but it had no door, and his accessibility became a signifier of the new company culture. In the first two years, he saw very little of his Italian and French homes. By the end of that time, the new generation of software was rolling out, several of the dormant projects were being activated, and the company's improved performance had attracted two new investors.

Coaches are highly effective at getting the best out of people, and get a great deal of personal satisfaction from developing and mentoring others. Consistently with this, they may find it hard to be tough when needed, and shy away from dealing with underperformance and difficult personal issues. They probably do *not* always represent the leadership archetype best suited to dealing with crises.

Working for coaches

- Realize that coaches may over-identify with people, and so may not always be prepared to make the kinds of tough decisions that are needed in a particular organizational situation. At times, this may mean you may have to take on the role of 'executioner.'
- Prevent them from protecting underperformers. Explain the negative implications of doing so.
- Prevent them from managing by guilt rather than giving honest, constructive feedback to underperformers.
- Create a greater sense of urgency about dealing with difficult interpersonal decisions.
- When they are overly optimistic about an executive's capacity to change, try to inject a greater dose of reality. Remind them of how many times the person in question has been given another chance. Help to establish realistic performance plans.

Managing coaches

- Appreciate their ability to get the best out of their people.
- Occasionally remind them to be more demanding of their people.
- Suggest other situations in the organization where their people development skills would be useful. Encourage them to use their talents and take on a mentoring role for high potential junior executives.
- Help them to be less idealistic, more political, and to feel comfortable with the dynamics of power.

THE COMMUNICATOR: LEADERSHIP AS STAGE MANAGEMENT

Communicators are great influencers, and have a considerable impact on their surroundings.

- Excellent at communicating broad themes/big picture
- Talented in using simple language/metaphors
- Not detail oriented
- Great presence/knowing how to attract the attention of others
- Impressive theatrical skills/creation of make-believe
- Capacity to reframe difficult situations positively
- Talent for influencing others
- Good networking skills/building alliances
- Excellent at managing various stakeholders
- Very effective in getting people to see their point of view
- Very effective in using 'experts'
- Not proud to ask for outside help/use advisors and consulting firms

Works best when influencing various organizational constituencies to overcome crisis situations.

Communicators have impressive theatrical skills and great presence. Optimistic and universally pleasant to those around them, their influence can be positive, even dazzling. However, their preference for looking at the big picture, rather than dealing with detail, can put pressure on others and attract accusations of superficiality.

Ronald Reagan, so media friendly that he was known as the 'Great Communicator,' was an outstanding speaker long before he became President of the United States. Funny, disarming, and gifted at drawing people out and towards himself, he was able to touch and inspire people individually at all levels. As president, he called on writers who crafted his speeches to suit his ability to deliver ideas and emotions simply and sincerely. Happy to delegate to advisors and his cabinet, Reagan took more time off from the White House than any of his predecessors. As President George W. Bush recalled in his funeral eulogy: 'He believed in taking a break now and then, because, as he said, there's nothing better for the inside of a man than the outside of a horse.' Peggy Noonan, one of Reagan's advisors and speechwriters, admired him greatly and wrote a famous tribute. Nevertheless, she noted: '[His] great flaw ... was his famous detachment, which was painful for his children and disorienting for his staff. No one around him quite understood it, the deep and emotional engagement in public events and public affairs, and the slight and seemingly formal interest in the lives of those around him. ... He would do in the nicest possible way what had to be done. He was as nice as he could be about it, but he knew where he was going, and if you were in the way you were gone.'

With their self-serving tendency to look for supporters and providers who can make them look good, organizational communicators are ideal clients for consulting firms. They need to be reminded that effective leadership is defined by results, not attributes. They need executives such as strategists and processors to make their dreams become reality.

Working for communicators

- Recognize that they are not good at dealing with detail. Be ready to support them with greater detail to clarify why what they are doing is necessary.
- Help them in the implementation of their broad ideas.
- Trust their instincts about how, when and where to communicate with the various organization's stakeholders.
- Make sure that their exposure to people is short. Communicators are not good at dealing with detailed follow-up questions.
- Ensure they receive multiple inputs to balance their ideas, and that experts do not try to run their own agendas.
- Prevent them from resorting to quick-fix solutions to organizational problems. Point out the longer-term ramifications of what they plan to do.
- Be realistic when dealing with them. Realize that communicators make many promises but do not necessarily deliver. Help them keep their promises. Engineer closure.
- Be aware that communicators may take credit for the work you have done. Actively build networks so that other people recognize your achievements. Make an effort to become independent from communicators.
- Prevent consulting firms from taking the company to the cleaners by asking communicators to explain exactly how they are using them.

Managing communicators

- Use communicators in situations where their talents are needed, such as taking on the communication role in crisis situations or dealing with various stakeholder groups.

- Be explicit about the kind of behavior and results you expect from them. Make them explain how they plan to meet your expectations and explain to them the consequences of not meeting your demands.
- Create a support system to help them with follow-up/implementation.
- Prevent them from excessive hiring of consulting firms or other advisors.
- Watch out for their taking advantage of the system, acquiring perks and other benefits.

MAPPING ARCHETYPES

So, what do we do with this new set of leadership archetypes? How do we build on this opportunity for self-knowledge and better perception of others? How can this knowledge be used to help leaders adapt their behavior to function well in a new role?

A key point is that archetypes result from an individual's response to the environment. Appropriate behavior in one situation will be unsuitable in another; obvious strengths in one role will handicap performance in others. Understanding personality make-up, competencies, and roles is a powerful tool in the hand of an organizational designer—as our clever general demonstrated. Understanding people's preferred style will be useful when building management teams, where members can help each other, leveraging their strengths and allowing colleagues to compensate for their weaknesses.

However, as mentioned before, identifying leadership behavior patterns is not easy. It can be a complex process. What's more, it triggers a sort of hypochondria. Just as junior doctors discover they have the symptoms of every new disease they study, we all start to recognize aspects of ourselves in the description of each archetype—and that's perfectly fine, because the truth is that most of us can be slotted into more than one archetype, and archetype identifications will change as our life changes. Assessing where and what we are is not a static, one-off, operation.

A substantial part of the LAQ analysis gives guidance on working for leaders who fit the eight leadership archetypes and managing others who align with them. Ideally, the LAQ will be completed by the individual, and also members of the core team(s) to which the person belongs (for example, colleagues from the same department, and fellow members of an executive team). A third category includes all interested others

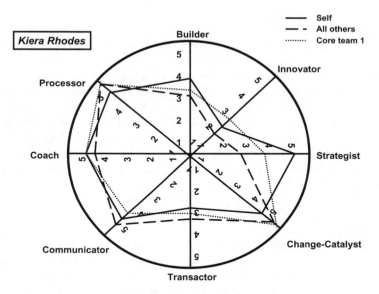

Figure 7.3   A leadership archetype profile

inside or outside the organization (for example, clients or people from other departments or subsidiaries). The self-score, core team score(s), and others' scores are then averaged and mapped on a spider web grid, where congruencies and discrepancies are immediately visible. To see how this works in practice, let's look at the mapping for Kiera Rhodes, who decided self-immolation was the only viable solution to her organization's crisis (see Figure 7.3).

Looking at her profile, the first observation is that her self-perception and the perception of others are quite close with the exception of the Strategist role. Her high Processor, Change-Catalyst and Coach scores noted by her department members and the other observers could explain why she was viewed as the person best suited to handling the downsizing project diplomatically. In addition, the high scores on the Communicator axis point out her effectiveness in getting the needed messages across. The divergence on the Strategist axis can be a consequence of the fact that this particular LAQ exercise was completed before she made herself and her whole department redundant. Although she was quite innovative in engaging in self-immolation, she is viewed as everything but the Innovator type.

Once an individual test-taker has had the opportunity to reflect on their results as shown on the spider web graph, the next part of the process is to consider the following questions. Ideally, these topics should be discussed with the person's executive team—when comparisons can be made with other members' scores and an analysis made of the overall team score to assess what competences are missing—but even if the thinking is done individually, it is still an invaluable exercise.

What executive role constellation is needed in your organization, given the environment it is operating in? What leadership behavior is needed for maximum effectiveness? What kind of behavior should be played down or changed given changes in the external environment?

What do you perceive as your most prominent style? If you have received multi-party feedback, what do others see as your most prominent style? How do you explain the divergences?

How does your leadership style fit the context in which your organization is operating? Could your style cause problems, and if so, what would they be?

What is the leadership style of your key subordinates? How do their styles fit with yours? Should you try to modify aspects of your style? What behavior should you avoid? What can your subordinates do to help you? Do you need to attract additional people who will compensate for the weaknesses in the team?

What is your superior's style? How does his or her style fit with yours? Should this person try to modify aspects of his or her style? What kind of behavior should he or she avoid? Is there any advice you can give your superior?

Given the importance of executive role constellations in teams, what changes need to be made to your team and the teams to which you belong?

What are we like?

What this discussion of leadership archetypes has demonstrated is that the ideal leader has the option of a repertoire of styles. Obviously, the higher the person rates on the various leadership archetypes, the better. Having the luxury of having more than one style to choose from will increase an executive's options in dealing with changing situations. It will be a rare leader, however, who rates high on all of the eight archetypes. But the identification of leadership archetypes may be the first step in expanding one's behavioral repertoire. In doing so, however, we need to be realistic. Certain roles will not come naturally. They just don't fit the scripts in our inner theater. We might not have the personality make-up for certain kinds of behavior. There will be problems if people are put into roles they are not suited for, particularly at senior levels in the organization. It is much better for an executive to maximize his or her strengths, and ask to work with others with complementary archetypes, rather than trying to do, or be, the impossible.

By recognizing the importance of specific leadership configurations, we will gain valuable insight into other people and how they operate. We will recognize the gaps that have to be filled in teams. And, most importantly, by looking at leadership as a set of complementarities, we can be more proactive at improving team effectiveness in a changing environment. Furthermore, executive teams that pay attention to individual differences in leadership styles will appreciate interdependencies and recognize how each member of the team can make the best contribution. It will help create a culture of mutual support and trust, reduce team stress and conflict, and make for more creative problem solving. In addition, increased trust will reduce the silo formation that is all too common in large organizations, and encourage effective knowledge management. In this way, building effective teams will contribute to the existence of boundaryless organizations, a factor that becomes truly a challenge in highly complex, matrix-like organizations. Most importantly, however, when executives take time to develop understanding of each other's strengths and weaknesses, they will have laid the foundation of a high-performance organization. Finding great executives is fairly easy. Getting them to play as a team is another story. We should never forget that one person can be a critical ingredient in a team, but one person cannot make a team.

PART 3

LEADERSHIP AND
CAREER DEVELOPMENT

INTRODUCTION

The common themes of all the chapters in the final part of this book are the vicissitudes of midlife and beyond. In general use, the term 'midlife crisis' is somewhat wildly applied to explain any random or uncharacteristic event or aberration on the part of anyone over the age of 40 or so. I take the term to signify what the student of human development Erik Erikson identified as the seventh stage in his theory of psychosocial development, middle adulthood, where the crisis is between generativity and stagnation.[1] Healthy progress from this stage to the next—late adulthood—will depend on our ability to accomplish some major adjustments in attitude and behavior. These include giving up our role in our children's lives, accepting the role reversal with our aging parents, coping with our physical changes and decline, and achieving a sense of satisfaction about our accomplishments. My focus is on how the events of midlife and beyond affect executives—but I extend my observations to embrace midlife as a critical stage in the human experience. I examine the changes that we face at the fulcrum of our life and career, a time when we have to confront loss and decline—of our looks, youth, dreams, family, and career possibilities.

Chapter 8 examines how this inexorable process of loss and change is experienced personally and professionally. At midlife, we begin to measure our life in terms of time-left-to-live, rather than time-since-birth. We begin to see life through a three-way mirror. One side of the mirror represents our children, bringing back many memories of our own childhood. Another side shows our parents, making us wonder whether we will become like them. The most frightening part of the mirror, however, is the one in which we see our self. Many people have a hard time looking at themselves in the mirror and dealing with the

[1] Erikson, E. (1963), *Childhood and Society*, New York: Norton.

ravages of time. Fortunately, we can be grateful to the mirror for showing us only our external appearance.

Managing 'the rest of your life' is a matter of challenging the negativity that the countdown of time-left-to-live often implies and finding ways to address the inevitable changes positively. In this chapter, I look at individual ways of coping with midlife and mid-career concerns and their implications for organizations. Ways of coping range from the constructive through a variety of increasingly negative mechanisms, culminating in a depressive, bitter response. I make a case for the institutionalization of leadership coaching and career monitoring, either through interventions from external individuals (psychoanalysts, psychotherapists, leadership coaches and consultants) or through integrated services within the organization.

In Chapter 9, I consolidate many of these issues around the concept of the CEO life cycle, which I touched on in my review of Vladimir Putin's role as the would-be CEO of Russia, Inc., described in Chapter 5 of this book. The CEO, or leader's, life cycle is a reductive and concentrated form of the cycle of life and can be divided into three stages: entry, consolidation, and decline. If we are not careful, the final, least creative and productive stage can prove to be the most long-drawn-out one. Knowing how to time and manage succession is a psychologically load-bearing issue for leaders. Leaders have more to lose in stepping down than most of us, and the prospect of no longer being in the spotlight can produce classic anxiety reactions. In this chapter I describe the darker, more destructive, responses that succession can inspire but argue that watchfulness, support and informed regulation by the board and other executive bodies can shine a much needed light on a very difficult process. CEOs, I argue, also have the blues but they do not always have the will, ability, or constructive encouragement to sing their way out of them. They cannot always tell when they have lost their audience and it is time to leave the stage. I propose some exit strategies that will be more edifying and satisfactory than hogging the stage for far too long, celebrating having done things 'My Way,' while the audience slips silently out of the fire doors.

In Chapter 10 I deal with the retirement syndrome—the imperative of letting go—through a series of case observations, and examine the personal, organizational, and societal ways in which we deal with retirement. Erik Erikson called this stage of life, usually the post-60 years, 'late adulthood,' a time when we are conflicted between what he terms 'ego integrity' (a sense of fulfillment and resolution within ourselves and with others) and despair. Failure to achieve this integration will lead to depression and a continued dread of death. Erikson sees this stage as having cultural as much as personal resonance, and—to bring this book full circle—I relate this to our need for special leadership development programs.

A key issue dealt with in this chapter is preparedness—but letting go is a necessity from which many of us turn in dread and denial. It is too much a reminder of our ultimate mortality but it is a lesson we all have to learn. 'Men must endure their going hence,' says Hamlet, 'even as their coming hither. Ripeness is all.'

In the concluding chapter I compare people who are 'once-born' to 'twice-borns,' using the terminology of the famous psychologist, William James.[2] According to James, once-borns are individuals who do not stray from the straight and narrow. They are tied to familiar territory where they have always felt comfortable. Conversely, twice-born people go to great lengths to reinvent themselves, having come to realize (for many different reasons) that life is too predictable, and that if they do not embark on some dramatic change in their life, they will sink to a state of living death. The implication is that twice-born people actively use difficult changes in their outer life to help them come to peace with their inner demons. Being twice-born means seeing the world in a different way. It means perceiving our relationships with other people and society differently. Twice-borns, inspired as they are by some great purpose, by something extraordinary, through their fantasies, dreams, and thoughts will be able to break the shackles that tie them down. They may discover themselves to be greater than they could have ever dreamt of being.

[2] James, W. (1902). *The Varieties of Religious Experience, a Study of Human Nature —A Psychology Classic on Religious Impulse.* New York: Exposure Publishers, 1988.

CHAPTER 8

MIDLIFE—STOP THE WORLD, I WANT TO GET OFF[1]

Dream as if you'll live forever, live as if you'll die today.

—*James Dean*

Turn your midlife crisis to your own advantage by making it a time for renewal of your body and mind, rather than stand by helplessly and watch them decline.

—*Jane Brody*

The great Swiss psychoanalyst, Carl Jung, described midlife as 'the moment of greatest unfolding, when a person still gives himself to his work with his whole strength and his whole will. But in this very moment evening is born, and the second half of life begins.'

> [I]nstead of looking forward one looks backward, most of the time involuntarily, and one begins to take stock, to see how one's life has developed up to this point. The real motivations are sought and real discoveries are made. The critical survey of himself and his fate enables a man to recognize his peculiarities. But these insights do not come too easily; they are gained only through the severest shocks. (Jung, 1983, p. 45)

Midlife is a time to look deeply inside ourselves; it is a time for inner questioning. As has been said, it is that awkward period when Father Time catches up with Mother Nature. Whether we plan for this or not, midlife can be a period of transition and reappraisal, when youth looks forward, old age looks back, and middle age looks very worried.

[1] Most of the material in this chapter has been taken from the article by Kets de Vries, M.F.R. (1978). 'The Mid-Career Conundrum,' *Organizational Dynamics*, 7 (2), 45–62.

This midlife transition described by Jung starts around our mid-thirties and continues for a number of years, the exact length of time varying with the individual. The onset of our so-called prime of life can be very stressful, as it is also often the period of our heaviest responsibilities. Men, as well as women, pass through a time of turmoil and unsettlement. For women this period is associated with the approaching menopause; for men, the term 'male climacteric' is occasionally used. Psychoneurotic and psychosomatic tendencies become more pronounced; divorce, health problems, and incidence of death peak suddenly. It is a time when careers are viewed in a different light. Goals and aspirations may turn into resignation or belated attempts at achievement.

It is possible that the mid-career crisis is peculiar to our achievement-oriented society, propelled by a residual 'Protestant' or better achievement ethic. This orientation implies that a career should be progressive—which means (given limited room at the top in the more classical pyramidal organizational forms) that many executives are likely to be disappointed in their ambitions. I believe that the prevention and reduction of these disappointments at mid-career can be an important contribution to the overall quality of people's working lives and will affect mental health and organizational effectiveness.

Executives passing the mid-point of their lives in organizations are often prone to anxiety and preoccupation with the meaning of the rest of their lives. In this chapter, I explore some of the psychological disturbances that can arise from the inescapable process of loss and change at midlife, and examine several common coping mechanisms.

WHAT HAS CHANGED?

An executive who had passed the midlife point—someone increasingly anxious about the kinds of challenges that were lying ahead of him—once recounted to me a distressing dream he had had. He described how, in his dream, he was sitting at his computer trying to finish a report. Things seemed to be going well when without warning he was overwhelmed by a sense of panic. When he looked at the computer screen the text he had been working on was no longer readable, but was 'dripping down.' Everything looked scrambled, making all the work he had done so far incomprehensible and useless. The dream took a terrifying turn as the screen changed into a kind of mirror in which he could see his own face, horribly distorted. He woke up sweating and very frightened.

While talking about his dream, the executive associated it with an increasing sense of meaninglessness he was experiencing at work. He felt his job was leading nowhere and he had begun to wonder what the point was of surpassing the annual plan one more time, beating the budget, or increasing the company's market share and profits. He also worried whether he would be able to keep up the pace he had been setting for himself. As the imagery of his dream implied, what he was really concerned about was the possibility that he might fall apart, and his sense of panic had been increased by chest pains from which he had recently been suffering. He had begun to wonder if he was suffering from a serious disease.

The executive's dream gives us some insight into the kind of issues that are important to us as we approach middle age.

A SERIES OF LOSSES

The aging body

To start with, and probably most importantly, midlife brings a greater awareness of aging, illness, and the resulting dependency that can accompany them. For the young, death is just a distant rumor. While you are under 40 it is easy to believe that these issues don't apply to you—and maybe it is better that way.

After midlife, things become quite different. Many of the executives on whose experiences I am drawing here begin to see time differently. They have a sense of life's finiteness. The idea of their own death becomes more of a reality, particularly as people to whom they are close have health problems and begin to die—in particular their parents. These people have been important figures in their inner theater, and their loss causes feelings of disquietude and sadness.

This point is brought home to all of us by the simple action of looking in the mirror and seeing how our face is changing. As the poet Jean Cocteau once said, 'The mirror is the place where one can see death.' Physical changes of necessity have psychological effects, because the self is tied inseparably to the body. The loss of attractiveness, health, and fitness strikes people as an assault on the self—one that can reawaken and reactivate feelings of insecurity and compensatory strivings that can be undigested memories of difficult childhood experiences. People in a leadership position feel the assault more than most people, because they generally have a heightened degree of narcissism. Narcissists especially (but all people to some extent) cling to a 'phantom age,' an age of success and attractiveness that they imagine they can hold on to forever. Unfortunately, the malfunctioning of the body reminds people forcibly and undeniably of their real age. Physical age is catching up with phantom age. In his memoirs, former French president Valéry Giscard d'Estaing describes with startling frankness the fear and unhappiness that the awareness of his aging brought him.

> It was while I was President of the Republic that I started to lose my looks. This development had started earlier, but insidiously. I have never completely accepted the way I look: too tall a stature, preventing a natural bearing; the hips too wide just below the belt; and, during adolescence, as the photographs show, something sweetly soft about my face, weakening its structural lines.
>
> I started to lose my hair when I was very young. I first noticed it in the bathroom of a hotel in a little German *Kurort*, which was lit by a window in the middle of the ceiling. The light was falling vertically, and I saw in the mirror how the light went through the crown of hair (each strand of which I could see separately), and fell directly on to the scalp. It filled me with a kind of terror ...
>
> Like all of nature, like every animal, I am the object of a slow process of decay ... But even if I am its object, I refused to be its witness and I try to avoid all its signs. I never look at myself in a mirror, except to shave, and even then I make sure that the light is as dim as possible. When I walk along the street, I take care never to look into shop windows which might reflect my image.
>
> During my seven years as President, whenever I was seated opposite a journalist or took a child in my arms in a crowd, I did not think for one second that they saw me as I had become. I was convinced that they saw me as I thought I had remained—a semi-young man of 35, with hair around my temples, firm and flexible muscles, barely hardened or matured by life, and only just rid of the physical softness of adolescence. I keep all my old suits. I go on wearing them indefinitely. As they hardly show the wear, they help keep me in the illusion in which I live—that of a body which the passage of time has not affected. (Giscard d'Estaing, 1991, p. 110).

The mirror forces us to acknowledge that certain things *are* happening to our body. The human ego is first and foremost a body ego. Bodily image (including the face) plays an important role in stabilizing identity. Physical transformations can have an enormous psychological impact and strongly affect our outlook on life. Physical aging leads to greater body monitoring and an increase in hypochondriacal anxiety.

Narcissistically predisposed women (but men are not excluded), who are inclined to rely greatly on their physical appearance for getting attention and managing their sense of self-esteem, find it particularly difficult to deal with the more noticeable effects of aging and the changes in their body image. They may try to fight it, and they may win a few early battles, but in the long run they will lose the war. A face can be lifted only a limited number of times.

Loss of potency

For men, the additional narcissistic injuries that come with aging (apart from facial changes) have to do with sexuality. Many men experience serious fears about their decrease or loss of sexual potency, discovering at midlife that they can no longer hold on to the fantasy of themselves as a kind of Don Juan or Casanova. Although they may not talk about such things in public, we get a sense of it through the joking behavior in the locker room where potency enhancing drugs like Viagra play an important role. Of course, where it is really spelled out is in an encounter with a psychoanalyst, psychiatrist, or psychotherapist.

Dealing with the loss of sexual potency is different for different individuals. It can be an underlying cause for diffuse feelings of irritation and anger, and may arouse envy toward the next generation, who seem unfairly free from such worries. As a consequence (and remembering that envy is one of the major equalizing forces in human life) some executives may displace their aggression and act out their feelings. This is one of the reasons I often say that the mythological King Laius— unfortunate father of the more infamous Oedipus—is alive and well and living in organizations. In a symbolic way, 'fathers' may want to kill their 'sons.' I have encountered quite a few senior executives who, upset about the things they cannot change (the aging process and their decreasing sexual prowess in particular) take out their frustration on younger executives. In this way, they show the world that they still have power, even if it is of another order.

So, when we come across an organization in which there is a high turnover of younger executives, where statements such as 'We give our younger executives lots of responsibility' turn out to be double-edged (since very few young executives pass their 'tests' and are proven worthy), we should suspect that the spirit of King Laius is on the loose.

The many dramatic succession stories we learn about in the financial media may also be related to similar psychodynamic difficulties. These stories are usually about senior executives who are reluctant to make way for the next generation. Instead, when the young rising stars are perceived as becoming too powerful, they are got rid of. I have regularly heard it being said that 'the first task of a CEO is to find his or her likely successor and kill the bastard!' To be the crown prince or princess in an organization can be a risky assignment. (I will say more about this phenomenon in the following chapters.)

A decrease in potency and the existence of generational envy relate closely to the very reasonable worry of some executives about whether they can continue to be effective in the workplace. They may experience an increasing fear of obsolescence and begin to feel imprisoned by routine; that they are no longer learning; they feel less productive. It is at this point in life that many executives become stuck. Some may rise to the personal challenge implicit in this situation and make a career change. Many, however, do not have the courage to take such a step, and hang on to their job, even at the cost of their mental health. External factors such as restructuring and downsizing, however, may force them to change.

Loss of interest

Another way in which some of these executives express their negative feelings is to say that they feel bored. Boredom can be viewed as one of the most socially devalued, noxious, frequently expressed, and frequently experienced human emotions. However, as any psychologist will tell you, boredom is a complex state of mind that can be a cover for many negative emotional feelings, including free-floating anxiety, restlessness, irritability, nervousness, and depression. Whatever the cause, such feelings are not conducive to happiness on the job and productivity.

Lack of vitality and creativity within an organization is often attributed to widespread boredom and the underlying lack of personal meaning members associate with their work process. Exploration of the causes of chronic patterns of boredom in organizational life is often blocked because of the inability of these people to discuss powerful negative feelings that surface with the experience of boredom and the repression of these feelings. We may hypothesize, however, that boredom serves as a very diffuse register of feelings of inadequacy and dis-ease. Arrogance and defensiveness are major contributors to boredom. Arrogance keeps us from being curious about unfamiliar experiences, situations, activities, and points of view. Defensiveness keeps us from learning more about ourselves.

Boredom can, paradoxically, provide people with a respite at times. It serves to give people a chance to do less desirable activities. Some people said that they took advantage of their boredom to study, repair things in the house, and do other chores. Boredom gives people a chance to be contemplative. Many executives have reported that when they were bored, they daydreamed, imagining alternative situations for themselves or planning future activities. Perhaps the most important aspect of boredom (comparable to an addict's occasional temporary withdrawal) is that it may reduce our tolerance level, so that we regain interest in situations that have become unstimulating. Whatever its causality, by developing a better understanding of the meaning of their boredom in organizations, executives can learn to confront this sense of discomfort constructively, expanding their awareness and unblocking repressed feelings.

Feeling like a phony

Some executives have another problem in that, somewhat ironically, as a direct result of their past success in the job they may start to feel fraudulent. Despite their evident and tangible achievements they begin to wonder whether they really are as good as other people think they are. They will attribute whatever success they have had to luck, compensatory hard work, or superficial factors such as physical attractiveness or likeability. People troubled by these irrational thought processes find it hard to accept their own talent and achievements. They have somehow absorbed the notion that they have fooled everyone around them. With success, however, comes the increasing dread that they will finally be found out. Such preoccupations will predictably cause a considerable amount of anxiety.

In Volume 1, Chapter 5 of this series I wrote about the neurotic impostor syndrome. I described how lingering in the background of people who feel like neurotic imposters are perfectionist attitudes about themselves. These feelings originate in the way they were treated while growing up. Perhaps parents dealt with the achievements of the developing child in the wrong way, causing confusion in the child's mind about the extent to which achievements were the result of his or her own efforts. As the child grew up, they began to distrust their own and their parents' perceptions. Achievements and capabilities were experienced as phony. No wonder that such children cannot enjoy their achievements, even as adults.

The matter may be further complicated (in particular for men), by an unconscious sense of anxiety about doing better than their fathers. This anxiety may be accompanied by an equally unconscious expectation that the father may become envious and retaliatory. In these cases the Oedipal stages of development seem never to have been satisfactorily resolved. Infantile fears about retaliatory envy, which may well contain a kernel of truth inferred from covert messages, may linger on into adulthood. These feelings may be exacerbated by the tendency for success to elevate the individual from the family background, raising realistic fears of separation, estrangement, and rejection. Thus, moving up the career ladder brings not pleasure but rather an intensifying amount of trepidation and anxiety.

Loss of family

Particular non-work issues begin to preoccupy many executives at this stage. Increasingly, many of them begin to worry about their relationship with their children and their spouse. They realize the balance of their attention has been lopsided, directed mainly toward their work. They feel that they are losing contact with their children. Some have a hard time dealing with their children's increasing independence. They do not always like what they see, nor how their children are turning out. Consequently, some of them make a desperate effort to change behavior they find unacceptable. But at this late stage, there is not much they can do about it. The time to act was earlier—when they were not around because they were too busy working on their career.

Asked about their relationships, most of the men (who have taken on the main breadwinner role) reveal a rather instrumental approach to their career. They seem to reason along the lines of: 'I am going to put a lot of effort into my career to start with, so that my wife and children will have it better later on.' Only the future seems to count. Many of these executives spend two or three times as much time and energy on their career as they do on their private life. This is a reality they don't like to admit, however. When questioned, they present figures that are much lower, to be (when asked) contradicted by wife and children. Under further questioning, they readily express concern about the quality of their private life and claim that they make a conscious effort to put time into it. But when their behavior is analyzed, many of their resolutions just pay lip service to a pleasant idea. The sad outcome of acting in this way is that they eventually find out that their wife and children are no longer around when they finally accomplish what they set out to do. When they finally do make time, the others no longer have time for them. In postponing gratification in this way—in mortgaging their lives—they miss intimate family moments that will never return. Now, far too late in the day, they want to make sudden changes and make up for lost time. But making changes in their family relationships and behavior of their children at this late stage is not going to be easy.

Tensions in the marital relationship frequently form part of this crisis. The children are leaving or have already left the house. Both partners may begin to worry what life will be like with only the two of them. Will they be able to manage without using the children as an excuse for not dealing with each other? Many couples experience great difficulties in handling such a situation. The house feels very different. The silence can be deafening. Not infrequently, and not necessarily consciously, such couples may create 'problem children' in order to have something to talk about. Moreover, these problem children may rise to the occasion, delay their departure, and stay at home longer. Some couples will do anything to avoid dealing with issues that are of real concern to each other. The outcome may be too painful.

Others may start new relationships, have affairs, and eventually divorce. Quite a few people choose this way of revitalizing themselves. Some men start affairs with younger women as a way of pushing away the aging process. These 'Peter Pans' may even start a new family, hoping that this time they will get things right. They are looking for a second chance. And, at times, it works, having learned a number of hard lessons from life.

Some men also find it hard to deal with the enthusiasm of their wives for their own activities. Many women married to high–flying, absentee executives in more traditional households (and societies) have little choice but to stop working when their children are born in order to spend time with them. Many are expected to be 'cheerleaders' for their husband's career. Once the children become more independent, they may then start picking up the threads of their previous career. Their renewed energy and interests can arouse the resentment and envy of their husbands, particularly if the men are tired and bored with their own job, and object to the reduced availability of their working wife.

An additional source of stress for individuals at this midlife point is the undeniable evidence that their parents are aging. Witnessing the mental and physical decline of our parents' abilities can be extremely distressing. Some people may interpret it as a harbinger of their own fate. As the Zen story goes: 'Grandfather dies, father dies, child dies'— life follows a specific pattern. With the death of our parents, we begin to realize that we are next in line. Furthermore, the increasing dependence of our parents also necessitates our assuming a new and different role. It is hard and upsetting to have to adjust to the reversal of the traditional roles of authority and submission *vis-à-vis* our parents. The realization of their impending death is a reminder of our own mortality.

Anniversary reactions

In addition, I have met a number of executives who suffer from an 'anniversary reaction'—an undefined form of anxiety that on closer analysis appears to be related to the anniversary of the death of a loved one. It is most commonly experienced as a state of depression. Basically, it is a strong emotional reaction to an earlier event occurring on the occasion of an annual celebration or remembrance. It is especially evident when a parent has died at a relatively young age. People wonder (not necessarily a conscious process) whether they will be the victim of the same fate, becoming more anxious as the date (and age) get nearer, sometimes precipitating a severe crisis. Some individuals may even experience symptoms similar to those of a deceased (usually same sex) parent, or another person important in their life. Deeply buried conflicts about rivalry and the realization of death wishes may be revived on these occasions. This, again, makes for complex feelings of unease.

THE END IN SIGHT

Critically, the time when we start to become aware of the crises and challenges of midlife coincides with a growing preoccupation with mid-career issues. The anguish and negativity associated with changes in our personal life are often accompanied by similar feelings about our professional life. We seem to be headed for nothing more than a rapid and inescapable decline.

Many executives, having reached a top position, begin to ask themselves, 'What next?' For some, finally reaching the position they have been striving for all their lives can come as a real let down. What they saw as their life's task has been achieved. Those who are unable to look for new challenges may become quite depressed.

Others, aware that most organizations are funnels (wide at the bottom and with very little room at the top), wonder if they will ever achieve the final step, the goal they set for themselves when they began their career. Their original target is within sight, but the competition is stiff. If they do not make it, how will they handle their disappointment? Will they get over it, or will they become seriously depressed?

Faced with this situation, they react with what the Germans call *Torschlusspanik*—panic at the closing of the gates. They may begin to work frantically, in a desperate bid to reach the end run. Aware of the fact that the career clock is ticking, they recognize that they are going through the last phase of their career. Will their dreams about career live up to the reality? It is now or never. Others, feeling that the cards have not been shuffled fairly, that they are not going to make it, become bitter. They may take their frustration out on people at work or at home.

Retirement is similarly and simultaneously becoming a reality that can no longer be ignored, and therefore yet another cause for worry. How adequately has retirement been prepared for? How can it best be dealt with? To those for whom their identity is bound up in their job, the idea of retirement can be very frightening. While financial concerns undoubtedly play an important part in these worries, the main problems have a different source. All too often executives fail to plan sufficiently for retirement, both financially and otherwise, because they simply do not want to think about it.

HOW TO MANAGE THE REST OF YOUR LIFE

Having read these observations, do *you* ever step back and think about your life? Or do you have no time for that kind of 'nonsense?' You can't engage in navel-gazing—you've got too many balls to keep juggling. And getting older hasn't made it any easier to keep those balls in the air. On the contrary, life has become increasingly complicated. Now you have to fight on so many fronts. But in spite of all this busyness, do you sometimes wonder whether you are still up to it?

If you are honest with yourself, you may recognize that these kinds of questions are beginning to take up more of your time. But what do you make of this change in your attitude? Do you know why you're becoming more reflective?

Your answer to these questions might be 'I don't know.' So let me change them slightly. Do you still feel alive when you are doing what you are doing, or do you experience an increasing sense of deadness? What has happened to the enthusiasm of your younger years? Is it still there? Do you have a disturbing feeling that not much new seems to be happening? That it takes a much greater effort to maintain the same level of enthusiasm you had in the past? Are you operating on automatic pilot?

A question that regularly comes up in my top executive seminars goes something like this: 'I'm 55 years old. I've been the president of this company for more than five years now. The idea that I will carry on doing the same thing for another ten years frightens me silly. What do you recommend I should do? Are there ways I can reinvent myself?' Clearly, there are no easy answers to this, although it is tempting just to say, 'Quit!' But quit to do what? And to go where?

For leaders, the relinquishing of power is especially difficult. The public recognition that accompanies their position at the top is a major dimension of their lives. It defines part of their sense of self. Just as trees need water and sunshine to flourish, many leaders need the admiration of their subordinates to feel truly alive. They crave an endless supply of narcissistic stimuli. For them, retreat into the private sphere represents an enormous reversal. They are suddenly deprived, at retirement, of what to them are essential nutrients: identification with an institution of great power; perks; influence over individuals, policies, finances, and the community; and constant affirmation of their importance as individuals and their role as a leader of others. The prospect of climbing down from the top of the heap and becoming a nobody holds little attraction for them. As former U.S. President Ronald Reagan once quipped: 'Two weeks ago I went into retirement. Am I glad that's over! I just didn't like it. Took all the fun out of Saturdays.'

Apart from the personal agendas of such people, (by which I mean what the job does to their mental health) other factors need to be considered. We all know that CEOs can have an enormous effect on the lives of other people in their organization. It is this fact that makes the question of how to assure that CEOs continue to function in a healthy, creative, and effective way so important.

Maybe you have begun to recognize these 'executive blues' in yourself. Maybe the routine is getting to you. Perhaps you need to admit (difficult though it may be) that you're growing bored with what you're doing. Midlife is a critical point and the decisions you make now will affect your ability to manage the rest of your life.

WAYS OF COPING WITH THE MIDLIFE CRISIS

Personality factors combined with external circumstances (partner and job satisfaction being the most important) will determine a person's style of coping with the midlife passage, in particular their way of dealing with the crises in career, marriage, and personal life that I described at the beginning of this chapter. I will isolate two dimensions (in the form of polarities) representing the executive's possible orientation to the external.

The first is the activity-passivity axis, indicating the pattern of activity and sense of dynamism with which the executive relates to the outside world. The second represents the degree of reality with which the individual interprets and perceives the external environment. Some executives accept reality, disturbing as it may be, and deal with substan-

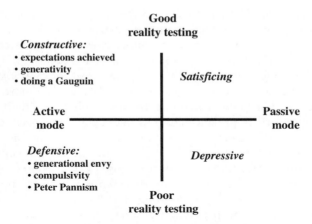

Figure 8.1 The midlife conundrum: coping strategies

tive issues. Others have not attained this more mature psychological state of mind and may resort to regressive, ritualistic, or even distorted activities. This polarity can be described as the 'reality' versus the 'distorted' world orientation. The first group has great reality testing; the second group deals with reality poorly.

By combining these two dimensions we can arrive at four major styles through which executives interact with their environment (see Figure 8.1): the constructive, the satisficing, the defensive, and the depressive. It's important to remember that these conceptualizations present 'ideal' types for purposes of clarification. In real life, the simultaneous manifestation of more than one style by one individual is not uncommon.

THE CONSTRUCTIVE STYLE

This style can be subdivided into several smaller groups.

Some executives have the ability to engage in realistic stock-taking and can restructure their experiences with new information and learning. They know how to reinvent themselves. They possess the sense of heightened reflection that comes with increased insight. They are able to share resources, skills, and creativity to support the development of the younger generations of management. For some, achievements at mid-career are essentially in line with earlier expectations and so this period in life is a time of self-confidence, satisfaction, and fulfillment. These people feel good in their skin. There is a feeling of being at maximum capacity and of being able to handle a highly complex environment. For these executives, the mid-career crisis turns into a rather uneventful transition, which lacks the sense of drama and trauma it can have for others.

Another subgroup basically has the same realistic outlook toward life, but for these executives the review at mid-career is a more difficult confrontation. They now realize the discrepancy between their original aspirations and their present achievement. They have been relatively successful in their career, but, despite their success, have not experienced the satisfaction they expected. The midlife review comes with a sense of an emotional letdown. But in spite of their feeling, they stay put, and manage to carry on. Given their sense of realism about abilities and opportunities, they are willing and able to settle for what they have. They possess the psychological strength and maturity to work through their feelings of disappointment while modifying whatever aspirations they may have had. A sense of concern for the next generation is integral to the behavior of this group. For example, taking a generativity stand by mentoring and coaching the next generation becomes a very constructive way to continue experiencing success vicariously.

Ian was a 45-year-old vice-president who gradually realized his lifelong ambition of becoming CEO of his company was unrealistic. Over the years, two younger executives who had skills more in line with company needs had reached vice-presidential positions. Although the decision did not come as a surprise, Ian was still disappointed when the president said that he would appoint one of these two as his successor. However, Ian understood the rationale of the decision and was able to deal with it emotionally. Soon after the new president was appointed, Ian could be seen devoting most of his energy to assisting the new man in overhauling company strategy. In addition, he began to fulfill a senior statesman's role at meetings of the executive committee, where his advice was eagerly sought, increasing his effectiveness and benefiting the organization.

In addition to these two subgroups, there is another form of the 'constructive style,' a more dramatic way of dealing with midlife and mid-career transition. Here we find the executives who may decide on a career change. These executives, who are realistic enough to realize that they will never meet their original aspirations in their present career, ask themselves whether their original career choice was ever the right one. They may conclude that their choice was wrong, but this group is willing to take the consequences. The simplest thing is to find a different role in the company that may give them renewed energy. Otherwise they will look for opportunities in other organizations. Most likely, if they choose a total career change, the individual has already thoroughly tested the requirements for success in the new field and possesses the necessary skills and experiences. I call this 'doing a Gauguin,' after the painter who gave up a banking career to become a painter on a Polynesian island.

Executives who belong to any of these subgroups that make up the constructive style show the highest degree of adjustment in coping with the mid-career transition. Their sense of reality testing is very stable. They show fewer stress symptoms, possess a sense of generativity, and are the executives who become the backbone of organizations, thus assuring continuation and growth.

THE SATISFICING STYLE

Using Nobel Prize winner Herbert Simon's term 'satisficing' (Simon, 1967), indicating attempts to meet criteria for adequacy, rather than to reach an optimal solution, some executives look at the environment in a basically realistic way but have a more passive mode of relating to the outside world. These are less achievement oriented, people with relatively lower aspirations (compared to the previous group), who are easily satisfied and whose lives are stable. They don't need to optimize; they are prepared to satisfice. Like the first sub-group of the constructive style, it's an exaggeration to talk about their having a mid-career crisis: usually, mid-career tends to pass without drama. We can assume that most organizations have a large number of individuals who are basically satisfied with what they are doing; they are not the highflyers.

Take, for example, a 40-year-old quality control executive in a large food company. When I asked him to comment on his life in the organization, I could discern his sense of satisfaction in his work because he enjoyed doing a good job (his job had been the same for the past five years) and felt comfortable in it. He very much liked his profession. He had a certain amount of autonomy, but was well aware of his limits. His relationships with people under and above him were excellent. This man was fairly unambitious in terms of salary or status and went out of his way to help people in the organization. Corporate careerism was strange to him. Other people described him as personable, friendly, and obedient to authority, without aggressiveness, a person who contributed considerably to a good working climate.

I found out that his marriage was very successful, based on mutual respect and comradeship. His family was extremely important to him and occupied a great deal of his time and energy. Other involvements outside the company included the building of model aircraft and gardening. During the interview, however, this man emerged as someone who did not have deep insights about himself and others, frequently unaware of his motivations for action.

Quite a few executives among this group in our achievement-oriented society would be considered 'plateau-ees,' 'shelf-sitters,' or 'retirees on the job.' While their situation might be stereotyped in terms of stagnation or lack of progress, these executives seem reasonably satisfied, accept their present status, and usually show few stress symptoms. Only a dramatic event, such as dismissal or demotion, will disrupt this tranquil state.

THE DEFENSIVE STYLE

Executives in this group combine the active mode with a distorted, unrealistic world orientation. Their reality testing seems to be somewhat impaired. Such people may suffer from stress symptoms and other dysfunctional patterns. Life is endured and often experienced as difficult. Here we find executives prone to a sense of panic when they realize that their lives may have been directed toward the wrong end. For some, their compulsive behavior—their capacity for working hard but not smart—leads to a dead-end. They have very little to show for their frantic work activity. Job obsolescence and burnout are fairly common among this group. Dismissal or demotion is not unusual. These people show a great resistance to change in their work behavior patterns and make little attempt to improve their leadership and technical skills.

In some instances, members of this group may place pleasure higher than job requirements. These people may have given up on the job and devote most of their time to outside activities. They may engage in Peter Pannism, denying—in spite of the inevitable march of time—that they have reached another stage in life. They may engage in sexual adventurism as a way of overcoming negative feelings about themselves and their job. This pattern may be accompanied by a reluctance and unwillingness to help develop the younger generation of management, which is often viewed with bitterness, spite, jealousy, and envy.

Mike, a 42-year-old director of finance of a medium-size electronics firm, began to complain about insomnia and stomach problems. Five years earlier, his career had been successful, marked by regular raises and steady promotions. Then his tranquility had been suddenly shattered by the arrival of a new and younger man in the organization. This new man was made vice-president of finance, a position Mike had coveted and expected. Some time later, Mike's health problems began to emerge but he kept them under control with medication. His behavior also changed noticeably. He started to dress differently, wearing stylish clothes aimed at a younger age group. At the same time, his colleagues started to complain about his moodiness and unpredictability. His irritability was reflected in the rapid succession of younger executives reporting to him. None seemed to live up to his standards. They all were fired or transferred. Although he spent more time than ever in the office, Mike's effectiveness decreased. Deadlines were frequently not met, and the quality of his work declined.

Closer investigation revealed that Mike's personal life was also suffering. His relationship with his wife had deteriorated substantially over the past five years. More and more after-work hours were spent at nightclubs until early morning. Eventually, a number of extramarital affairs led to divorce. He developed a drinking problem that became increasingly noticeable, leading to his dismissal.

Mike's example demonstrates a number of prominent modes that can be discerned among executives who display the defensive style—the most common being scapegoating, denial, and obsessional behavior. These defensive modes are ways of acting out generational envy (a topic further developed in the following chapters), Peter Pannism, and compulsive behavior.

Generational envy

Some executives are unwilling or unable to accept that their unrealistic ambitions are not going to be achieved. They become angry at their situation and blame others for their misfortunes. Unable to reconcile themselves to their lack of appreciable gain, they fall back into paranoiac hostility, adult delinquency, or take flight into illness.

Executives who resort to this mode often target the younger generation in the organization, who represent new skills and leadership techniques. The mixture of envy, rivalry, and anger that they feel toward the coming generation can prompt older executives to abuse their power. Under various disguises they may set up younger executives to fail, giving them responsibilities beyond their current abilities. High turnover of talented junior executives working under specific senior executives can frequently be explained, after close investigation, by the executive's use of this mode of operating. Not only are these senior executives able to destroy career paths of others working under them, but their actions also have a negative effect on organizational morale.

Peter Pannism

Executives in denial refuse to admit their inability to actualize their unrealistic goals at mid-career, and escape into alcoholism, drugs, sexual promiscuity, and psychosomatic illness. Affairs with younger women and hypochondriacal concerns over health and physical appearance become ways of denying the aging process. Manic activity can make them increasingly ineffective in work and social roles. These executives try to ignore the fact that they have reached plateaus in their careers or have been demoted. A sense of unreality emerges, of participation without involvement. Pretending becomes their way of life. Organizational life turns into one of role-playing and acting and often combines denial with elements of the compulsive mode.

Compulsive behavior

A very similar behavior pattern characterizes a subgroup of defensive executives who resort predominantly to compulsive modes. These executives resort to the manic defense. They come across as living machines: hyperactive, but forever unable to reach their desired goals. They are the classic examples of coronary-prone, Type A individuals. Also, for some of them, compulsive work activity becomes an escape from unsatisfying family interaction.

However, even success in the careers of these executives will not bring relief from their hyperactive, overcompensatory behavior. In fact, their sense of weariness and joylessness may actually increase. Success can make them more anxious. Not only does Nemesis in one form or another loom for such people, but they also feel they need to pursue other, even more unrealistic goals. This pattern of behavior can be viewed as the sign of a threatening depression and mental breakdown.

THE DEPRESSIVE STYLE

The depressive style is an outflow of the defensive style, being a combination of the passive mode and a distorted orientation to life. Many of the frantic activities of the executives resorting to this style are efforts (often subconscious) to mask the approach of a mental breakdown. Self-denigration, a sense of failure, and pessimism characterize these executives, who feel that their life course has been pursued in vain, and that they lack a reason for continued existence. They are not confident enough to make new departures or lack a belief in their ability to continue learning and developing. They experience a strong sense of doubt about ever being appreciated. For them, the mid-career point brings a sense of 'too late.' They start to dwell more in the past. Ambition, optimism, satisfaction, and good health are now exchanged for a lack of hope and optimism, a sense of isolation, purposelessness, and psychosomatic disorders. This sense of helplessness and hopelessness may lead to inactivity, work impairment, and dismissal. In some cases it may end in suicide.

IMPLICATIONS OF MIDLIFE TRANSITIONS FOR ORGANIZATIONS

With increasing life expectancy likely to lengthen our potential working life, in the future there will be an ever-larger proportion of executives in the middle and later age groups. Commitment to one organization may become a less common phenomenon, with a trend toward more flexible and varied careers. I believe society in general as well as organizations could use this change in career patterns to harness the wealth of talent and skills that the middle-aged and older have to offer at work, within the family, and in a community—a wealth that is currently being wasted. The mid-career passage could become an opportunity for reassessment, re-evaluation, *and* positive action.

But despite its costs in human anguish and lowered organizational productivity, the issue of midlife transition in executives has received little attention. By making a few suggestions that might benefit executives at the critical transition point of mid-career, I hope I can suggest ways of preventing, or at least reducing, unsatisfactory coping reactions and symptom formation.

The need for leadership coaching

In view of the many problems executives encounter at midlife and mid-career, I believe there is a great need for the provision of leadership coaching to help break unsatisfactory established behavior patterns. By this I mean coaching initiated by the organization's senior executives, which, apart from dealing with knotty organizational problems, can include discussions about more personal matters, such as issues involving family members and friends.

In advocating a greater use of leadership coaching, I am thinking not only of intervention in instances of a severe crisis, but also of a more preventive form of coaching at times when 'repair' is less difficult. Far too often, leadership coaching is sought in cases of breakdown, but no steps are taken to help the much larger number of people who are mostly suffering from demoralization and general discomfort. To facilitate the life coaching process, periods of high risk for career (and family) should be identified and the appropriate steps taken. In this context, leadership coaching means not only inventory taking and redirection, but also learning to deal with mastering disappointment, grief, and restitution; it implies dealing with general life issues.

Leadership coaching can also play an important educational role, in that it can teach executives the importance of helping the younger management generation to progress and develop in the organization. Mentoring or coaching the younger generation can do wonders for one's mental health. There is something to be said for an altruistic motive (Kets de Vries, 2009). For the executive at mid-career, this gen-erativity can be a positive counterbalance to their own personal change process.

Leadership coaching can also play a major role in helping executives learn how to learn, to acquire new skills and competences to become better at problem solving, and remain open to new challenges. The notion that education is limited to what we do in the first 20 years of our life is hopelessly outdated. Given the rapid changes we are exposed to, lifelong learning will be a *sine qua non*. This makes leadership coach-ing even more important. Access to lifelong learning opportunities, an appropriate atmosphere of support and confidence, and the recognition of midlife change at home and in the organization can all help prevent rut-formation and redundancy (Dotlich, Noel and Walker, 2004).

Career monitoring throughout the life cycle

There is now a greater awareness that—as far as leadership development is concerned—the major emphasis and the bulk of resources have been directed to the career entry point. Some attention has been given to mid-career but only very recently has the idea of mid-career and pre-retirement coaching taken hold. With increasing knowledge of the problems associated with mid-career, more attention needs to be given to the notion of mid-career life coaching clinics and career redirection workshops. Not only would such 'clinics' provide individuals with a chance to assess their abilities, interests, and opportunities, but they also serve as outlets for information exchange that can help executives in their decision-making. Within these workshops, the goals of work life can be re-examined and appropriate modifications in career direction made.

In this context, I also believe that leadership coaches should become better prepared to help people handle multiple careers. As the psychological contract between individual and organization has been broken, multiple careers will be the norm. Dealing effectively with multiple careers will necessitate both vision and a search for alternatives going beyond narrow company boundaries. As I have indicated before, regular career changes are becoming more the rule than the exception. We are increasingly likely to see dramatic career changes taken not only by executives who are stuck in their job and are becoming redundant, but also by relatively successful executives looking for new avenues for development and growth. Organizations need to become more aware of these phenomena and better prepared to deal with these changes—which will involve their making greater effort to retain their talent.

Furthermore, the increasing tendency toward dual-career families will also necessitate employers making concessions to executives' commitment toward their family: there is a growing reluctance on the part of executives to sacrifice personal and family gratifications for the sake of career.

Prevention of obsolescence

Executive obsolescence and burnout are side-effects of the rapid increase in knowledge and information through changes in technology, managerial practices, and occupations. The knowledge revolution is another reason why leadership development is important throughout the career life cycle. Executives, whose skills have lost their relevance, are often demoted, transferred into positions where they can do limited damage, or fired. Some of the more 'lucky' ones are kicked upstairs; others may be forced into early retirement. These problems of obsolescence, burnout and leveling off can be prevented through the upgrading of skills or retraining for new careers in related or even unrelated fields. An increasing number of executives are looking for ways to reinvent themselves.

Given the callousness of many organizations toward their obsolescent or redundant executives, and their unwillingness to take some of the responsibility, it is only natural that feelings of bitterness are common, particularly among middle-level executives. Not all obsolescent or potentially redundant executives are able to express their distress and discontent, however, since in their eyes this can imply the admission of defeat. Sometimes, they are not even consciously aware of what is happening to them, although their body may tell a different story. These executives may express a sense of satisfaction with their careers, but are troubled by a higher than normal incidence of physiological stress symptoms.

For many executives their dissatisfaction with their company's attitude toward career and personal development is probably related to the fact that continuing talent management within organizations is usually directed toward a handful of crown princes or princesses, rather than the large majority of executives. Apart from the question of how this kind of allocation of resources will affect the overall morale of the company, another tricky question is how many crown princes or princesses an organization can actually afford? It may be better to redirect resources to enable potentially redundant executives to be re-educated for positions more in line with their talents and interests.

Self-help   Naturally, executives themselves have a strong responsibility to deal constructively with their mid-career transition and prevent their own obsolescence and redundancy. It has become quite clear that we live in an age where companies give executives opportunities, but executives have to manage their own career. Owning our own life and career involves a continuing, realistic assessment and evaluation of goals and opportunities and alertness to signs of possible obsolescence, redundancy, or burnout because of changes in the company and its environment. Only through such involvement will people be able to appraise the future outlook of their current situation and take appropriate action. For example, reduced profits, top management changes, mergers, excess hiring, technological transformations, and changes in market needs need to be watched carefully.

Stress symptoms can also act as a prompt to make changes in how executives deal with their family or work environment. Sir William Osler, the father of modern medicine, once stated that one of the surest guarantees for a long life was to have a mild heart attack at life's midpoint. The shock is likely to make the individual more receptive to a change in life pattern. However, one would hope that continuing personal assessment and frank self-evaluation might avoid such a crisis occurring.

As I mentioned earlier, there will be an increased prominence of second or third careers. In this day and age, careers will be shaped by the needs of the individual more than by the organization and may be subjected to regular redirection, depending on the life changes experienced by the executive. With greater work-related flexibility and individual self-confrontation, executives will be better equipped to manage their transition at mid-career and beyond, and minimize any dysfunctional effects it has on them.

CONCLUSIONS

My exploration over many years of the various impacts many individuals experience at midlife and beyond, and their ways of dealing with them, has reinforced my belief that the answer to midlife dysfunctionality lies in the provision of leadership coaching, mentoring, and counseling at this critical time. I would also stress the need for executives to take avoiding action against career obsolescence and burnout by being less rigid about their career orientation and reassessing, on a regular basis, the satisfaction and pleasure they derive from both their career and personal life.

Timely attention paid to these matters can transform the mid-career experience into a station on a route to greater personal growth and generativity, rather than the start-point of a decline into boredom, frustration, and stagnation. Remember, as long as we are capable of self-renewal, we are alive—and as long as we practice the art of renewal all the time we can dream and are prepared to be adventurous.

CHAPTER 9

THE CEO LIFE CYCLE[1]

All the art of living lies in the fine mingling of letting go and holding on.
—*Henry Ellis*

Retirement is the ugliest word in the language.
—*Ernest Hemingway*

When I let go of what I am, I become what I might be.
—*Lao Tzu*

In many companies, CEOs are bound by tradition or policy to step down at a certain age, and plan accordingly. Many have enough vision and insight to overcome any momentary desire to stay on, and, indeed, take pleasure in mentoring and developing the next generation of managers. Most CEOs and most board members manage the CEO's succession well. However, some CEOs have a very hard time dealing with succession and retirement. And other key players, including members of the board and top managers—willingly or not—may also avoid taking real action or pay only lip service to change, thereby sabotaging a succession.

Consider the following disguised composites of different actual cases.

- At a directors' meeting of Wooten, a diversified paper products company, the agenda featured the selection committee report presented by Bob Reed, chairman and CEO. The board members had expected to receive a list of the candidates to succeed Bob, who was

[1] Most of the material in this chapter is based on Kets de Vries, M.F.R. (1995). 'The Life Cycles of CEOs,' *Across the Board*, 32, (8), 32–37, and Kets de Vries, M. F. R. (1994).'CEOs Also Have the Blues,' *European Management Journal*, 12 (3), 259–264.

past retirement age. However, Bob informed the board that, despite an extensive search, the selection committee had determined that no candidate was qualified: the three insiders needed at least four to six years' seasoning, while the outsiders (in spite of their outstanding track records) lacked the kind of expertise that would fit the future needs of the company. The board agreed that Bob should postpone his retirement for another four years. But several directors felt troubled. Something wasn't quite right. Were there really no competent external candidates? And why did no one in the company qualify? What had happened to leadership development all these years? Or was it possible that the selection committee, knowing Bob's attachment to his job and his reluctance to release the reins, was colluding with the CEO?

- After much discussion with his board and friends, Harold Jackson, the retiring CEO of a small-tool manufacturing company, decided to appoint his second-in-command, Phil Conti, to replace him. Phil understood the workings of the business, knew the small-tool industry inside out, and would continue with the plans Jackson had initiated. Jackson had considered bringing in an outsider recommended by a member of his board, but he always felt so comfortable with Conti (in whom he saw a younger version of himself) and was confident he would carry on well. Five years after Jackson's retirement, it became clear how well Conti had carried on. No new product lines had been developed, the manufacturing plant was approaching museum quality, and the company was attracting very little young talent. Reluctantly, the board decided that Conti had to be replaced.

- When Bill Hoffman took control at a computer company much like the one he'd just left, he knew exactly what he wanted to do. His subordinates, relieved that the ex-CEO had finally been put out to pasture, assured him they would help him further his ideas. For the first six months or so, Bill's plans moved ahead nicely. Because he knew all the right ropes to pull and backs to pat, he had little difficulty launching some fairly radical changes necessary to come up with innovative new products in the ever-changing computer industry. Some time into the second half of that year, however, Bill noticed a subtle change in the way his lieutenants were treating him: they were resisting his ideas for reasons he couldn't fathom. Then he discovered that some of them were holding meetings he didn't know about and they were managing things around him. As these incidents increased, Bill began to see himself losing control of the situation and unable to push through his ideas. By the end of his first year as top executive, Bill was seriously considering looking for another job.

As these examples show, the succession process does not always run smoothly. Underlying each disruption I have described here is a psychological drama of which the key actors were unaware or only subliminally aware. A leadership change in a company can trigger a number of psychological forces with which these players—the CEO, board members, and other top managers—must cope.

STEPPING DOWN

The first point at which the CEO and the board should be alert to possible trouble is when the CEO approaches retirement age and, for the first time, must acknowledge that some day his or her association with the company will end. To accept this truth gracefully, the CEO must overcome some hidden fears that plague us all.

The denial of death

The realization that one must give up power threatens the deep-seated wish to believe in one's own immortality. In one case I know of, the president of an apparel company who was also its founder refused to accept his physical decline. He had suffered a minor stroke, but it was taboo in the company to talk about replacing him. Fearful of his violent temper, senior executives did not dare bring up the matter. The non-executive board members were made up of loyal friends who were unwilling to tackle the problem. Eventually a second stroke permanently incapacitated the president. At the time, even the number two man was not ready to step into his shoes. After a lengthy period of upheaval, during which the company suffered serious financial losses, a competitor acquired the company at a bargain-basement price.

Founders like this—who see their companies as symbols of their success and as extensions of their own personalities—often have a particularly hard time letting go. Relinquishing power is a kind of death for people who have long been accustomed to great power, so they avoid thinking about it, and senior subordinates and board members often oblige by avoiding the issue, too (Kets de Vries, 1996; Kets de Vries, Carlock, and Florent, 2007). They may fear that the boss will interpret their talk of succession as a hostile act—evincing a none-too-subtle desire for the CEO's demise—to which the boss will retaliate.

Another reason for this particular founder-president's refusal to deal with succession may have been a profound wish to leave a legacy.

Leaving behind a reminder of one's accomplishments can be viewed as a symbolic way of defeating death. Although the legacy can take physical form, like an office building or factory, most often it is an intangible of corporate culture, like a management philosophy, an idiosyncratic interpretation of organization policy, or a particular way of doing things. When the time comes to hand over power, the outgoing CEO may worry that a successor will disrespect the legacy and destroy what he or she has painstakingly built up over the years.

To ensure their particular legacy's survival, the CEO may seek a successor who will carry on in exactly the same way. But this search for a clone often carries the seeds of its own failure. Given the changing needs of the company, what is right for the present may be a disastrous course in the future (Levinson, 1974). The external environment is likely to be different. Some CEOs even secretly (and not always consciously) nourish the hope that their successor will fail and supply further proof of their own indispensability. They may even take steps, unconsciously or not, to set the successor up for failure.

Loss of power

Sometimes the best interests of the company are no match for the CEO's need to stay in power and control. Having stepped down, some CEOs change their mind and launch a campaign against a chosen successor. (See Chapter 10 for a further discussion of this topic.) While the attack has all the earmarks of rationality, in truth it is based on the fear of losing power.

Working with an officially designated successor can be too difficult a task for some CEOs. The deep loss that having a successor represents may be much too painful to bear. One response is to keep the situation ambiguous and maintain the boss's power base. A symptom of this stonewalling is the rapid entrance and removal of crown princes in an organization. Although former business tycoons like William Paley of CBS, Peter Grace of W.R. Grace & Company, and Armand Hammer of Occidental Petroleum Corporation were special cases—they were either founders or inheritors—they tenaciously held on to power, making succession extremely difficult. More recently, Disney's former CEO Michael Eisner has been known to fire his likely successors.

Generational envy—in other words, envy of the next generation—is common in organizational settings, with senior managers acting vindictively toward younger executives. The bitterness they feel at not having succeeded where the younger manager might may induce them to set up traps and impediments to block the younger person's career. There can be a no more unhappy creature than an ill-natured senior executive, who is neither capable of experiencing pleasure nor of conferring pleasure on others. Their spiteful tactics are frequently subtle: under the guise of giving newcomers ample opportunities to prove themselves, they create parallel excuses for handicapping the progress of these individuals. Crown princes, ostensibly groomed specifically for the leading role, come to a bad end, having aroused the envy of their boss.

The succession saga of Larry Ellison at Oracle is a more recent example of such a drama. In Oracle's history some executives have been named as possible successors to Ellison, but all predictions have proved very wrong. Many of Ellison's would-be heirs have come and gone, forced out or obliged to leave when they clashed with their boss or (worse) stepped too far into his spotlight. To illustrate, in 1993 Larry hired Ray Lane, a well-respected executive, as president and COO. He was so effective that for several years Ellison even disengaged from the company's day-to-day management. But, given his controlling personality, that situation could not last. He couldn't tolerate Lane's success for too long. As expected, he became interested in the company once more. To highlight his position as the only alpha male at Oracle, he named himself head of applications, the beginning of a process to remove Lane's responsibilities. In June 2000, Lane left. A few months later, Oracle executive vice president Gary Bloom, Ellison's other most likely in-house successor, also quit. Today, Ellison is still the main person in the company he founded. It has been said that his two most senior aides are ill-suited for the job (Symonds, 2003).

The psychology of power is peculiar. When subordinates learn that a new person is to take up the reins, they shift loyalties quickly. Subtle changes occur in relationships. New power networks spring up. Suddenly, the outgoing CEO no longer feels in control. When a CEO comments that the succession problem has been resolved—in spite of overwhelming evidence to the contrary—one can be sure that these powerful psychological forces are at work. Such comments are often mere rationalizations to cover up a reluctance to let go.

SELECTING THE SUCCESSOR

The choice facing the CEO when he or she has decided who will be the new star is whether to go for an insider or an outsider. On the surface, chief executives make this choice according to what they think the company needs in the future, e.g. globalization, greater financial control or a new marketing orientation, and which candidate they perceive as being most likely to meet those ends. In reality, however, the choice between an insider or outsider is frequently determined by the forces of self-interest.

High-ranking corporate officers and board members may lobby to influence the decision and may even covet the position themselves. These executives will bear in mind that an insider is less likely to replace them than an outsider. Compromise, the containment of group conflict, and maintenance of the informal social network may be their prime concerns. Whether this preoccupation with stability and conservation is wise depends on the state of the company's environment. However, beside these rational explanations, other hidden factors also affect the choice and carry on the succession drama.

The dilemma of choice

The ties that bind leaders and followers are based on people's tendency to identify with those around them. Followers see their peers as similar to them but they also identify with their leaders. This is what creates a group. Seeing others as alike nourishes a feeling of unity and belonging, and provides a sense of direction and purpose. The precondition for the successful operation of this identification process is the illusion that it is mutual and that the leader hands out favors equally and loves everyone in the same way (Freud, 1921).

To single out someone from the group as a successor can look like favoritism, which promises to shatter the illusion of togetherness that all have relied on. To avoid making the painful decision and thus having to deal with the anger of the group—not to mention the disappointment of the candidates not chosen—CEOs often try to maintain this illusion at all costs.

One example was a head of an electronics company who had surrounded himself with a group of executives with very uneven talents. Although it was easy for outsiders to spot the stars, the CEO could not face the necessity of choosing one of them. He would smooth over the mistakes of the more incompetent and resist praising the stars for their stellar performance. As time went by, disgruntled about this treatment, several of his best people resigned. Why they left remained a puzzle to the boss; he thought he had been fair by treating everyone equally. To avoid accusations of favoritism, he eventually went outside the company for a successor. The successor was not the 'messiah reincarnated' and only lasted a year. His hiring and firing were costly affairs for the company.

Usually, the political forces inside a company favor selection of an insider. In large, complex corporations, an insider causes less disruption to the structure than an outsider, and an insider is less likely to build a whole new executive team. As mentioned earlier, insiders also may have the best chance because of the CEO's need to leave a legacy. An insider knows how things work in the organization and already has a commitment to the predecessor's way of doing things. Indeed, some CEOs pick an insider simply to perpetuate their own connection with the company.

The wish for the perfect solution

Selection of an outsider often signals the board's desire for a radical change in the company's direction. Sometimes there is a good reason behind the wish, like an industry shake-up or an economic shift. But sometimes the wish for a different kind of leader is based on psychological forces like jealousy, envy, or resentment on the part of known successors. Rather than hand over the reins to a known quantity, boards (and the chief executives who control them) have been known to fling their companies into the hands of near strangers.

The CEO of the financially battered Willet Bank & Trust Company[2] had nearly driven himself and the board crazy with his inability to choose an heir. No insider measured up to his standards. Furthermore, as he had been chosen above every one of them in the past, they clearly lacked what it would take to succeed in that office. Finally, in desperation, the board persuaded the CEO to bring in an outsider, Tom Langdon, who, the board knew, would impose stringent controls to improve the quality of the loans, which was the source of the trouble.

Langdon came on board but lasted only three years. He ignored the company's corporate culture completely, and his rigidity in upgrading loan quality led to the loss of several important customers. His poor performance, plus the resentment he drew from a number of senior executives, became the basis for his removal from the top job. Again, the board was at a loss what to do about the succession issue. As before, they had been ineffective in monitoring the talent pool in the organization. They had done a poor job in encouraging the CEOs in the company to groom possible successors.

CEOs are wise to spread the responsibility for choosing their successors. Acting alone, they are likely to sabotage the process (not neces-

[2] Names disguised.

sarily a conscious process) and choose badly. Non-executive board members should therefore play a key role in deciding on a future candidate, and whether the new CEO should be an insider or an outsider. If planned well, an insider's succession will hold fewer surprises for the organization. Unfortunately, none of us is loved at home as much as we are abroad. And the board may likewise stress an insider's weaknesses while taking the virtues for granted. Thus even if there are capable insiders around, the board may not choose them.

Not surprisingly, failing companies go outside more often than successful enterprises do. As we all know, when we want evolution, an insider is most suited. For a revolution, an outsider is the best choice. In many cases, an inside-outsider—someone who is not in the core business but who knows the business well (or comes from elsewhere in the same business)—may be the best choice.

THE FINAL ACT

Eventually the succession takes place, initiating a period of change. The status quo is disrupted. As might be expected, the company's new leadership orders strategic replacements that affect the organization's structure and transform reporting relationships. But here too, psychological forces come into play that can derail a new CEO's ability to manage the transition period and take firm control.

Romancing the past

One powerful force facing any new CEO is the tendency of people to idealize the past. We are all inclined to screen out painful, anxiety-provoking thoughts or events. Pleasant memories sometimes function as a shield to conceal a related painful memory. People under stress become victims of a struggle between the defensive process of denial and forces of memory.

This phenomenon has been named the 'Rebecca myth,' because in Daphne Du Maurier's novel *Rebecca,* a young woman who marries a widower is haunted by people's idealized memories of his first wife's endless virtues (Gouldner, 1964). In truth, the dead wife was a monster. Replacing or superseding an absent person can be a formidable task for the person attempting it. The newcomer has to replace a person whom everyone else likes to remember as perfect and who represents an ideal that the outsider fears can never be met. When people remember an absent person, any fantasy can become the truth. There is always the tendency to see the past as *la vie en rose*.

Furthermore, most people's behavior is influenced by strong conservative forces. Wary of the new, we cling to the familiar. Corporate executives and board members often block out the excesses of the old regime and maintain that things were much better before. The successor is in for an uphill battle to overcome this handicap.

The unacceptable reality

Inevitably, a considerable amount of anxiety accompanies even a well-planned succession. People have to sort out many changes and ambiguities. The uncertainties make them long for direction and leadership, and it is now that the CEO's symbolic role becomes very important. The new executive feels suddenly transformed into some kind of messiah, who will solve all problems. Understandably, not many CEOs can live up to this ideal.

The tendency of anxious people to need strong leaders explains why CEOs usually have more influence during a crisis than during normal times, and why incoming bosses enjoy a honeymoon period of enthusiasm and commitment. Some of them take advantage of the momentum this creates to very good effect. But how long can a honeymoon last? Very soon reality sets in—and with reality comes disappointment.

THE CEO LIFECYCLE: HOW LONG IS LONG ENOUGH?

I have often wondered what the optimum time is for a top executive to be effective on the job and it is not easy to find agreement on the point, particularly among CEOs. Responses tend to vary widely. After all, the answers depend on so many variables. For example, are you operating in a highly turbulent or a relatively stable environment? What kind of pressures are you under from the different stakeholders (the board, institutional shareholders, the stock market, banks, customers, or private equity)? Are you working for a family-controlled firm? (If so, that can make quite a difference. Owners may have quite another outlook as far as commitment and motivation are concerned.)

Nevertheless, the most common response I usually have from CEOs asked about the optimum time for doing what they are doing is ten years, plus or minus two. We should bear in mind that the figures can be very different when we look at family-controlled or entrepreneurial firms. In some instances, a family member or entrepreneur may become a CEO at a fairly young age, and they may hang in there for extremely long periods of time. Think of the executives I mentioned earlier, such as the late Armand Hammer of Occidental Petroleum and William Paley of CBS. These people almost had to be carried out of their respective organizations in their coffins. A time limit was not part of their personal agenda. Personally, I tend to favor the magical number eight. In my opinion, eight years is probably the period of maximum effectiveness for most people in what can be a very stressful job. However, the reality is that CEO jobs have become increasingly shorter—and as a matter of fact, far too short.

Usually, someone becomes CEO when he (and unfortunately, most CEOs do still tend to be men) is in his early fifties. A considerable number of potentially productive years lie ahead of him. The question is how many of these years are going to be really productive. How long can a CEO really be effective in leading his people—making the organization dance by stimulating creativity, innovation, and productivity?

THE VIEW FROM THE TOP

New CEOs quickly realize that being top dog changes many things. Life is suddenly quite different from what it was before. In many instances, there is no longer a higher step on the career ladder. Authority figures (if we forget the board) are no longer leaning over your shoulder. It is now entirely up to you to make something out of it. That being the case, you find yourself at times feeling quite alone, anxious, fearful, insecure, and wondering whether you will be able to handle the new responsibilities that come with the job. Many CEOs, although they may be reluctant to admit it, worry whether they will be able to hack it. They wonder if they haven't reached their level of incompetence. But for most new CEOs, such concerns are only distant clouds on the horizon. There are usually other, more overriding diversions when they are new to the job.

However, it's interesting to consider whether there is such a thing as a life cycle for CEOs. Does the position follow a certain pattern? And if so, what is the sequence of stages? How does it all unfold? I believe there is such a life cycle and in this chapter I describe the stages it moves through. (I touched upon this issue in Chapter 5, when discussing Vladimir Putin's time as president of Russia.)

Just as there is such a thing as a product life cycle (a time period during which a product will secure sales and profits), I would argue that the same cycle applies to the 'returns' produced by a CEO. Product and technology life cycles have become shorter and shorter, putting enormous pressure on CEOs to keep up with events. No wonder that the cycle for CEOs has become so short.

Conceptually, I see CEOs as passing through three stages while in the position: a period of entry, when lots of experimentation may take place; a period of consolidation; and a period of decline.

The entry period

Having reached the top position, what is the first action you would take as CEO? Obviously, the single most important thing is to gain the confidence of the people who wanted you in the job in the first place. You have to prove yourself and achieve successes to consolidate your position. You want to establish a power base. That means that you have to win the support of the board and the respect and loyalty of your troops.

From this point on, many different scenarios are possible. Immediately after entry, having won the confidence of your main constituencies, a honeymoon period begins—the time during your entire tenure as CEO when you are most open to new ideas. It is a period when you are willing to learn and to experiment. You are ready to absorb a lot of critical knowledge as rapidly as possible. It is the point at which you are prepared to make major changes, particularly if you are brought in as an outsider.

Important questions to ask at this stage are: What exactly do the people who helped you to get the job expect from you? What changes (if any) would they like to see made? What do they feel is currently wrong with the company? What special talents do they think *you* can offer them in order to change the present situation?

For example, it is possible that they feel the company is lacking in innovation and needs someone with a solid track record in high technology. Or they might consider that the company is not cost effective, and that they need someone with experience in cost cutting. Or, again, they may want a person with human relations or talent management skills, an individual with the ability to bring people together after the company has been through years of turmoil. Then again, global marketing may be a top priority, hence the appointment of someone with a solid background in international marketing, and so on and so on. Thus it is wise to make your first moves concordant with the expectations of the people who appointed you.

However, their expectations and your preoccupations may not necessarily be a match made in heaven. And in spite of the openness to new impressions that characterizes the first stage of the CEO life cycle, there is always the potential for regression. Because this period of entry can be highly stressful, and because of the level of anxiety you are experiencing, you may fall back on the things you think you are best at; you may rely on the old repertoire that has served you so well in the past. This orientation, however, may very well be the wrong one for the company at this particular time. Decisions made in haste, based on previous expertise, may be particularly difficult to reverse, given the loss of face that a change of mind might involve. You may later be reluctant to take another direction and admit that you have made a mistake.

During this time of experimentation your performance as CEO may not yet live up to expectations, particularly if you have been brought in from the outside. After all, so many new things have to be learned: you have to make sense of your new environment; you have to get to know your various constituencies; and you have to select your key lieutenants, the people who will help you make it happen. You may have to 'kill' wounded princes—executives in the organization who expected the position.

Consolidation

After a new CEO has established a particular theme that signifies important aspects of his personality—a theme that seems to strike a chord with the forces of the external environment—the second phase, the period of consolidation, sets in. You have gone through the rites of passage and proved yourself. As you are able to demonstrate good results, you begin to feel more secure in the job. Company performance is improving and your own performance is about to peak.

By this stage, if everything has gone well, you have forged effective alliances with your various constituencies. Your executives are committed to the course you have chosen. You have built up a good working relationship with your board, which is confident of your abilities. If things have not gone well, of course, you may find yourself out of a job. And this trend about being out of a job is growing as boards become increasingly preoccupied with performance and less patient with ineffective CEOs.

But let us suppose things have worked out well. The people who count are pleased with your performance, and you are building up credit with your various constituencies. With the consolidation of your power base, you are increasingly in a position to actualize the preoccupations derived from your inner theater—the dream you have for the organization. As time goes by, you may focus more and more on one particular theme, a pattern that may reflect something that has been a thread running through your life.

One way of looking at this is to view it as an attempt to deal with an issue that has never really been completely resolved, something the CEO is still struggling with, consciously or unconsciously. What is worrisome, however, is that any deviation from this theme may no longer be welcome; rigidity starts to set in. Consequently, substantial new initiatives are no longer to be expected.

Decline

This stage can be said to start around the time when, from the CEO's point of view, the excitement of mastering new things starts to wane. As far as change is concerned, we are now only talking about incremental changes. The only thing that counts is the fine-tuning of this major theme and people who question that do so at their peril.

One sign that a CEO has reached the final phase in the career cycle might be that there is not much change in the product portfolio. No new products are planned for the near future. The composition of the existing customer base seems static, and no initiatives are forthcoming to recruit new ones. Furthermore, there is no new blood coming into the organization. The company sticks to the same tired old group of senior executives who are committed to the particular orientation of the CEO. Another indicator is that the company is accumulating too much cash. Top executives are running out of ideas about how to use the available money.

It is during this third phase that problems can snowball. What is happening to the CEO? You may be too settled and stopped listening to points of view at odds with your own. In fact, you are likely to come down heavily on the opposition. Moreover, the job itself no longer gives you enough stimulation. The routine is getting to you, and your performance may be slacking off.

For a good example of this sort of behavior we only have to look at the story of the legendary Henry Ford, manufacturer of the Model T car. What was originally an extremely bold idea (an affordable car for the masses) almost became the company's downfall because of Ford's unwillingness to make adjustments to the design. The model stayed the same from 1908 to 1927, despite changes in market conditions and loss of market share to General Motors. Ford was unable to stray from his obsession to make cheap cars. His deep-seated preoccupation (which reveals much about his rather ambivalent relationship to his father, who was a farmer) was to help farmers by providing a means of transport from remote and isolated farms.

A similar monomania appeared in a CEO called Sewell Lee Avery, once the chairman of Montgomery Ward, a large U.S. department store chain. Avery was preoccupied with cost cutting and liquidity (he feared an imminent depression), a theme that had been effective when he held other positions. Unfortunately, at Montgomery Ward that obsession led Avery to turn the company into a bank with a department store front. His particular preoccupation left customers with very little to buy, which did nothing to further the interests of the company.

Ken Olson, the founder and former chairman of DEC, provides another example. One of the pioneers of the computer business, Olson had a vision of the computer industry that was once exactly in tune with the needs of the consumer. However, his continued preoccupation with technical perfectionism and failure to pay much attention to changing consumer needs, led to rigidity, and poor adaptation to the market. Ultimately this hurt profits tremendously and led to his forced retirement. His unfortunate statement that 'there is no reason for an individual to have a computer in his home,' made him quite famous.

Observing the behavior of media mogul, Summer Redstone, many industry observers wonder how much longer Viacom insiders can put off a shareholders' revolt. Unlocking the languishing value of stock in his media company by splitting it into two entities may not be the answer. Furthermore, Redstone's behavior has appeared troublesome. During an interview with Larry King, he said, 'The people who fear dying are people who are going to die. I'm not going to die. I'm going to live forever. ... I feel as if I was 20, in every way, even sexually.' (Redstone, born in 1923, had just married a woman 40 years younger than himself.) Unfortunately, his deluded claim that he is immortal appears to be more of a threat than a promise for the shareholders of the troubled company. Luckily for Redstone, in Hollywood most media companies seem to be run more like private fiefdoms than real businesses. If Viacom had been a troubled bank, car company, or newspaper, Redstone would be long gone. But even in an entertainment world, Viacom no longer has the luxury of having a leader who lives in the past, acting like an aging member of the Rat Pack, ogling showgirls at a Vegas casino. With the media tycoon in charge—and given the company's poor results—Redstone may no longer be able to hold on to his vast empire.

For various reasons these CEOs found it very hard to adjust to changes in the external environment. The stubbornness of some in clinging to one particular theme, whose time rapidly passed, led to their downfall. Naturally, such a mismatch is more immediately noticeable in industries characterized by a highly dynamic, turbulent environment. Executives who operate in a relatively stable environment can get away with rigidity of action for longer.

CEOs can find it very hard to admit to themselves that they are losing their effectiveness, that the time has come to look for new horizons and do something else. Too much of their sense of self may be tied up with the job. They are likely to have become attached to the power of their position and possibly addicted to being in the limelight. Deciding when enough is enough is easier said than done. This third phase—decline—can have a devastating effect on the company. Holding on to a theme that has become outmoded or redundant can be disastrous. In some cases it may even bring the company to bankruptcy.

However, many alternative scenarios are also possible. Some CEOs start to distance themselves from day-to-day company activities, becoming even more remote. Needing new mental stimuli, they become interested in other things while maintaining their old routines. They may begin to spend more time outside the office. They may start to pursue different, more glamorous interests, spending a lot of time on social or sporting events. All this would be perfectly acceptable in a CEO who is capable of delegating and letting go. Unfortunately, lessened involvement with the nitty-gritty of the business does not always go hand-in-hand with increased delegation. Delegation might mean that people start to question the theme the CEO is pursuing and discover that it is no longer appropriate.

Other CEOs may squander scarce company resources on company airplanes, clubs and other perks, retreats, or special events. Some may become involved in risky new ventures. They may see the merger and acquisition route as a solution to their sense of inner unrest and anxiety (and boredom), however costly it turns out to be. Consequently, they spend the company's resources on rather ineffective efforts at empire building. Others (commendably) may become more involved in social concerns, such as sponsorship of the arts or special sports events. This is quite all right, as long as it does not detract from the running of the business.

Lee Iacocca's well-publicized and time-consuming external activities—fund-raising for the Statue of Liberty, and toying with the idea of becoming a presidential candidate at a time when Chrysler needed all the help it could get to stay afloat—are an illustration of good ideas that were badly timed. Jan Carlson, a former CEO of SAS, also became preoccupied with the acquisition game and his presence in the media.

With both men, people began to ask who was actually running the company and taking care of the day-to-day business. When these kinds of behavior are combined with an unwillingness to change a previous successful theme, decline can accelerate.

This period of decline may also worsen if the board does not execute its review functions properly. As you prove yourself, the board may have given you increasing latitude. Over time you may even have filled the board with people indebted to you, who do not really take their review function seriously. It does not help that in many instances board members over-identify with the problems of the CEO. After all, many of them will have been CEOs themselves at some point. It is not easy to ask a close colleague to change his or her act or get out. Thus many boards have a tendency to turn a blind eye, taking action only when things become really catastrophic—by which time it is often too late.

GAINING SELF-AWARENESS

So, what advice can we give CEOs who find themselves stuck in their job, fearful of no longer being effective? The best thing, of course, is if these executives themselves realize what is happening, acknowledge their increasing ineffectiveness, and look for new horizons when the going is still good. A graceful exit is always a preferable choice and is often in everybody's best interest. Painful as the decision may be, it may prove to be the wisest one ever made. Stepping down may give you the jolt you need to become more effective, albeit in another situation.

Leader and leadership development programs can provide another form of stock taking. The time taken for reflection and comparison—to study 'the leader within'—can lead to a feeling of renewal, arresting a downswing in effectiveness. Such programs are great opportunities to exchange ideas with colleagues who find themselves in a similar situation. It may become the impetus to leave the organization and try another job.

Taking time out

Going one step further, the CEO can consider the possibility of taking a sabbatical—an option that is, in fact, rarely taken, given the reality of organizational politics. Many top executives find it too risky to be out of circulation for too long. They worry (and rightly so) that their job may no longer be there when they come back. However, some CEOs who have taken the plunge, and organized their companies in such a way that they continued functioning in an effective manner in their absence, found doing so a very rejuvenating, enriching experience.

Handing it on

Other CEOs obtain great pleasure from their role as mentor or leadership coach—seeing younger executives standing on their own two feet, taking risks and making decisions. Of course, this approach to learning only works if a CEO has created a culture of trust and true dialogue within the company, where existing assumptions can be challenged. Mentoring and leadership coaching are ways of establishing continuity in the organization.

CEOs who take this route help the organization learn from their own experience and adapt successfully to changes in the environment. CEOs can create a culture that helps executives anticipate the demands of the external environment, exploit new opportunities, evolve continuously, and avoid becoming stuck in dysfunctional learning patterns.

THE MOMENT FOR CHANGE

The major challenge for many CEOs is to recognize when the moment has come to change course—when, if they fail to regenerate themselves, they are likely to become one of the walking dead. Because (to pursue my rather morbid metaphor) if they continue in the direction they are headed, they will leave a graveyard behind. The prayer devised by American theologian Reinhold Niebuhr, now regularly used in many 12-step rehabilitation programs, asks:

> Give me the serenity to accept things I cannot change, the courage to change things I can, and the wisdom to know the difference.

Wise CEOs are those who know what is meant by this.

CHAPTER 10

THE RETIREMENT SYNDROME: THE PSYCHOLOGY OF LETTING GO[1]

The years teach much which the days never know.

Ralph Waldo Emerson

Do not go gentle into that good night,
Old age should burn and rage at the close of day,
Rage, rage against the dying of the light.

Dylan Thomas

Growing old isn't so bad when you consider the alternative.

Maurice Chevalier

In the bleak, Oscar-nominated comedy *About Schmidt*, Jack Nicholson stars as Warren Schmidt, a 67-year-old insurance executive from Omaha, Nebraska, who is set adrift following retirement. The film is the character study of a sad, aging man who is face to face with mortality and the emptiness of a life near its end. His retirement party is the first of the movie's painfully sour-sweet ceremonies. The 'party' shows quite

---

[1] The material for this chapter has appeared elsewhere in print in the following sources:

Kets de Vries, M. F. R. (2003). 'The Retirement Syndrome: The psychology of letting go,' *European Management Journal*, 21(6), 707–716; Kets de Vries, M. F. R. (1979). 'Is there life after retirement?,' *California Management Review*, XXII(1), 69–76, and Kets de Vries, M. F. R. (1994). 'Can You Manage the Rest of Your Life?' *European Management Journal*, 12 (2), 133–137.

clearly that Schmidt isn't looking forward to retirement. He is at a loss why he has to go through such an event. He doesn't respect the person who has become his successor. The future holds no promise of a golden sunset for him. Schmidt seems to have cultivated no interests outside work. On retirement, he reassesses his life, wondering whether his job, marriage, and family life were ever what he had hoped for. The situation is exacerbated by his loathing for his dowdy wife ('Who is this old woman living in my house?'). His treasured but alienated daughter lives in Denver, barely speaks to him, and is set to marry a man he regards as a total nincompoop. Searching for some kind of meaning, Schmidt decides to contribute $22 a month to the welfare of an African 'foster' child. His frank letters to six-year-old Ndugu appear to be the only place where he is able to establish human contact; where there seems to be a degree of authenticity. When his wife suddenly keels over while vacuuming their home, the rest of his world falls apart. Unable to take care of himself, he begins to deteriorate physically. Not only does he neglect his appearance, it doesn't take very long before his home is messier than a pigsty.

On an impulse, Schmidt—uncertain about his future as well as his past—packs up his 30-foot Winnebago (which his wife has nagged him into buying) to set out on a cross-country journey to stop his daughter's wedding. Along the way—no longer shielded by the work environment or his wife—he tries to connect to other people, efforts that turn out disastrously. He makes a depressive visit to his childhood home which has been turned into a tire store, and tries to strike up a friendship with a trailer-park couple that ends abruptly when he makes a clumsy pass at the wife. His daughter's future relatives represent Schmidt's worst nightmare: a rowdy clan of counterculture refugees and wannabes. His future son-in-law sells 'top of the line' waterbeds and wears his long, thinning hair in a ponytail. His son-in-law's mother is the ultimate lewd old gal, who cajoles him into a hot tub (even joining him in the nude) and tells him far more than he would ever like to know about her sex life while spouting psychobabble. Her intrusiveness is an anathema to Schmidt, who has wasted away in the insurance industry for decades; whose sterile, middle-class life was micro-managed by his wife; and whose controlled behavior probably drove his uptight daughter to a guy like his future son-in-law in the first place. During his mini-quest across the Midwest, we see a man gradually stripped of all his illusions about his past career, his marriage, his daughter, and his life. Schmidt seems destined to end his life as he lived it: a failure, going through life with a tight little smile, born of obtuseness, isolation, depression, and terror. Probably, if he would have known that life would turn out like this, he might have taken care of himself in another way; he would have managed his life quite differently.

Schmidt ends up full of regrets, a sorry example of poor career and life management. As the story unfolds, *About Schmidt* turns into a cautionary tale about life. It reaffirms the wise counsel not to put all our eggs in one basket. If we want to live life to the fullest, we have to invest in matters other than work—and not start when we retire. A solo ride to work can be a ride into nowhere. What this film makes us realize is that people who grow old with grace are quite rare. For too many of us, retirement comes as an unexpected realization for which we have been very poorly prepared. But as the example of Schmidt illustrates all too depressingly, sooner or later, people in positions of power and authority have to let go.

THE CHALLENGE OF LETTING GO

It has often been said that as we grow old, we have to give up certain things. I prefer to reframe this statement and say that we grow old if we *fail* to give up certain things. As we live in a society where many people no longer only have one, but a series of careers, the challenge, of course, is knowing what to give up, how to do so, and what next. If we want to live life to the fullest in our later years, we have to give up, decades earlier, our single-minded devotion to work (or one line of work) and the mighty dollar. We also have to invest in other things than work. Hopefully, we have discovered that the most important things to invest in are relationships. If we invest in relationships, for example, we will create good memories with people close to us that will sustain us in difficult times. Life is not just about letting go, but also starting new beginnings.

The extent to which letting go of one line of work is a positive or negative experience will depend very much on the individual and his or her particular circumstances. Letting go has a devastating effect on some people; they perceive it as a hostile act, whether it happens at a prearranged stage in life (at retirement), through voluntary or imposed redundancy, through an organizational or political *coup d'état*, or through ill health.

Apart from the high price organizations pay when senior executives hang on beyond their 'best before date,' we should also be aware on a personal level of the darker side of power holding—its ability to detach the individual from the realities of life outside, its diminution of a personal life, its tendency to warp the responses of both leader and followers, its propensity to enmesh a leader in isolation, its over-reliance on external symbols of success rather than inner stability. We should not forget that real aging takes place when regrets take over from dreams, when we desert our ideals. Worry, doubt, self-interest, and despair are the furies that destroy a person's spirit. We need to go beyond Benjamin Disraeli's lament that 'Youth is a blunder; manhood a struggle; old age a regret.'

FAMILIAL AND SOCIETAL ATTITUDES TOWARD RETIREES

The reason why growing old and retirement are often negative experiences is well illustrated by an old German folk tale.

> Once upon a time there was a very old man who was no longer able to earn his daily bread and lived with his son and daughter-in-law. His eyes had grown dim, his hearing was not what it used to be, and his hands were no longer steady. At mealtimes he had difficulty holding his spoon and would spill food on the clean tablecloth. This maddened his son and daughter-in-law, who finally placed him out of sight, in a corner behind the stove. At mealtimes the old man would look sadly at the table with tears in his eyes thinking of happier times. One day, his earthenware bowl dropped out of his trembling hands and broke into pieces. His daughter-in-law scolded him and replaced it with a wooden bowl, from which he ate from then on.
>
> One day, seeing his small son busily nailing some pieces of wood together in front of the stove, the boy's father asked, 'What are you doing?' 'I'm making a trough for you and mother to eat out of when I'm grown up,' said the little boy, happily. His father and mother burst into tears and, weeping, kissed the grandfather and brought him back to the table. There he ate until the end of his days and nothing was ever said, even when he spilled his food on the beautiful, snow-white tablecloth.

The point of this tale is not whether the family lived happily ever after, but our fundamental denial of aging, contempt for old age, and the bitter aftertaste they leave. The moral of the tale centers on our fear of role reversal: what I do to you, you might do to me. As children, we are dependent. As we grow up we have an ambivalent attitude toward the elderly. On the one hand, we express love and affection for them; on the other, we may demonstrate hostility and resentment, informed by our memories of confrontations with the power older people once had over us. We live in a youth-oriented culture where the retired are the new survivors and reverence for the elderly a low priority item.

Because we no longer kill our kings or high priests when their power wanes does not mean that we have put aside our bias against the elderly.

But the number of retired people in society has risen, a consequence of increased life expectancy and, until recently, of ever earlier retirement ages. It is a cause of worry from a socio-economic perspective. Who will pay for their retirement, given the new demographics? Can societies really afford it? In the past, retirement was only justified when an individual was physically or mentally unable to continue work. It is now a luxury of western society to which we are gradually growing accustomed. Given the magnitude of this new social phenomenon, the process of retirement is becoming an increasingly important issue for individuals, organizations, and society.

Rites of exit

Retirement can be viewed as a transition point, a rite of passage guiding the individual from one social position to the next. It is a symbol of old age. This psycho-social transition point can be celebrated with a banquet, a commemorative gift, or special treatment of an employee during the last day or days on the job. Within an organization the purpose of these rites is to help people define and accept their new role as a retiree. Through these rites someone's change in role and position is announced to the outside world through differential treatment and a celebration of past accomplishments, accompanied by declarations of gratitude for services rendered. The emphasis is on the past. Unfortunately, too often, little is said about new beginnings, future challenges, and opportunities.

Congratulations and pleasantries cannot hide the fact, however, that someone is being divorced from a job, a world of work, and a career. Feelings of separation and loss are aroused during these rites of exit. Retirement is often experienced as a period of mourning and exile hidden under a thin veneer of smiles, handshakes, and tokens of appreciation.

ENDING IT ALL

There is a clear semantic distinction between the active statement 'I am retiring' and the passive 'I am being retired,' but the fact is, whatever the terminology used, most people do not have much of a choice. The decision is made for them—they *are* being retired. To many, retirement takes on the meaning of a symbolic rejection and intensifies awareness of a wider process now occurring, which is reversing many of the developments that took place in childhood, adolescence, and young adulthood. Unlike the rapid physiological transformation that occurs during adolescence, aging is a gradual process. The realization of change occurs in a different way: we may feel old because of the way others label us and the position we occupy on the social clock.

Letting go is so difficult for some leaders that they insist on remaining in a position of power—even when they know they have accomplished all they can, are no longer happy with their performance, feel isolated or empty or unfulfilled, have exhausted the challenges, and no longer have a clear sense of direction. I call this the 'retirement syndrome.'

CEOs who reach the top at a relatively early age and, once there, enjoy a long tenure are hit particularly hard by retirement syndrome. Unlike peers who entered the most senior positions later in life, many have lost their initial sense of excitement and adventure. Their worldly success and physical attractiveness coincided early on, making the downhill run much longer and more treacherous than the uphill struggle. Retirement leaves them wanting to surpass past achievements but unsure what course to take. It begs the question whether we should have 'beauty' and 'power' at the same time or consecutively.

Hank DeWit,[2] one-time CEO of an information technology company who stepped down at age 39, knows that feeling of decline well:

> I felt wiped out all the time and spent most of my energy sweating over whether other people would notice my exhaustion and lack of concentration—which made both problems worse. It wasn't a healthy sort of tiredness, the kind where a shot of adrenalin carries you through. I'd lost any sense of excitement; everything had become a chore. I sat through meetings but couldn't have told you the first thing about what we'd discussed afterwards. I'd been so good, but I'd lost it. People did notice, of course. Gossip filtered up. I started to get paranoid about it, watching my back, avoiding certain people. I felt I was hanging on to the whole thing by my fingertips. I used to say to myself, 'Hang on there; you've got years to go yet.' I was terrified I'd used myself up so soon; there didn't seem to be anything of me left. Driving in the morning, I'd have to fight the impulse to turn and head straight back home. When the company started to lose market share, I knew my state of mind had to be responsible—at least, I couldn't see any way out, which amounted to the same thing. I realized I wanted to run away, but it was a while before I could see myself getting out in more positive terms, for me and for the company. It was too much, too soon.

---

[2] All names disguised.

Getting out and heading in another direction was a practical option for a relatively young executive like Hank, who peaked early in his career. People like him can change industry, try out a new venture, be a non-executive board director, become involved in a nonprofit organization, join the public sector, or go back to university to pursue learning opportunities earlier discarded as unrealistic. For these people there are still a lot of new opportunities and adventures to look forward to.

But what about older leaders looking (or forced) to leave their job? Faced with the question of what to do next, they know that the answer is retirement—and they generally don't like that prospect. Sure, they could step into a non-executive director position, do volunteer work, play golf, or work in their garden, but those options don't promise the same degree of gratification. An imminent retirement date brings older leaders up hard against a number of painful realities that come with the consciousness of letting go: loss of work (a critical activity in life as it has implications for the purpose of self-esteem) and possible loss of health and vitality, as well as loss of public exposure and public contact; and loss of influence, power, attention, and admiration. In addition, they face the prospect of spending time at home with a partner who may have become a virtual stranger—and they know that modes of relating that worked with that partner at 20 may not work so well now, as they become reacquainted.

Awareness of these real and potential losses and the need for a changed lifestyle are frequently exacerbated by the consciousness of what was lost years earlier, on the way to the top—a fulfilling personal life; good relationships with spouse or partner, children and friends; and time to develop outside contacts and interests. Facing retirement, many CEOs prefer clinging to power rather than confronting these painful realities, preferring action over reflection (with its tendency to give way to depressive thoughts). They do anything and everything within their power to postpone the day of reckoning, perhaps fearing that Malcolm Forbes was right when he observed that 'retirement kills more people than hard work ever did.'

In addition to these personal conflicts, people facing retirement also have to deal with financial and social concerns. In more traditional companies (excluding the excesses of people in the financial sector), retirement benefits are typically lower than full CEO income, and the sooner one leaves the firm, the lower the benefits. Accustomed to socializing with people who have comparably high disposable incomes, and wanting to stay in familiar social circles, many leaders feel financial pressure to remain in the job, or are looking for new ones. Additional pressure to remain in the job market may come from spouses and children who are used to the perks and reflected glory that comes with a top leadership position.

Yet these constraints, realistic though they may be (and prominent though they may seem to figure in decision-making) are only the tip of the iceberg. The crisis of letting go also hinges on a hidden but potent mass of psychological and emotional factors. We turn to those now.

THE PHYSICAL AND PSYCHOLOGICAL EFFECTS OF AGING

Despite the inevitability of aging and death, many people are surprised to see evidence of physical decline in themselves. When the face frowning back from the mirror shows the ravages of age, they feel as if, as one wit put it, they're being penalized for a crime that they didn't commit.

Self-consciousness about the deterioration of the body can stimulate the search for outlets that can substitute for attractiveness and virility. For some people—and CEOs are prime candidates, given the prestigious position they occupy—the wielding of power is an important substitute; symbolically if not actually, having power becomes a replacement for having looks. Henry Kissinger, former U.S. Secretary of State, even hinted at a compensatory relationship between power and sexuality when he said ambiguously, 'Power is the greatest aphrodisiac.' Kissinger was well aware of the sexual attractiveness of power to members of the opposite sex, but his comment also suggests that power turns on the power-holder as well.

An explicit example of the perceived relationship between the body, genitalia or sexuality, and power is illustrated by a tradition—a real anthropological curiosity—that existed in an Indian Hindu kingdom until the turn of the seventeenth century.

It has been the custom of the Maharaja of Patiala to appear once a year before his subjects naked except for his diamond breastplate (composed of 1,001 brilliantly matched blue-white diamonds), his organ in full and glorious erection. His performance was adjudged a kind of temporal manifestation of the shivaling, the phallic representation of Lord Shiva's organ. As the Maharaja walked about, his subjects gleefully applauded, their cheers acknowledging both the dimensions of the princely organ and the fact that it was supposed to be radiating magic powers from the land (Cath, Gurwitt, and Ross, 1982, p. 524).

Leaders may lose their looks, but if they still have their power, they have an allure nonetheless. No wonder so many leaders are reluctant to let go.

The experience of nothingness

It has been said that one grows old by living. I would argue that, on the contrary, people grow old by losing interest in living. People so preoccupied by loss and personal vulnerability that they have no hope for the future often become imprisoned by depressive thoughts. The idea of letting go of power and responsibility (and compounding their vulnerability) is particularly unattractive to these people. They sometime act out in foolish ways as they fight the inevitability of change. If the power of position is the only thing a leader has left, he or she may display great single-mindedness and persistence in maintaining that power base. The threat of going from being somebody to nobody overnight, of being a nonentity experiencing nothingness, generates an enormous amount of anxiety. President Harry Truman confronted this threat candidly when he said, shortly after leaving office, 'Two hours ago I could have said five words and been quoted in every capital of the world. Now, I could talk for two hours and nobody would give a damn' (Graff, 1988, p. 5). Many leaders—given their narcissistic disposition—dread this change in status. As long as they can hold on to their power, they at least have personal contact with sycophants and yes-men.

The U.S. President Lyndon Johnson provides an illustration of the psychological stresses involved in the process of letting go. Since early childhood, Johnson suffered from nightmares about paralysis:

> He would see himself sitting absolutely still, in a big straight chair ... The chair stood in the middle of the great, open plains. A stampede of cattle was coming towards him. He tried to move, but he could not. He cried out again and again for his mother, but no one came. (Kearns, 1976, p. 32)

Strokes were not uncommon in Johnson's family. His grandmother had been paralyzed from the neck down by a stroke and sat in a chair like the one in his dream. It is interesting to speculate how far Johnson's childhood terror of paralysis, demonstrated by this dream, influenced his later behavior and actions—to what extent his search for power was a compensatory reaction to his fear of helplessness. And yet even after he had become successful beyond his wildest dreams—as President of the United States, he was arguably the most powerful person in the world—he *still* had a fear of becoming paralyzed. (Incidentally, two previous presidents, Franklin Roosevelt and Woodrow Wilson had in fact suffered from a similar condition as Johnson's grandmother.)

Did the two images—Johnson's of his grandmother and those of the previous two presidents—become mixed up in Johnson's mind? Later events suggest that they may have. In the late 1960s, Johnson realized that his time as president was running out. His health was suffering; he was embroiled in political crises; it was becoming clear that the Vietnam War could not be won with conventional weapons; and he could no longer depend on his usual congressional allies; the chances of his winning a second term were remote. As his presidency drew to a close, the old nightmare returned in different form:

> This time he was lying in a bed in the Red Room of the White House, instead of sitting in a chair in the middle of the open plains. His head was still his, but from the neck down his body was the thin, paralyzed body that had been the affliction of both Woodrow Wilson and his own grandmother in their final years. All his presidential assistants were in the next room. He could hear them actively fighting with one another to divide up his power ... He could hear them, but he could not command them, for he could neither talk nor walk. He was sick and stilled, but not a single aide tried to protect him. (Kearns, 1976, p. 342)

Johnson would wake up so terrified from this dream that he was too afraid to fall asleep again and risk experiencing a repeat of it. He could soothe himself only by going through a specific ritual. He would get out of bed and walk through the White House until he reached the portrait of Woodrow Wilson. After touching the picture, he would be able to return to bed and sleep. It was almost as if Johnson needed to make this symbolic gesture in order to reassure himself that he was still alive and not paralyzed, that it was Wilson who was dead. The symbolism of paralysis and the need to overcome it are significant indications of Johnson's mental state. Faced with the imminent loss of power, his delicate psychic equilibrium, which cost him so much to maintain, wavered. Powerlessness, in his world view, meant paralysis—nothingness, and death.

The edifice complex

The fear of nothingness and the depression that accompanies it are accentuated by the need all of us have to leave behind a legacy. A common preoccupation of leaders is whether their successors can be relied on to respect the 'monument'—the actualization of the 'dream'—that took them so long to build. Many leaders suffer from what can be described as an 'edifice complex.' The fear that their legacy will be destroyed can motivate them to hold on to power for as long as possible. On a more fundamental level, leaving behind a reminder of one's accomplishment can be equated symbolically with defeating death. French presidents have excelled in doing so, exemplified by Georges Pompidou's center for modern art, François Mitterand's grand arch at La Défense and pyramid at the Louvre, and Jacques Chirac's Quai Branly museum of indigenous art. A continuing personal presence can be an expression of a leader's personal difficulty in facing mortality, the inescapable necessity of letting go in the final sense. It may indicate the fear that without him or her, the monument will be destroyed.

The retiring leader, already burdened by conflicting emotions, facing an uncertain future for the first time in perhaps many years, also has to resign the vision or dream that has not only been a personal motivation but also the driving force behind an entire organization. Furthermore, when passing the baton, the leader may have to witness the systematic rejection of this vision by emerging leaders and be considered part of an inferior past, with no place in the future. The anointing of a crown prince or crown princess can have a devastating impact on the outgoing CEO as the power dynamics begin to shift. Someone else may replace whatever dream he or she had about the future of the organization, contributing to anger, sadness, and depression. It will be most difficult for CEOs for whom work was the center of their life to accept this change. With impending retirement, they experience a sense of panic realizing that their time is almost up. They may have the strong conviction—however convoluted—that there is still so much unfinished business to be dealt with. Thus, not surprisingly—and far too often—if the situation permits, CEOs may have second thoughts. They will resort to any excuse to hang on.

There can be another scenario, however. Taking great pride in what one has accomplished will go a long way to make the disengagement process easier. There can be pride in having contributed to the development of a capable successor—vicarious gratification can be a facilitating factor in the disengagement process. The key is whether the 'dream' has been accomplished—whether the next generation has bought into the dream. If reconciliation and acceptance are absent, it is all too easy for envy and anger to be generated. The retiring leader may direct his or her anger at the ungrateful next generation, society at large, and the aging process itself, all of which are tearing down what took a lifetime to build up. The famous words of Louis XIV, '*Après moi, le déluge,*' are well worth remembering. Old men can be dangerous; they may harbor little concern about what happens to the world afterward.

The talion principle

Another complicating factor for those faced with the prospect of relinquishing power is the *lex talionis*, or talion principle, which derives from early Babylonian law and states that criminals should receive as punishment exactly the injuries they inflicted on their victims. This eye-for-an-eye retribution has been the law of many societies throughout history. Although modern society has found other systems and forms of justice to compensate for injury, the ancient law of an eye for an eye and a tooth for a tooth still operates in the collective and individual unconscious. It is manifested in feelings of guilt, a general fear of retribution, the everyday language of revenge (e.g. 'settling a score' and 'getting even') slips of the tongue, and symptoms such as general anxiety, stress, depression, and bad dreams.

The talion principle is highly significant in relation to retirement. Leadership involves the making of difficult decisions that affect the life and happiness of others—sometimes positively, more often negatively. Because of their unconscious belief in the talion principle, leaders file all those decisions in a memory bank and, as the number of 'victims' mounts, increasingly expect retaliation. As a result, leadership is frequently accompanied by paranoia. While paranoia can strike anyone, leaders are especially vulnerable, because they do in fact face many dangers, both obvious and hidden, in the form of opponents who would like to berate them (but have to hold their tongue to hold on to their job). One simply cannot be an effective leader without rubbing some people up the wrong way. There will always be followers who feel stepped upon and dream of (or enact) retaliation, just as there will always be followers who envy a leader's power and plot to attain it (especially when the time comes for succession).

Leaders, as their achievement of a position at the top testifies, are extremely adept at the power game. Sensitive to any shift in their power base, they bridle when power shifts even slightly toward potential successors. They may lash out, attempting to put ambitious ladder-climbers in their place. For leaders, then, ideas of persecution are a rational response to a world populated by real, not just imagined, enemies. With no place for leaders to hide, they tend to be mistrustful, guarded, hypersensitive, and unusually vigilant. Sensitive to signals of danger and hostility, their primary mode of reaction becomes defensiveness. Given the very real dangers that leaders face, healthy suspiciousness is an effective adaptive mechanism. Being vigilant in the presence of perceived or likely danger is simply an extension of their wish to survive.

The anxiety that many leaders feel over the prospect of retaliation after loss of power can trap them in an escalation of aggression: they take pre-emptive action, initiating destructive measures to crush real and/or imagined opponents even before there is any indication that those opponents intend to retaliate. Such behavior is clearly not in the organization's best interests.

One CEO of a company in the insurance industry did everything in her power to postpone retirement. For decades, she had been known for her abrasive personality, and she had made many enemies. During her tenure at the helm, she had called for many purges of top executives, and she had repeatedly engaged in questionable re-engineering efforts that had led to the dismissal of thousands of employees. With that history, she dreaded the mandatory retirement date that loomed in the near future. In an unguarded moment, she referred to 'those SOBs' who would finally 'get a chance to get at her' when she retired. She feared that after retirement she would be more vulnerable to lawsuits from people who felt wronged by her. That fear colored not only her rational thoughts but also her dream life. A repetitive dream had started haunting her sometime earlier. She was lost in a swamp, overcome with feelings of anxiety about things to come; from far away, she heard the barking of hounds, and she started to run, fearful of being attacked. The dream left her with a sense of dread—a dread not unlike that which she felt about her upcoming retirement.

Because images of danger dominated her inner life, this woman went through a number of convoluted steps to try to get the non-executive members of the board to negate the mandatory retirement date. With the help of a headhunting firm, she tried to persuade the board that no one within the company or available outside was ready to take over the reins at this critical juncture in the history of the organization. Her efforts increased the level of paranoid anxiety on the part of the non-executive board members. They bought into her argument that grave dangers would fall on the company if she were no longer there, and thus they agreed to have her stay on for a few more years to shepherd the company while preparing a successor to take over.

THE ORGANIZATION'S ROLE IN RETIREMENT

It is clear that the problems of the retirement syndrome have to be addressed on both an individual and an organizational level, yet organizations are notoriously negligent in this regard. People on the verge of retirement are all too often abandoned to sink or swim, without help or preparation from the organization.

John Simon was a leading executive with an investment bank. His experience of letting go reflects many of the negative and damaging effects that lack of personal preparation can have:

Well, of course I didn't want to go. Nobody ever does. They might talk a lot of rubbish about looking forward to retirement, but they're only trying to make the best of it.

They had the cheek to offer me early retirement when I was 55. I thought it was a joke at first and couldn't believe it when I realized they were serious. They didn't push it once I made it clear how I felt. Then when my 59th birthday was coming up, they suggested I might like to reconsider. The human resources people had spent God knows how long preparing an in-house brochure on retirement strategy, and I remember them handing it to me as if it was some kind of prize. I made up my mind right then that I was going to stay on as long as I could. Nobody else knew as much about the business as I did. I thought they were ignoring everything I'd done over the years. I mean, I hadn't put all that into my work just to turn it over to some business-school graduate with a silly haircut because HR thought I should.

I didn't think about retirement at all. Toward the end, I cut down the amount of traveling I did, but that was because the company decentralized a lot of operations and much of what we handled went directly to the regional offices. I didn't feel any more tired at 59 than I had done during the previous 15 years. At times I felt a bit out on a limb. Nearly all my colleagues had gone and my division—like the rest of the company—was full of much younger men and women. They seemed very cliquey and I didn't have much to do with them.

I was very friendly with the outgoing CEO. We'd joined the company at the same time back in the 1970s. Our wives were friends and we all met socially. He stayed until his 65th birthday, then came in twice a week in a consultancy capacity for a further 15 months. I assumed I'd do much the same thing; at least, I certainly didn't think that at 59 that would be it, finished, the end. When nobody said anything about consultancy, I mentioned it myself, and that's when they dropped the bombshell about dismantling the division. They tried to do it nicely. HR said it wouldn't be 'viable' anyhow once I left; the company was getting behind the off shoring policy and opening more offices overseas. But I got the impression they thought I was taking up space. I seemed to be the only person to whom it came as a surprise. I felt stabbed in the back.

I know I was bitter. It didn't help that I started to get ill for the first time in my life. Just aches and pains—the doctor couldn't find anything seriously wrong—but I had to have a series of tests and got into a depression. I refused their offer of a leaving celebration; it seemed such a sham. Who was celebrating what? Now I regret that a bit because I left under a cloud, after more than 25 years in the place.

That was three years ago. I feel better now. I'm off the antidepressants and quite by accident last year I discovered a real passion for gardening. We've got a large garden but I'd never really done anything in it—just used to pay the gardener. Then last summer he was off with a bad back for several weeks and I had to take the place in hand. Now we're really making it into something special. It's practically a full-time job. Things are better with my wife as well. It was misery when I first was at home. She's an artist, very wrapped up in what she does, and of course there's no retirement ceiling in her kind of work. I don't think she understood what I went through when I retired. It was ironic that the same week I left the company she had her first solo exhibition. We're the same age and there she was, getting all the accolades, still pushing ahead, when I felt pushed aside. We talked about it. It wasn't easy. Last month I was 63 and she gave me an oil painting she'd done of my favorite part of the garden. I hadn't known she'd done it; it was a fantastic surprise. It seemed to round everything off, somehow.

John Simon came to terms with his position, but the emotional costs were high. Though his personality contributed greatly to his problems, they were exacerbated by the insensitivity with which his company dealt with him. Although the firm's efforts to confront the issue of executive retirement had been well meaning, they had not gone far enough to be effective.

Contrast Simon's experience with that of another retiring executive, in much the same situation. Victor Carlotti was managing director of a chemical division of a large multinational company:

When I was in my early sixties, the company was taken over and the parent company began intervening more in our operations. Shortly afterwards my old Group CEO left and the atmosphere changed overnight. I became increasingly unhappy with the changes and on my suggestion my early retirement (albeit only one year early) was accepted. My pension was unaffected, the company continued to pay me until my 65th birthday, and I received a small bonus.

I'd begun thinking about how I'd manage my retirement at least three or four years earlier. I knew I'd have to try and structure life after retirement in the same way I'd structured it in business. I knew I'd need a certain amount of discipline, and as far as possible I planned things in advance. I wanted to do some charity work, and I had that lined up for the time when I left the company. I finalized all those details about six months before I finished work. I took a couple of courses on post-retirement. They were organized by a local organization. I also took a leadership coach to help me manage the transition and explore various options. The company was very helpful in providing me with one.

As the time grew nearer, I had generally very positive feelings about retirement. I suppose I felt apprehensive about some aspects, but basically I took it philosophically, if not 100 percent enthusiastically. The company's attitude helped; they were happy for me to work from home several days a week. I wasn't too bothered about the loss of responsibility and decision-making. I was most worried about having nothing to do, which is why I put so much preparatory effort into restructuring my life. I was prepared to manage on less income and in fact we moved to a smaller house about a year before I retired, as our old house was starting to need a lot of maintenance. With the children out of the house, it had become far too big for us.

I knew the person who took over from me quite well. As a matter of fact, I had trained her for the present position. In the last couple of months, I took her around, introduced her to my major customers, and did a certain amount of handover work with her. I felt proud of how effective she proved to be.

Initially, I did think about taking on another position, some sort of con-sultancy. I made some inquiries and talked to a few people. But with all our children and grandchildren living abroad, I knew we'd be doing a lot of traveling and that really ruled out that sort of commitment. We spend at least four months of the year out of the country. When we're in England, my voluntary work for the cancer society regularly takes up two mornings a week, with some occasional meetings on top of that. I'm on two boards as non-executive director—that doesn't take too much of my time. Most of our friends are also retired, so we see more of them. I read more, and enjoy it more, swim and walk a great deal, and go to the theater, an opera or to a concert at least once a week. We've also made it a habit to take two major trips a year. The most recent were one to India, and 18 months later, a tour around the world, something my wife and I have always wanted to do. My wife and all my family were very helpful and positive about my retirement. In the end, we were all looking forward to it.

Now, three years on, I can genuinely say that I feel contented and very much engaged with life. I've met many people who feel that they've lost a lot with retirement, but that's not the case with me. I did wonder before whether I'd feel resentful, whether I'd feel I was missing out, or left high and dry. I know plenty of people who do. Would I get back now? Well, a couple of years after I'd left, my old company approached me with the offer to become the interim COO. I was very flattered, very pleased; it did mean a lot to have been asked. But the office has relocated, and we travel so much ... it wasn't too difficult to decide to turn it down.

In the end, the most important things for me were that I was both fortunate and determined: fortunate that I found it easy to adjust first of all to the idea of retirement, then to retirement itself, and determined that I was going to make it work. And of course, I had my wife with me all the way, encouraging me to see retirement as a new phase in life, rather than as the end of something.

For Victor, retirement was an event, and a positive one at that. But not everyone has Victor's foresight and up-front approach, and not everyone facing the necessity of letting go has either the time or the inclination to prepare as he did. Furthermore, not every company is as helpful as his was at easing the retirement process.

In most companies, however, retirement planning—starting new beginnings—is viewed largely as a personal concern, and management provides little or no feedback or guidance. In view of the negative effect poorly managed executive departures can have on company morale, this policy is dangerously shortsighted. It may reflect a company philosophy that is equally blinkered. Today, organizations are tempted to ease out senior people at relatively early ages for several reasons. Early-retirement policies can be seen as a way to rejuvenate the organization, as an alternative to laying off people during downturns, as a way of saving money (older people are generally more expensive to employ), as an alternative to firing because of poor performance, and as a way of unclogging employment channels to create promotion opportunities for younger people. However, early retirements can create critical shortages of experienced people who are culture carriers; the loss of senior people may affect the organizational 'memory' (its cultural values), which in turn can have negative effects on morale and performance. Organizations have to face several major issues: how to recognize and maximize the value and quality of experienced executives; how to anticipate and contain the emotional and psychological costs of retirement and redundancy; and how to balance the psychological needs of executives with good policy for the company. The development of strategies to meet these issues can greatly ease the stresses of the retirement syndrome.

No one can avoid aging, but aging productively is something else. Organizational retirement policies should be enabling, allowing executives to address the adjustments they need to make when counting down to retirement. One such policy is phased retirement, where individuals can control their own gradual reduction in working time. Phased retirement can have the additional benefit to the organization of encouraging talented people to remain in some kind of part-time capacity. Although they may be paid more, the cost of retaining older executives is far less than recruiting, selecting, training, and motivating younger people with less work experience. Giving outgoing executives the opportunity to serve as a consultant to the company for some time makes the retirement process less painful and may facilitate a more graceful exit. Cutting down hours, phasing in the company pension, job sharing, and working from home—a gradual process of letting go—can help to cushion the shock that might otherwise come with the abrupt leaving of work. The feeling of still being needed will only reinforce executive morale and promote a positive attitude toward the future. Companies that facilitate personal adjustment toward leaving give people the opportunity to look beyond work and enhance their quality of life after retirement.

If this plan seems too idealistic, given today's economic and social realities, it might be useful to remember that sooner or later we are all going to have to confront our time to let go, with all the psychological weight that moment of realization carries. Intelligent and sensitive organizational policies should recognize that necessity; room and time should be built into the organizational culture to deal with it. Creating 'beautiful exits' for executives—departures with grace—will have a positive effect on the working atmosphere. It will make the organization a better place to work.

For many, retirement and old age may seem a long way off. But on the day it comes, it will be too late to do anything about it. It seems rather foolish to sow little but weeds at the height of one's career, and expect to harvest a valuable crop. We need to invest in life as we live it. We need to own our own lives. And to have this kind of ownership, we need to diversify our interests; we need to keep on learning. Wasn't it Aristotle who said, 'Education is the best provision for old age'? Retirement can be something other than a terminal state anticipated with despair and hopelessness. Retirement from one organization can be the beginning of a new one. There are many ways of dealing creatively with this phase of the career clock. Second or even third careers, new interests, sport, travel, volunteer work, educational ventures, new friendships, and grandchildren can all help to add a new phase to the social clock of time. Perhaps the greatest way in which we can help ourselves confront retirement is conscious preparation: planning ahead, valuing our relationships, continuing to learn, and, above all else, allowing ourselves to let go. Apart from pursuing new interests, it is most important to invest in meaningful relationships.

To create more pleasant endings, it is important to create and cherish happy moments—to find situations where we 'touch' people. Good memories create a sense of aliveness. And these memories will make a fine cushion in old age. Only by making these kinds of investments can we follow a different route from that of Warren Schmidt, the tragic hero whose story I told at the beginning of this chapter. Although getting old is not for sissies, wisdom is all about knowing how to grow old in a dignified way. When we accept that life is full of tension; when we are no longer tormented by childhood guilt; when we are able to avoid tragic adult traps; when we are able to forego short-term pleasures for the sake of long-term values; when we are able to use judgment in the right manner; we will be on the road to wisdom. Attaining this kind of wisdom—a search that may start earlier than we think—is one of the most difficult chapters in the book of life.

CONCLUSION: THE TWICE-BORN EXPERIENCE

Carpe diem! Rejoice while you are alive; enjoy the day; live life to the fullest; make the most of what you have. It is later than you think.

—*Horace*

When it's time to die, let us not discover that we have never lived.

—*Henry David Thoreau*

Many peoples' tombstones should read 'Died at 30, buried at 60.'

—*Nicholas Murray Butler*

I already know as much about my fate as I need to know. The day will come when I will die. So the only matter of consequence before me is what I will do with my allotted time. I can remain on shore, paralyzed with fear, or I can raise my sails and dip and soar in the breeze.

—Richard Bode

At the beginning of the twentieth century, the psychologist and philosopher William James first distinguished people as being either 'once-born' or 'twice-born' (James, 1902). According to James, once-borns are individuals who do not stray from the straight and narrow. They are tied to familiar territory where they have always felt comfortable. Conversely, twice-born people go to great lengths to reinvent themselves, having come to realize (for many different reasons) that life is too predictable, and that if they do not embark on some dramatic change in their life, they will sink to a state of living death. The implication is that twice-born people actively use difficult changes in their visible life to help them come to peace with their hidden inner demons. The tragedy of life is that we wait so long to begin it.

Whether we turn out to be once- or twice-born is determined by how we deal with having to work through those hardships and misfortunes that force us to turn inward and tackle internal changes, leading to a 'second birth.' Obviously, were we to die early, or have a near-death experience, we may live more intensely. We may want to live each of our remaining days to the fullest. Life is very short; we have to take time to look around once in a while, otherwise we may never live.

Within organizational life, once-borns are individuals who want to fit in and do what is expected of them (Zaleznik, 1977; MacGregor Burns, 1978). They are well-socialized conformists, ideal organization men and women, who prefer to stick to the tried and tested. They are obedient to authority and follow orders, reluctant to question the rules and regulations to which they are subjected. The relations of once-born leaders and their followers are transactional, that is, one thing is exchanged for another. Once-borns create structures that make it clear what is required of their subordinates, and what rewards the latter will receive for following orders. Once-born leaders are self-conscious people who worry what others think about them. They do not have innovative or creative responses to life events; they behave like creatures of habit. Life for these people (who are usually unconscious of the way they deal with it), is limited and uneventful. Sadly enough, once-borns have created this world of self-limitations for themselves; they have become their own jailers. Once-borns, for the sake of making a living, forget to live. They treat life like a never-ending bank account. They talk about 'killing time,' while time is killing them.

In contrast, twice-borns have the ability to turn adversity, and associated depressive reactions, to their advantage, awakening their inner life. Betrayal, illness, divorce, the loss of a long-cherished dream, retirement, separation, the death of a loved one—all these distressing incidents can be initiations to a deeper, more meaningful life. When these people have to cope with tough breaks, they go into action mode. Twice-borns turn crises to their own advantage by making them a time for renewal, rather than stand by helplessly and watch their own decline. Instead of framing their experience as a catastrophe, they reframe it as an opportunity for a new beginning. They prepare themselves to challenge life themes that they had always taken for granted. They come to the realization that whether they are experiencing the worst or best time in life, it is the only time they have got.

Those who make the journey from once-born to twice-born have at some point in their life arrived at a crossroads where they realize that the old ways of doing things are no longer working. In an organizational setting, once-borns wake up to the sense that they are stuck and going nowhere; what's more (given their mindset), the same might be said of their company. Disturbingly, they realize that they are bored with what they are doing, a feeling they keep very close to their chest or attempt to deal with in fantasy terms—perhaps there's a better way of living, somewhere over the rainbow, at the far edge of a dark wood, or on a distant shore? However, the real question is, will they take the bait? Will they go for it? Considerably greater distress may be needed before they are forced out of their comfort zone.

Twice-borns react quickly and positively to challenges for personal growth and development. They are not fooled by the calendar. They know that there are only as many days in the year as we make use of. William James wrote about the links between religious experience and mental abnormality, referring to depressive reactions that are not uncommon among twice-borns. Despite the stigma that is attached to depressive reactions, a modicum of depression can in fact encourage reflectivity and contribute to deep insight. James suggested that profound depression must be accompanied by a powerful desire to make sense out of things. Pushing on through, without learning from the pain of depression, will not contribute to new solutions. James took the writer Leo Tolstoy as an example, explaining that the Russian novelist's successful efforts to restore himself to mental health led to more than a return to his original condition. As Tolstoy himself said, 'Everyone thinks of changing the world, but no one thinks of changing himself.' The novelist asserted, 'Without knowing what I am and why I am here, life is impossible.' Twice-borns try to enter a new and higher plane through reflective processes. The process is one of redemption, not merely a reversion to a previous state; the sufferer, when saved, experiences a second birth, having attained a deeper kind of consciousness. It's almost as if the individual has to pass through an unreal life before being born into a life that feels truly real.

THE ROAD LESS TRAVELLED

Beyond the dark wood

The following lines begin Dante Alighieri's great poem, *The Divine Comedy*. Dante wrote it at a time when he was in great confusion about his future.

> Midway in our life's journey, I went astray
> from the straight road and woke to find myself
> alone in a dark wood. How shall I say

> what wood that was! I never saw so drear,
> so rank, so arduous a wilderness!
> Its very memory gives a shape to fear.

In medieval Italy, Dante was the victim of a change in the volatile power politics that characterized that time. In exile in Rome, he was condemned to death in his absence, should he ever attempt to return to his native Florence. Dante was 35 years old, and had reached midlife, according to the biblical assessment of the human lifespan: 'The days of our lives are 70 years' (Psalm 90:10). He was certainly lost in a dark wood. And it was at this point in his life that he embarked on his tale of an epic journey to Heaven through Hell and Purgatory, with the poet Virgil as his guide.

Sailing beyond the sunset

Another epic hero, Ulysses, is depicted in a similar state of crisis in a poem by the Victorian English poet Alfred, Lord Tennyson. In the poem, published in 1842 when Tennyson was 33 (but written earlier), Ulysses is presented as an older man, a sailor-king reflecting on a lifetime of travel. He reveals his restlessness, having returned to the kingdom of Ithaca after years of voyaging. As he grows older, and despite being reunited with his wife and son, Ulysses yearns for the old years of exploration. He only felt truly alive during his adventuring: the contrast between the heroic deeds of his past and his present peaceful life eventually becomes unbearable. He determines to make one more journey, with the risk that it will be his last. He tries to persuade his old traveling companions to join him:

> ... Come my friends,
> 'Tis not too late to seek a newer world.
> Push off, and sitting well in order smite
> The sounding furrows; for my purpose holds
> To sail beyond the sunset, and the baths
> Of all the western stars, until I die.
> It may be the gulfs will wash us down:
> It may be we shall touch the Happy Isles.

As a lifelong traveler, Ulysses has failed to assimilate the responsibilities of being a father, husband, and a king. Yes, it was great to get back to Ithaca; yes, it was wonderful to be with his wife and son again; but the bliss was brief and soon wore off. Ulysses is still full of vigor, dismayed to find himself 'match'd with an aged wife' and detached from his 'decent,' hard-working son. Ulysses' particular brand of boredom strikes a chord with many executives whom I meet in the course of my work (although they are reluctant to express it).

Tennyson draws us into Ulysses' predicament by connecting us to his adventurous spirit, awakening the hero or heroine in us all. He teases us to release our suppressed conviction that we can do so much better. Ulysses has no time for the tried and tested. What he wants most of all is to feel alive. His last new voyage is a flight into action.

Tennyson's poem leaves us with the encouraging message (one that should be gender neutral—not having the woman at home taking care of the chores while the husband goes on adventures) that whatever our physical age, the wish to reinvent ourselves lives on: we never lose the possibility of being twice-born. Ulysses empathizes with those who fight the stultifying boredom that comes with routine, with doing the same thing day in and day out. He emphasizes the need for new experiences, never to settle for the ordinary and to seek something new. Life, he says, is too short:

> How dull it is to pause, to make an end,
> To rust unburnish'd, not to shine in use!
> As tho' to breathe were life! Life piled on life
> Were all too little, and of one to me
> Little remains ...

Once-born people may go through life without ever knowing what is happening beyond the dark woods, or even worse not seeing the woods at all. It wouldn't cross the mind of once-born people to join Ulysses on his travels. That's not to say that there isn't the possibility that a once-born person will wake up one morning and see the finger of fate pointing at some disturbing questions, the most distressing of which is likely to be, 'Is this all that you want from life?'

Twice-borns, on the other hand, are likely to grab the finger of fate and twist it hard. Instead of standing by helplessly and watching their decline, they turn their discontent to their own advantage by recognizing it as an opportunity for renewal of their body and mind. Twice-borns would shudder at T. S. Eliot's *The Love Song of J. Alfred Prufrock*, whose hero has 'measured out my life with coffee spoons.' Whether through choice or calamity, twice-borns walk deliberately into the dark woods, leap on board Ulysses' ship, deviate from the straight path, make mistakes, suffer losses, and confront what they need to change within themselves in order to live a more authentic life.

Twice-borns prefer to trade the safety of the known for the power of the unknown.

Crossing the abyss

Once-born or twice-born, how do we respond to this call to authenticity when it comes? What can we do to awaken our passion and to feel truly alive? How do we learn to extend our dreams beyond our self-imposed boundaries?

One common experience recounted in the executive seminars I run is the moment when the familiar begins to seem strange, and people feel a need to distance themselves from the ordinary world of others. This leave-taking need not be actual; it can be symbolic. For example, one of the participants—let's call him Pierre—had made a conscious decision to leave his company a year before he actually did so. It was not a particularly difficult decision because Pierre had been disillusioned with the organization for far too long. But despite his awareness that the company's activities were affecting his mental health, he failed to act. Unfortunately (and I have seen this frequently), inertia is a very powerful force that can perpetuate misery for a long time. Of course, other considerations play their part—the mortgage, tuition fees, car payments, and so on. These obligations act like Band-Aids, covering but not healing deep wounds. My discussions with business leaders have taught me that they miss or delay many opportunities to change their life. It is not always easy to create a tipping point and really make a difference. The tipping point for Pierre was a diagnosis of colon cancer, which fortunately was discovered at an early and treatable stage. Lying in a hospital for the first time in his life, he had time to confront what was happening to him, instead of brushing his awareness of the tedium of his life to one side, as he had done before.

Pierre was fortunate to have the support of a good friend, who visited him regularly, taking on the role of sparring partner. During their discussions Pierre realized how accomplished he had been at ignoring the pain of his existence, continuing to do a job he didn't like, for a company whose ethics he abhorred, while living with a woman with whom he had very little in common. The insights that these conversations provided made Pierre aware of the full extent of the false, meaningless, and irrelevant existence he had been leading. He had never thought about the purpose of his life or indulged in inner contemplation. He realized that he had no idea what his deepest values and beliefs actually were.

As he became more engaged in his inner journey, Pierre took stock of his limiting, self-sabotaging beliefs. It had taken a serious threat to his health to make him question the life he had chosen and understand the person he had become. Now he was listening to his inner voices, which were becoming insistent, challenging him to engage in things that made him feel really alive. Pierre began to feel impatient to take action, while delighting in his new-found reflectiveness. These contra-dictory impulses made him aware that self-discovery was going to be an evolving process. Pierre decided to close one door at a time. Under-standing his life would be an unfolding inner awakening that would transform his understanding and insight. Pierre wanted to live his life to the full; he was no longer interested in operating on automatic pilot.

Pierre discovered that the realization of the relative meaninglessness of his position freed an enormous amount of emotional energy, which had previously been diverted into intense frustration about his job. Now this energy was channeled productively into thinking about ways of reinventing himself. But what were the implications of this? What choices would he have? Although his present position was far from what he had dreamt of when he started his career, it did provide security, safety, and a high standard of living for his family. These thoughts made him feel that he was poised on the edge of an abyss. He was worried about losing control. But Pierre also understood that he had already faced the first and most difficult risk—being honest with himself. It was normal to be afraid of the unknown. And the fear could even be valu-able, because it would give him something to push against.

Pierre began to ask himself what truly mattered to him, and what his talents, strengths, abilities, and passions were. Passion and natural ability in a certain area can be a good indication of what is truly impor-tant in life. Pierre knew he was cautious and would have to start to move toward realizing the big dreams that would change his life with small steps. But the most important thing was to get started. Pierre believed he was capable of change and resisted the idea to wait until conditions were perfect. He decided to take action.

Some actions were obvious. His job would be the first thing to go. Pierre wanted to work for an organization with purpose and to do something that provided meaning. A friend gave him an attractive opportunity to build up a leading teaching hospital complex, a project with real meaning. Dealing with his marriage was less straightforward. He and his wife had been living separate lives. They no longer talked and their sex life was non-existent. But Pierre decided he wanted to give their relationship a chance. Family counseling helped to restart a very ritualistic relationship but Pierre went one step further by engaging a

psychotherapist, to help him avoid slipping back into his previous dysfunctional behavior. With each step Pierre took, he felt stronger, more
skilled, more self-confident, and more successful in his work and his
relationship.

In my work with senior executives, I have found that they rarely
adopt a purposeful approach to their work without having first worked
through a major life event. Pierre took the bait but only because of a
calamitous life event. Unfortunately, far too many people endure one
traumatic event after another without slowing down enough to make
the critical change that would make for a fuller life. They get up every
day and engage in the same manic defense—running without ever
asking themselves where they are running to or why, afraid to pause and
be forced to reflect on their behavior. Pierre, through a combination of
factors that he could not ignore, realized that he could no longer continue life as usual. He found reflective space through serious illness. In
order to do the important work of contemplating our truest selves we
all need that kind of space. When we begin to listen to our calling and
act on it, we are responding to the deepest wisdom and guidance available to us. We listen to the themes in our inner theater that are most
important to us. We are then ready to make the transition toward being
twice-born. So are there ways to accelerate the once-born to twice-born
transition, apart from the kind of trauma and suffering I have described?
Are there institutional ways in which one can speed up the process?

CATALYSTS FOR TRANSFORMATION

Although William James popularized the terms, this concept of once- or
twice-born has an ancient pedigree, rooted in the concept of socio-
religious or developmental rebirth. Many religions have provided the
context for these transformations. Shamanism is the accumulation of
traditional beliefs and practices about communication with the spirit
world. Many shamans engage in trance-inducing processes like singing,
dancing, drug-taking, meditation, and drumming. The notion is that,
while in a state of trance, the shaman's spirit leaves the body and enters
the supernatural world.

Drug-taking, however, has always been the royal road to enhanced
and altered consciousness. The introduction of modern hallucinogenic
drugs like LSD saw a remarkable cultural rapprochement between
eastern mysticism, twentieth-century pharmacology, messianic politics,
and nineteenth-century romanticism. The writer Aldous Huxley, in his
book *The Doors of Perception* (1954), wrote about his experience of taking

mescaline. He borrowed the title of his book from William Blake's *The Marriage of Heaven and Hell* (1793), saying, 'If the doors of perception were cleansed every thing would appear to man as it is, infinite.' The high priest of LSD, the American writer and psychoanalyst Timothy Leary, made great claims for the spiritual and therapeutic value of the drug, which he maintained enlarged human consciousness and opened the mind.

Mind-altering drugs can create states of mind in which novel or even enduring perceptions can arise, unhindered by the mental filters and processes of everyday life. Users have intense emotional experiences during these experiments, resulting in spiritual revelations that contribute to personal transformation and could facilitate the transition from once-born to twice-born. These experiences, however, are challenged by scientific investigation.

The established religions have also looked at ways of engineering rebirth. For example, the initiation sacraments of upper-caste Hindus are regarded as a second or spiritual birth, an actual event in a person's life that is analogous to physical birth, with the objective of activating their spiritual self—which then passes through stages of growth, as a child does. The individual is born again as a competent adult, functioning rationally and leaving childhood behind.

In a similar way, many Protestant sects (evangelicals, Pentecostals, Seventh-Day Adventists), and Islamic sects such as the Sufi or Kharijites, have indoctrination techniques that trigger forms of rebirth. Occult and esoteric groups use the same techniques, which stop short of well-documented processes of brainwashing, as do secret societies such as the Freemasons, the Order of the Oriental Templars, Gnostics, Scientologists, and Rosicrucians.

For those who want to experience therapeutic rebirth without resorting to shamanism, or through means of religious experience it may be sufficient for them to harness the midlife crisis so many of us experience. The example of Pierre, and William James's observations, indicate that any form of psychological breakdown can provide the opportunity for radical transformation.

Going beyond the midlife point is often a catastrophe for some people because they have ignored their real feelings for years. Eventually, some become aware of the disparity between the person they really want to be and the person they feel constrained to be by societal pressures. If we think in terms of being twice-born, midlife may in fact be the right stage in time to listen to what these out-of-awareness processes have to tell us. Typically, this is the period when people's inner questioning happens (Jaques, 1965). Whatever else can be said about reaching midlife, there is one truism: many of us are poorly prepared for the fact that time is running out.

Perhaps the deepest angst we have in our middle years and beyond (as my examples have shown) is over the sense of not having realized our full potential. This is what wakes us in the middle of the night and disturbs the tranquility of our days. It is the greatest concern of my executives. Most of them want to leave a legacy; they want to have had a life of meaning. Their challenge is to have an opportunity to re-orient their personalities, and reinvent themselves.

Coming back to Dante and Tennyson (I am assuming that Tennyson's Ulysses was some kind of alter ego for the poet), we see how both men intended to introduce the notion of being lost to evoke the destiny of all of us: the struggle to come to grips with our own mortality.

Signs of trouble

When the disparity between where we are and where we want to be becomes unacceptable (and the effort to hide the resultant distress becomes insupportable), we face another danger: of being lured into the action trap. This can lead people to look for sudden, even dramatic, solutions. Stories of people taking unlikely or even desperate steps are legion: we have affairs, get divorced, get depressed, start taking Prozac, buy a sports car, have plastic surgery, decide to run a bed and breakfast, become a scuba diving instructor, and so on.

However, despite these dangers, a worse outcome of passing the midlife point is doing nothing. When confronted with feelings of stress, anxiety and depression, once-borns may prefer to ignore the warning signs. Dealing with the underlying, semi-conscious, disturbing thoughts that contribute to feelings of discontent is too frightening.

In the short term, their strategy of simple negation may be successful. The lingering feeling that things are not really fine may just go away. Unfortunately, the mind is more subtle than that. A more likely scenario is that these feelings have merely submerged. Furthermore, people who indulge in willful ignorance often discover that when disturbing feelings resurface at the next stress point, they have become much more intense and overwhelming during their time underground.

By listening to my executives, I have learned to identify many signs that indicate someone is in the process of moving from a once-born to a twice-born state. For example, there is preoccupation with the aging of the body—a sense of one's own mortality—which plays a major role in the process. People may experience feelings of turmoil, despair, helplessness, distress, dread, disappointment, and fear, often feeling trapped in unwelcome, restrictive career or family roles; or experience boredom or discontent with previously fulfilling activities or parts of their lives. Their children may ask them disturbing questions or display signs of worry—making them more aware of the transience of things. There may be the issue of job loss or of disappointment with a career that has plateau-ed. Lingering in the background are the unfulfilled dreams of youth, questioning the correctness of their life path, and the turmoil associated with marital disharmony, separation, or divorce.

All these feelings of discontent may result in various forms of 'acting out' behavior, setting the stage for a tipping point that, in turn, sets in motion the process of moving from once-born to twice-born behavior. The more obvious behavior patterns are:

* the need for a life 'makeover,' a process whereby a marriage or career is tossed out the window;
* a total change of lifestyle reflecting the wish to do something completely different, including changing career, going back to study, or engaging in extensive travel;
* trying to overcome boredom with things, people (including a partner) or activities that used to be central to a person's life, including once-valued material possessions, such as houses, cars, and other must-haves; and serious questioning of one's previous accomplishments—were they really worth all the time and effort?

These reflections lead to the perennial existential questions: 'Who am I?' 'Where am I going?' 'Where do I want to be?'

Stylistic differences

An important point to make here is that, while midlife is a sort of *rite de passage* for all of us, there seems to be a difference between the way men and women seem to respond to it. My observations of male and female participants in my seminars for senior executives reveal a variety of attitudes, on a spectrum that ranges from pragmatic to angst-laden, with women sitting toward the former end, while the latter could be labeled 'mainly men.' It can sometimes seem that men have reserved these life transitions for their exclusive use (and excuse), yet it is clearly not a male biological preserve. In particular, at midlife women face the menopause, the physical and psychological effects of which can drag on for several years. For those who have had families, there is the additional factor of having to let go of their growing children: the empty nest is both a real and emotional void, when the home they go back to, and the absence of a focus for their emotional attention, suddenly seem much too large. One could speculate at length about why women seem better equipped to deal with the anxieties of midlife and beyond, but perhaps one explanation could be women's greater capacity for compromise and multiple interests. As one workshop participant put it, 'I think most men define themselves by what they do, rather than what they are, whereas when somebody asks me "What do you do?" my answer will probably depend on *what I'm doing at the time*. So at work, I'm the VP Administration for my company, at home I'm so-and-so's wife or mother—and if you ask me when I'm out, I'm doing my shopping.' Another woman, the co-owner of a publishing company, said: 'I don't think women are really built for the same kind of excitement as men, at least not once we've obeyed the biological imperative. We get suspicious of it. When we feel fed-up, bored, or frustrated we tend just to shut up and get on with it. But women do reinvent themselves, despite the domestic balls and chains. If someone had told me a few years ago, when I was rolling around in leggings on a rubber mat with small children singing "The Wheels on the Bus," that I would later start my own business, I would have been incredulous.'

Twice-born: a new way of life?

Being twice-born simply means seeing the world in a different way. It means perceiving our relationships with other people and society differently. It means re-ordering our values—from external to internal richness, from a sense of separation to a sense of connection and interdependence, from a short-term to a much longer-term focus.

Our lives are made up of personal narratives that give shape and meaning to our life and are central to how we make sense of ourselves, culturally as well as individually. Our individual world view determines how we write and color these narratives. Even events over which we seem to have no control can be interpreted in an infinite number of ways. We can allow others to impose their truth on us—or we can create our own truth. If we don't take control over our life and refuse to question authority, we are likely to remain in a state of suspended animation.

Unfortunately, for those of us in Generation X, born in the shadow of World War II, and growing up through the Cold War, a reluctance to take the initiative is likely to have been reinforced during our school days, when we solved problems identified by others, read what we were told to read, and wrote the kind of essays that others wanted. Personal initiative was discouraged. Gradually, passivity and reactiveness became a way of life. Fitting in and being accepted became more important than self-actualization. We learned that the way to succeed was to play the teachers' game rather than our own. We actually fight change because acceding to it would feel like stepping off a cliff into an abyss.

However, at middle age, many of us outgrow our pretences and drop the passive roles we have played since our school days. Women who submerged their identity while their children were growing up may feel a sense of liberation once they are older. Many men may have begun by committing to marriage and raising a family, but 25 years on, with the children out of the house, be struck by the irrelevance of their situation. The idea of making dramatic changes becomes more attractive.

There is no telling what legacy Generations Y and Z will leave as they reinvent what it means to grow older and apply their many blessings and ingenuity to the pursuit of health and happiness. These generations are better informed and in better shape than their progenitors. Most likely, they will possess a different work style than the generations before them. They will have different goals, different ideas, and require a different leadership approach to retain them. They are less accepting of what they are told. They are living too long and too well to stay settled even in a contented state for more than a few years at a time. And with experience, each new life cycle crisis they will face will stand a better chance of looking like just another chance to start all over again. The detective writer Agatha Christie (1977) wrote in her autobiography: 'I have enjoyed greatly the second blooming that comes when you finish the life of the emotions and of personal relations; and suddenly find—at the age of 50, say—that a whole new life has opened before you, filled with things you can think about, study, or read about. ... It is as if a fresh sap of ideas and thoughts was rising in you' (p. 21). We should all hope to be able to say the same. As we grow older, the only things we regret are the things we didn't do. We have very little control over birth and death, but we have some control over the time in between. When the time comes to die, we have to make sure that dying is all we have left to do. In the words of the philosopher Seneca, 'Life well lived, is long enough.'

REFERENCES

Ackerman, N. W. (1958) *The Psychodynamics of Family Life*. New York: Basic Books.

Adler, A. (1956). *The Individual Psychology of Alfred Adler*. H. L. Ansbacher and R. R. Ansbacher (eds). New York: Harper Torchbooks.

American Psychiatric Association (1994). *Diagnostic and Statistical Manual of the Mental Disorders, DSM-IV*. Washington, D.C.: American Psychiatric Association.

American Psychiatric Association. (2000) *Diagnostic and statistical manual of the mental disorders, DSM-IV-TR*. (4th edn) Washington, D.C.: American Psychiatric Association.

Auletta, K. (1994) 'The Human Factor.' *New Yorker*, September, pp. 54–69.

Baker, P. and Glasser, S. (2007) *Kremlin Rising: Vladimir Putin's Russia and the End of Revolution*. Dulles: Potomac Books.

Balint, A. and Balint, M. (1939) 'On Transference and Countertransference.' *International Journal of Psychoanalysis*, 20, 223–230.

Bass, Bernard M. (1960) *Leadership, Psychology, and Organizational Behavior*, New York: Harper.

Bass, B. M. (1981) *Stogdill's Handbook of Leadership*. New York: The Free Press.

Bass, B. M. (1985) *Leadership and Performance Beyond Expectations*. New York: Free Press.

Bass, B. M. and Avolo, B. J. (1994) *Improving Organizational Effectiveness through Transformational Leadership*. Thousand Oaks, C.A.: Sage Publications.

Baumeister, R. F. (1989) *Masochism and the Self*. Hillsdale, N.J.: Lawrence Erlbaum.

Belbin, R. M. (1996) *Team Roles at Work*. Oxford: Butterworth Heinemann.

Belbin, R. M. (2003) *Management Teams: Why they Succeed or Fail*. Oxford: Butterworth Heinemann.

Bion, W. R. (1959) *Experiences in Groups*. London: Tavistock.

Bion, W. R. (1970) *Attention and Interpretation*. London, Tavistock.

Blake, R. R. and Mouton, J. S. (1985) *The Managerial Grid III: The Key to Leadership Excellence*. Houston: Gulf Publishing Company.

Bollas, C. (1987) *Shadow of the Object: Psychoanalysis of the Unthought Known*. London, Free Associations Books.

Borgatta, E. F., Couch, A. S., and Bales, R. F. (1954) 'Some Findings relevant to the Great Man Theory of Leadership'. *American Sociological Review*, 19(6), 755–759.

Bowlby, J. (1969) *Attachment and Loss. Vol. I: Attachment.* New York: Basic Books.

Bowlby, J. (1973) *Attachment and Loss. Vol. II: Separation: Anxiety and Anger.* New York: Basic Books.

Breuer, J. and Freud, S. (1895) *Studies on Hysteria. The Standard Edition of the Complete Psychological Works of Sigmund Freud.* J. Strachey. London: Hogarth Press and the Institute of Psychoanalysis. 2, 3–311.

Burns, J. M. (1978) *Leadership,* New York: Harper and Row.

Camus, A. (1991) *The Myth of Sisyphus.* New York: Vintage.

Carver, C. S. and Scheier, M. F. (2001) *Perspectives on Personality.* New York: Allyn & Bacon.

Casement, P. (1985) *On Learning from the Patient.* London, Tavistock.

Cath, S. H., Gurwitt, A. R., and Ross, J. M. (eds) (1982) *Father and Child.* Boston: Little, Brown.

Christie, A. (1977) *An Autobiography.* New York: Collins.

Dean Parsons, R., and Wicks, R. J. (eds) (1975) *Passive-Aggressiveness: Theory and Practice.* New York: Brunner/Mazel.

De Gaulle, Charles. (1975) *The Edge of the Sword,* Westport, Conn: Greenwood Press.

Deutsch, H. (1965) *Neuroses and Character Types.* New York: International Universities Press.

Dicks, H. V. (1967) *Marital Tensions: Clinical Studies Toward a Psychological Theory of Interaction.* New York: Basic Books.

Dotlich, D., Noel, J., and Walker, N. (2004) *Leadership Passages: The Personal and Professional Transitions that Make or Break a Leader.* San Francisco: Jossey-Bass.

Dumas, A. (2004) *The Count of Monte Cristo.* New York: Barnes & Nobles Classics.

Epstein, L. and Feiner, A. H. (eds) (1979) *Countertransference.* New York, Jason Aronson.

Erikson, E. H. (1963) *Childhood and Society.* New York: W. W. Norton and Co.

Erikson, E. H. (1978) *Life History and the Historical Moment.* New York: W. W. Norton & Co.

Fairbairn, W. R. D. (1952) *An Object-relations Theory of Personality,* New York: Basic Books.

Ferenczi, S. (1988) *The Clinical Diary of Sandor Ferenczi.* Cambridge MA, Harvard University Press.

Fiedler, F. E. (1967) *A Theory of Leadership Effectiveness.* New York: McGraw-Hill.

Freud, S. (1899) 'Interpretation of dreams' (*The Standard Edition of the Complete Psychological Works of Sigmund Freud*), Vol. 4. London: The Hogarth Press and the Institute of Psychoanalysis.

Freud, S. (1915) *Observations on Transference Love.* London, The Hogarth Press and the Institute of Psychoanalysis.

Freud, S. (1917) *A Childhood Recollection from Dichtung and Wahrheit. The standard edition of the complete psychological works of Sigmund Freud* (Vol. XVII). London: The Hogarth Press and the Institute of Psychoanalysis.

Freud, S. (1921) *Group Psychology and the Analysis of the Ego. The standard edition of the complete psychological works of Sigmund Freud* (Vol. XVIII). London: The Hogarth Press and the Institute of Psychoanalysis.

Freud, S. (1953) 'Some character-types met in psychoanalytic work,' *The Standard Edition of the Complete Psychological Works of Sigmund Freud*, Vol. 14. London: The Hogarth Press and the Institute of Psychoanalysis.

Gabbard, G. O. (ed.) (1999) *Countertransference Issues in Psychiatric Treatment.* Washington D.C.: American Psychiatric Press.

Geertz, C. (1973) *The Interpretation of Cultures.* New York: Basic Books.

Geertz, C. (1983) *Local Knowledge.* New York: Basic Books.

Glick, R. A. and Meyers, D. I. (1988) *Masochism: Current Psychoanalytic Perspectives.* Hillsdale, N.J.: Analytic Press.

Goethe, J. W. (1994) *Faust.* New York: Oxford University Press.

Goldstein, W. N. and Goldberg, S. T. (2004). *Using the Transference in Therapy.* New York, Jason Aronson.

Goleman, D. (1995) *Emotional Intelligence.* London: Bloomsbury.

Gouldner, A. (1964) *Patterns of Industrial Democracy.* New York: The Free Press.

Graff, H. F. (1988) 'When the term's up, it's better to go gracefully.' *International Herald Tribune*, 26 January, p. 5.

Greenberg, J. R. and Mitchell, S. A. (1983) *Object Relations in Psychoanalytic Theory.* Cambridge, M.A.: Harvard University Press.

Greenson, R. R. (1967) *The Technique and Practice of Psychoanalysis.* New York: International University Press.

Grossman, W. (1986) 'Notes on Masochism: A Discussion of the History and Development of a Psychoanalytic Concept.' *Psychoanalytic Quarterly*, 55, 379–413.

Grover, R. (1994) 'Jeffrey Katzenberg: No More Mr. Tough Guy?' *Business Week*, January 31, p. 46.

Guntrip, H. (1969) *Schizoid Phenomena, Object Relations and the Self.* New York: International Universities Press.

Hedges, L. (1987) *Interpreting the Countertransference.* Northvale N.J., Jason Aronson.

Heimann, P. (1950) 'On Countertransference.' *International Journal of Psychoanalysis*, 31, 81–84.

Hinshelwood, R. D. (1999) 'Countertransference.' *International Journal of Psychoanalysis*, 80, 797–818.

Hoffman, Stanley (1967) 'Heroic Leadership: The Case of Modern France.' In: Lewis J. Edinger (ed.), *Political Leadership in Industrialized Societies*, New York: John Wiley and Sons Inc.

Hoffman, E. (1994) *The Drive for Self: Alfred Adler and the Founding of Individual Psychology.* Boston: Addison-Wesley.

Horowitz, M. J. (ed.) (1991) *Person Schemas and Maladaptive Interpersonal Patterns.* Chicago: University of Chicago Press.

House, Robert J. (1977) 'A 1976 Theory of Charismatic Leadership' in *Leadership: The Cutting Edge*, James G. Hunt and Lars L. Larson (eds). Carbondale, Ill: Southern Illinois University Press.

House, R. J. and Baetz, M. L. (1979) 'Leadership: Some empirical generalisations and new research directions.' *Research in Organizational Behavior*, I, 341–423.

House, R. J. and Shamir, B. (1993) 'Toward the Integration of Charismatic, Transformational, Inspirational, and Visionary Theories of Leadership.' In: M. Chemmers and R. Ayman (eds), *Leadership Theory and Research Perspectives and Directions* (pp. 81–107). New York: Academic Press Inc.

Huy, J. (1995) 'Eisner Explains Everything.' *Fortune*, April 17, pp. 33–48.

Huxley, A. (1954) *The Doors of Perception*. New York: Harper & Brothers.

Isenberg, Daniel J. (1984) 'How Senior Managers Think.' *Harvard Business Review*, November–December.

IJzendoorn, V. (1995) 'Adult Attachment Representations, Parental Responsiveness, and Infant Attachment: A Meta-analysis on the Predictive Validity of the Adult Attachment Interview.' *Psychological Bulletin*, 117, 387–483.

Jack, A. (2005) *Inside Putin's Russia: Can There Be Reform Without Democracy?* New York: Oxford University Press.

Jacobi, J. (1971) *Complex/Archetype/Symbol in the Psychology of C.G. Jung*. Princeton: Princeton University Press.

Jacobson, E. (1964) *The Self and the Object World*. New York: International Universities Press.

Jaques, E. (1965) 'Death and the Mid-Life Crisis.' *International Journal of Psychoanalysis*. XLVI, pp. 502–514.

James, W. (1902) *The Varieties of Religious Experience, a Study of Human Nature— A Psychology Classic on Religious Impulse* (2008). New York: Exposure Publishers.

Jardim, Anne. (1970) *The First Henry Ford: A Study in Personality and Business Leadership*. Cambridge, Mass: MIT Press.

Jennings, Eugene E. (1960) *An Anatomy of Leadership: Princes, Heroes, and Supermen*. New York: Harper.

John, O. P., Robins, R. W., and Pervin, L. A. (2008) *Handbook of Personality: Theory and Research* (3rd edition). New York: The Guilford Press.

Jung, C. G. (1923) *Psychological Types*. New York: Harcourt, Brace, Jovanovich.

Jung, C. G. (1971a) 'Psychological Types', (*Collected Works of C. G. Jung*), Volume 6. Princeton: Princeton University Press.

Jung, C. G. (1971b) 'Description of the Archetypes and the Collective Unconscious' (*The Collected Works of C. G. Jung*), Vol. 9. Princeton: Princeton University Press.

Jung, C. G. (1983) *Aspects of the Feminine*. G. Adler and R. F. C. Hull (Translators). Princeton: Princeton University Press.

Kearns, D. (1976) *Lyndon Johnson and the American Dream*. New York: HarperCollins.

Kernberg, O. (1975) *Borderline Conditions and Pathological Narcissism.* New York: Jason Aronson.

Kernberg, O. (1976) *Object Relations Theory and Clinical Psychoanalysis.* New York: Jason Aronson.

Kernberg, O. (1979) 'Regression in organizational leadership.' *Psychiatry,* 42, 29–39.

Kernberg, O. (1985) *Internal World and External Reality.* New York: Jason Aronson.

Kernberg, O. (1988) 'Clinical Dimensions of Masochism'. *Journal of the American Psychoanalytic Association,* 36, 1005–1029.

Kets de Vries, Manfred F. R. (1978) 'Folie à Deux: Acting Out Your Subordinates' Fantasies.' *Human Relations,* 31(10), 905–924.

Kets de Vries, M. F. R. (1979). 'Managers can Drive their Subordinates Mad.' *Harvard Business Review,* 125–134.

Kets de Vries, M. F. R. (1987) 'Interpreting Organizational Texts.' *Journal of Management Studies,* 24(3), 233–247.

Kets de Vries, M. F. R. (1989) *Prisoners of Leadership.* New York: Wiley.

Kets de Vries, M. F. R. (1991) *Organizations on the Couch.* San Francisco: Jossey-Bass.

Kets de Vries, M. F. R. (1993) *Leaders, Fools, and Impostors.* San Francisco: Jossey-Bass.

Kets de Vries, M. F. R. (1995) *Life and Death in the Executive Fast Lane: Essays on Irrational Organizations and Leadership.* San Francisco: Jossey-Bass.

Kets de Vries, M. F. R. (1996) *Family Business: Human Dilemmas in the Family Firm.* London: International Thompson Business Press.

Kets de Vries, M. F. R. (2001) *The Leadership Mystique.* London: Financial Times/Prentice Hall.

Kets de Vries, M. F. R. (2006) *The Leader on the Couch.* Chichester: Jossey Bass.

Kets de Vries, M. F. R. (2007). 'The Leadership Assessment Questionnaire.' INSEAD Working Paper, Fontainebleau.

Kets de Vries, M. F. R. (2009) *Sex, Money, Happiness, and Death: The Quest for Authenticity.* Basingstoke: Palgrave.

Kets de Vries, M. F. R., Carlock, R., and Florent, E. (2007) *Family Business on the Couch: A Psychological Perspective.* Chichester: John Wiley and Sons Ltd.

Kets de Vries, M. F. R. and Miller, D. (1984) *The Neurotic Organization: Diagnosing and Changing Counterproductive Styles of Management.* San Francisco: Jossey Bass.

Kets de Vries, M. F. R. and Miller, D. (1985) 'Narcissism and Leadership: An Object Relations Perspective.' *Human Relations,* 38(6), 583–601.

Kets de Vries, M. F. R., and Miller, D. (1987) *Unstable at the Top.* New York: New American Library.

Kets de Vries, M. F. R. and Perzow, S. (1991) *Handbook of Character Studies.* Madison, Conn.: International Universities Press.

Kets de Vries, M. F. R., Sheksnia, S., Korotov, K., and Florent-Treacy, E. (2004) *The New Russian Business Leaders.* Cheltenham: Edwar Elgar.

Klein, M. (1946) *Notes on some Schizoid Mechanisms. The Writings of Melanie Klein.* (Vol. 3). H. Segal. London, The Hogarth Press.

Klein, M. (1948) *Contributions to Psychoanalysis, 1921–1945.* London: The Hogarth Press.

Kobasa, Suzanne R. (1979) 'Stress Life Events, Personality and Health: An Inquiry into Hardiness.' *Journal of Personality and Social Psychology*, 37(1), 1–11

Kohut, H. (1971) *The Analysis of the Self.* New York: International Universities Press.

Kohut, H. (1977) *The Restoration of the Self.* New York: International Universities Press.

Kohut. H. (1978) 'Creativeness, charisma, group psychology.' In Paul H. Ornstein (ed) *The Search for the Self* (Vol. 2). New York: International Universities Press.

Kohut, H. and Wolf, E. S. (1978) 'The disorders of the self and their treatment: An outline.' *The International Journal of Psychoanalysis*, 59, 413–426.

Kotter, John P. (1982) *The General Managers*, New York: The Free Press.

Lachkar, J. (1992) *The Narcissistic/Borderline Couple.* New York: Brunner/Mazel.

Langs, R. and Searles H. F. (1980). *Intrapsychic and Interpersonal Dimensions of Treatment: A Clinical Dialogue.* New York, Jason Aronson.

Levinson, Harry (1980) 'Criteria for choosing Chief Executives.' *Harvard Business Review*, July–August, 113–120.

Likert, R. (1961) *New Patterns of Management.* New York: McGraw-Hill.

Lipowski, Z. J. (1975) 'Sensory and Information Inputs Overload: Behavioral Effects.' *Comprehensive Psychiatry*, 16(3), 199–221.

Luborsky, L. P. (1990) *Understanding Transference.* New York: Basic Books.

Luborsky, L. P., Crits-Christoph, P., Minz, J., and Auerbach, A. (1988) *Who Will Benefit from Psychotherapy?* New York: Basic Books.

Luborsky, L. and Crits-Cristoph P. (1998). *Understanding Transference: The Core Conflictual Relationship Theme Method.* Washington: American Psychological Organization.

Luthans, Fred, Rosenkrantz, Stuart A., and Hennessey, Harry W. (1985) 'What Do Successful Managers Really Do? An Observation Study of Managerial Activities.' *The Journal of Applied Behavioral Science*, 21(3), 255–270.

MacArthur, Douglas (1964), *Reminiscences*, New York: Da Capo Press.

MacGregor Burns, James (1978), *Leadership*, New York: Harper Colophon.

Mahler, M. S., Pine, F., and Bergman, A. (1975) *The Psychological Birth of the Human Infant.* New York: Basic Books.

Manchester, William (1978), *American Caesar.* Boston: Little, Brown and Company.

Maroda, K. J. (2004). *The Power of Countertransference.* Hillsdale, N.J.: The Analytic Press.

Marshall, R. J. and Marshall S. V. (1988). *The Transference-countertransference Matrix.* New York: Columbia University Press.

Masterson, J. F. (1981) *The Narcissistic and Borderline Disorders.* New York: Brunner/Mazel.

McCall Jr., Morgan W. (1976), 'Leadership Research: Choosing Gods and Devils on the Run.' *Journal of Occupational Psychology*, 49, 139–153.

McCall Jr., Morgan W. and Lombardo, Michael M. (1983), 'What Makes a Top Executive.' *Psychology Today*, February, pp. 26–31.

McClelland, David C. (1961), *The Achieving Society*. Princeton: Van Nostrand.

McDougall, J. (1985) *Theaters of the Mind*. New York: Basic Books.

McGregor, D. (1960) *The Human Side of Enterprise*. New York: McGraw-Hill.

McKinley Runyan, W. (1982) *Life Histories and Psychobiography*. New York: Oxford University Press.

McWilliams, N. (1994) *Psychoanalytic Diagnosis*. New York: The Guilford Press.

Meissner, W. W. (1978) *The Paranoid Process*. New York: Jason Aronson.

Meltzer, D. (1967) *The Psychoanalytic Process*. London: Heinemann.

Miller, A. (1975) *Prisoners of Childhood: The Drama of the Gifted Child and the Search for the True Self*. New York: Basic Books.

Miller, A. (1981) *Prisoners of Childhood*. New York: Basic Books.

Miller, D. and Friesen, P. H. (1980) 'Momentum and revolution in organizational adaptation.' *Academy of Management Journal*, 24, 591–614.

Miller, D. and Freisen, P. H. (1984) *Organizations: A quantum view*. Englewood Cliffs, N. J.: Prentice-Hall.

Millon, T. (1981) *Disorders of Personality*. New York: John Wiley and Sons Inc.

Millon, T. (1996) *Disorders of Personality: DSM IV and Beyond*. New York, John Wiley and Sons Inc.

Mintzberg, H. (1973) *The Nature of Managerial Work*. New York: Harper & Row.

Minuchin, S. (1974) *Families and Family Therapy*. Cambridge: Harvard University Press.

Monnet, Jean (1976) *Mémoires*. Paris: Fayard.

Mumford, E. (1909) *The Origins of Leadership*. Chicago: University of Chicago Press.

Murphey, A. J. (1941) 'A Study of the Leadership Process.' *American Sociological Review*, 6, 674–687.

Neustadt, Richard (1960) *Presidential Power*. New York: John Wiley and Sons Inc.

Ogden, T. H. (1982) *Projective Identification and Psychotherapeutic Technique*. New York: Jason Aronson.

Pervin, L. and Oliver, J. E. (eds) (2001) *Handbook of Personality: Theory and Research*. New York: The Guilford Press.

Petrie, A. (1967) *Individuality in Pain and Suffering*. Chicago: University of Chicago Press.

Pfeffer, Jeffrey (1977) 'The Ambiguity of Leadership.' *Academy of Management Review*, 104–111.

Pfeffer, J. and Salancik, Gerald R. (1978) *The External Control of Organizations: A Resource Dependency Perspective*. New York: Harper and Row.

Putin, V., Gevorkyan, N., Timakova, N., and Kolesnikov, A. (2000) *First Person: An Astonishingly Frank Self-Portrait by Russia's President Vladimir Putin*. Moscow: Publicaffairs.

Racker, H. (1968) *Transference and Countertransference*. New York: International Universities Press.

Reich, W. (1949) *Character Analysis*. New York: Farrar, Straus and Giroux.

Reik, T. (1983) *Listening with the Third Ear*. New York: Farrar, Straus and Giroux.

Rizzolatti, G. and Fogassi, L. et al. (2001) 'Neurophysiological Mechanisms Underlying the Understanding and Imitation of Action.' *Nature Reviews. Neuroscience*, 2(9), 661–670.

Rotter, Julian B. (1966) 'Generalized Expectancies for Internal versus External Control of Reinforcement.' *Psychological Monographs*, 80 (1, Whole No. 609).

Ruszczynski, S. (ed.) (1993) *Psychotherapy with Couples*. London: Karnac Books.

Ruszczynzki, S. (1995) 'Narcissistic Object Relating.' In S. Ruszczynski and P. Fisher (eds), *Intrusiveness and Intimacy in the Couple*. London: Karnac Books.

Sager, C. J. (1991) 'Couples Therapy and Marriage Contracts.' In A. S. Gurman and D. P. Knisper (eds), *Handbook of Family Therapy*, Vol. 1. New York: Brunner/Mazel.

Sakwa, R. (2004) *Putin: Russia's Choice*. New York: Routledge.

Salzman, L. (1980) *Treatment of the Obsessive Personality*. New York: Jason Aronson.

Schore, A. N. (1994) *Affect Regulation and the Origin of the Self: The Neurobiology of Emotional Development*. Mahweh, N.J.: Erlbaum.

Searles, R. (1979). *Countertransference and Related Subjects. Selected Papers*. New York: International Universities Press.

Shapiro, D. (1965) *Neurotic Styles*. New York: Basic Books.

Sharpe, S. A. (1981) 'The Symbiotic Marriage: A Diagnostic Profile.' *Bulletin of the Menninger Clinic*, 45(2), 89–114.

Sharpe, S. A. (1992) 'The Oppositional Couple: A Developmental Object Relations Approach to Diagnosis and Treatment.' In R. A. Nemiroff and C. A. Colarusso (eds), *New Dimensions in Adult Development*. New York: Basic Books.

Simon, Herbert A. (1967) *Administrative Behavior*, (3rd edn), New York: The Free Press.

Smith, S. (1977) 'The Golden Fantasy: A Regressive Reaction to Separation Anxiety.' *International Journal of Psychoanalysis*, 58(3), 311–324.

Stern, D. N. (2004) *The Present Moment in Psychotherapy and Everday Life*. New York: W.W. Norton.

Storr, A. (1979) *The Art of Psychotherapy*. New York: Methuen.

Stogdill, Ralph M. (1948) 'Personal Factors Associated with Leadership: A Survey of the Literature'. *The Journal of Psychology*, 25(2), 35–11.

Strean, H. S. (1985) *Resolving Marital Conflict: A Psychodynamic Perspective*. New York: John Wiley and Sons Inc.

Suedfeld, Peter and Rank, A. Dennis (1976), 'Revolutionary Leaders: Long-term Success as a Function of Changes in Conceptual Complexity.' *Journal of Personality and Social Psychology*, 34(2), 169–178.

Sullivan, H. S. (1953) *The Interpersonal Theory of Psychiatry.* New York: Norton.

Symonds, M. (2003) *Softwar: An Intimate Portrait of Larry Ellison and Oracle.* New York, Simon & Schuster.

Tannenbaum, R. and Schmidt, W. (1958) 'How to Choose a Leadership Pattern.' *Harvard Business Review,* 36, 95–101.

Trevarthen, C. (1999/2000) 'Musicality and the Intrinsic Motive Pulse: Evidence from Human Psychobiology and Infant Communication.' *Musicae Scientiae:* Special Issue, Rhythm, Musical Narrative, and the Origin of Human Communication: 155–211.

Tucker, Robert C. (1981) *Politics as Leadership.* Columbia: University of Missouri Press.

Valéry Giscard d'Estaing (1991) *Le Pouvoir et la Vie,* Vol. 11: *L'affrontement.* Paris: France Loisirs, quoted in *The Economist,* June 8, 1991, p. 110.

Weber, M. (1947) *The Theory of Social and Economic Organizations.* New York: Oxford University Press.

Weber, Max (1964) *The Theory of Social and Economic Organizations.* New York: The Free Press.

Weick, Karl E. (1979) *The Social Psychology of Organising* (2nd edn). Reading, Mass: Addison-Wesley Publishing Co.

Whittaker, C. A. (1958) 'Psychotherapy with Couples.' *American Journal of Psychotherapy,* 12(1), 18–23.

Wildavsky, Aaron (1980) *The New York Times Book Review,* April 27.

Willi, J. (1984) *Dynamics of Couples Therapy.* Northvale, N. J.: Jason Aronson.

Willner, Ann R. (1984) *The Spellbinders,* New Haven: Yale University Press.

Wilson, M. (2003) *The Difference Between God and Larry Ellison: God Doesn't Think He's Larry Ellison.* New York: Collins Business.

Winnicott, D. W. (1975) *Through Paediatrics to Psycho-analysis.* New York: Basic Books.

Wolfe, T. (1988) *The Bonfire of the Vanities.* London: Bantam.

Wolstein, B. (ed.) (1988) *Essential Papers on Countertransference.* New York: New York University Press.

Zaleznik, Abraham (1977) 'Managers and Leaders: Are They Different?' *Harvard Business Review,* 55, 67–78.

Zaleznik, A. (1990) *Executive's Guide to Motivating People.* Chicago: Bonus Books.

Zaleznik, A. and Kets de Vries, M. F. R. (1975) *Power and the Corporate Mind.* Boston: Houghton Mifflin.

Zaleznik, A. and Kets de Vries, M. F. R (1985) *Power and the Corporate Mind* (rev. edn). Chicago: Bonus Books.

INDEX

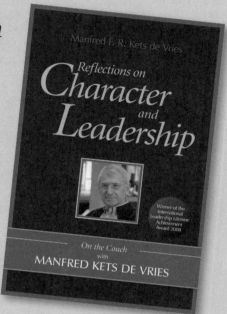